# Outsider Blues
## A Voice from the Shadows

Clifton Ruggles
and Olivia Rovinescu

T0204827

Fernwood Publishing

Halifax

Articles published in this book are reprinted from the *Montreal Gazette*, *Community
Contact*, *Serai*, and the *Mirror*.

Editing: Brenda Conroy and Douglas Beall
Design and production: Beverley Rach
Cover painting: Clifton Ruggles
Photography and paintings: All photos, unless otherwise credited, by Clifton Ruggles.
All paintings are by Clifton Ruggles. Shadowlands photoessay photos by Clifton
Ruggles with exception of page 18, 2 top photos by Olivia Rovinescu and page 20 top
photo by Ian Cameron. Personal Biography photoessay photographs by Clifton
Ruggles and Olivia Rovinescu as well as a collection of old family photos. Other
photographers are Olivia Rovinescu, Marcos Townsend, Ian Cameron and Eric
Ourique.
Printed and bound in Canada by: Hignell Printing Limited

A publication of:
Fernwood Publishing
Box 9409, Station A
Halifax, Nova Scotia
B3K 5S3

Fernwood Publishing Company Limited gratefully acknowledges the financial
assistance of the Book Publishing Industry Development Program and the
Multiculturalism Programs of the Department of Canadian Heritage and the
Nova Scotia Department of Recreation and Culture.

**Canadian Cataloguing in Publication Data**

Ruggles, Clifton

Outsider blues

Includes bibliographical references.
ISBN 1-8956686-65-2

1. Racism -- Canada. 2. Canada -- Race relations. 3. Black Canadians.*
I. Rovinescu, Olivia. II. Title.

FC106.B6R83 1996    305.896'071    C95-950334-X    F1035.N3R83 1996

# Contents

# Outsider Blues: A Voice from the Shadows
## In the way of an introduction
Clifton Ruggles

The articles that appear in this book originate in the shadows—those marginal spaces that Black people have been forced to inhabit ever since the first slaves reached the shores of North America, weighted in the chains of captivity. The stories have their roots in the dark pungent holds of slave ships where Black bodies were piled one on top of the other. They have their beginnings in fields where slaves toiled under the merciless lash of the overseers; in the lynching trees where the spectre of dead Black bodies dangled in deafening silence; from the shadows of the dark hiding places where the shiny Black faces of escaped slaves gleamed with the fear of being caught and the hope of freedom; in the kitchens and laundry rooms where Black women toiled from the first rays of morning light until long after the sun had gone down, when they would trudge the long way home with sore feet and blistered hands; in the nurseries where Black nannies cared for other people's children while often their own lay sick and alone; on the platforms of train stations where porters and redcaps, under the weight of passengers' luggage, were forced to flash that shiny-toothed, "Yes Sir, Mr. Charlie" grin, in the hope of getting a better tip. The stories have their beginnings on the dusty dirt roads that stopped where the paved road to the white part of town began and behind the walls of the run-down shacks that stood only metres from the train tracks, homes whose floorboards rattled threateningly every time a train rumbled passed, where there was no running water and where you had to wear your coat and boots to bed because it got too damn cold. They originate in the churches where the voices of Black preachers thundered and the Black people sang praises to the Lord in the hope of finding a better world in the next life. They emerge from the shadows of juke joints where Black music spoke of the pain and the joys of Black life, and where the shadows held hushed whispers of things that could not be spoken. At times the voices in these stories are like the lonely distant anguished shrill of a jazz trumpet in whose music is retained the haunting sadness of collective Black memory. The voices tell the story of a people who have lived an ambiguous existence, who have had voice but have gone unheard, who are both visible and invisible, a people whose history has been obfuscated.

I experienced what I call the "shadowlands" while working in the back rooms of restaurants and hotels and on the trains, when people looked through me and didn't see me. Black writers throughout the years have used a variety of terms to describe the many facets of the shadowlands. James Baldwin (1990: 25) described the Black in America "as a series of shadows, self created, intertwining, which now we helplessly battle." Ralph Ellison (1947) referred to it as "invisibility," bell hooks (1990) and other Black feminist writers have referred to it as the "margins." Richard Wright's "native son" certainly knew of it and so did Claude Brown's (1966) "manchild in the promised land."

The stories, which have shaped my worldview, have to do with the history of my exclusion. However this exclusion has also had an empowering effect on me. Marginalization can be liberating in that it gives one the freedom to see other possibilities and to experience other ways of being which can both inform the dominant discourse and help transform it. bell hooks echoes similar views when she says that marginality "is more than a site of deprivation." It is also the site of radical possibility, a space of resistance that "one stays in, clings to even, because it nourishes one's capacity to resist" (1990: 147).

When I was a young boy I used to draw in the margins of my exercise books. The margins were outside the jurisdiction of the teacher. I was no longer confined to that space whose limits had been defined by a Eurocentric educational system. The margins were my own and I could do with them what I wanted. There I was both architect and artist. I was free to explore the full range of my ideas. The margins provided me the space for creativity and self-expression. The space was not finite but filled with possibilities, continually expanding, shifting and reshaping itself. It was in the invisible space of the margins that I developed a critical way of viewing the world.

My family's history in Canada is one of the many untold stories buried in the margins. My parents migrated to Montreal in the 1940s from areas in Nova Scotia that were economically depressed. They came seeking a better life for themselves and their children but soon discovered that, for Black people, life anywhere in Canada was one of racial discrimination and lack of opportunity.

Life in Nova Scotia had been a daily struggle for survival—unemployment, segregation, lack of education, alcoholism and a general condition of despair had engulfed many of the Nova Scotian Black communities. I saw the toll it took on successive generations in my family. It left a bitterness that would haunt many of my relatives for the rest of their lives, and many sought to escape the disillusionment and hardships of life through the "demon" bottle that finally destroyed them.

My mother's father died young, leaving my grandmother with ten children to raise. Poverty had a familiar face for the Eskins family. They lived in a shack in Yarmouth, only steps from the railway tracks, overlooking the dump, the mud flats and the fish plant. Singer Lou Rawls must have been thinking of my grandmother's house when he sang the song "Dead End Street," for it sure fit the description. In an attempt to make ends meet my grandmother did laundry and other odd jobs and, even though space was scarce, took in the occasional boarder who shared a room with her children. Her sons quit school at an early age to carry hundred-pound bags of coal to houses in the area. The hardship of my grandmother's life killed her by the time she reached her mid forties.

My father's family were descendants of the Black Loyalists who fought on the side of the British during the American Revolution in the late 1700s and who were given land by the British for their loyalty. My grandmother, Buela Ruggles, owned a small farm in the Annapolis Valley, Nova Scotia, the site of one of the first Black settlements in Canada. She was a stern, bible-toting woman who was a strict disciplinarian. My father often told me how she'd beat him daily, just in case he'd done something he shouldn't have. But he loved her anyway and, when she couldn't run the farm anymore because of her rheumatism, she moved in with us. This move caused great consternation for my mother, as she and my grandmother did not see eye-to-eye on child-rearing. My grandmother had old fashioned ideas regarding lightness and darkness of skin colour and treated her children and grandchildren accordingly. You couldn't use the word "Black" in her presence because she would say, "If you're Black, you ain't no grandson of mine." As far as she was concerned, she was Negro and all her grandsons were "brown." She would never fail to remind us that there was some "white blood" on her side of the family and for this reason she reckoned that she was better than other Black people. Even though she probably thought my father married a woman from "the wrong side of the tracks," she was most likely pleased that he'd married a light-skinned woman who would produce light-skinned children.

My mother was part Black, part white and part Native, and was quite fair, with long wavy hair. Colour, it seems, was not an issue in her household as the children came in many hues. My mother's grandfather was Cherokee and her grandmother was Mi'kmaq. My Native ancestry is clearly visible as it is etched in the features of my aunts and uncles on my mother's side of the family. The early forging of Native/Black relationships is understandable given the times. Both groups were oppressed, and the Black parts of town and the reserves were often in close proximity to each other. In the United States, where my great grandfather was born, many of the Native American tribes gave refuge to escaped slaves.

Every summer my parents would send us "down-home" where we stayed with our relatives. This term was used by many Blacks from Nova Scotia for whom places like Montreal, Toronto and Winnipeg became a second home. The real home was still down-home. It was there that we learned the old folks' ways and the customs of the these Black Maritimers who were our forebears. I worked side-by-side with my uncles in the fish plant, cutting up the cod fish, boxing it and sending it west. When the fishing boats came in, we'd go down to meet the fishers, who gave us huge slices of swordfish or tuna, and we'd go home and have us a fish fry.

It was a great place and life seemed so simple. It made me wonder why my parents had left what appeared to us kids to be such a great life. It wasn't that I didn't notice the poverty—it was hard not to notice the conditions that some of my relatives lived in—but as a kid, these things didn't really seem to matter. It was only later that I understood why my father joined the army. It was an opportunity to get employment, learn a trade and get his family out of depressed economic conditions.

My father was very proud of his time in the army. He would tell us kids many stories of his experiences overseas and how he marched with the liberation forces in Holland. He came home and took my mother with him to Montreal to start a new life. He became one of the CPR sleeping-car porters working out of Montreal's Windsor Station. Sometimes my mother would take us down to the station to meet him. He looked so proud and so dapper in his freshly pressed uniform. The station always appeared to be such a mysterious place, with smoke rising from the powerful snorting steam engines. My father loved trains, and toy trains were his favourite Christmas presents to us.

I can't say I always wanted to be a writer. There were no positive role models that a poor, Black child could aspire to. My expectations were very limited. Careers in writing or in the arts were not considered practical, given the lack of opportunities available to Blacks. Even though I had artistic talent (I was quite a good artist), I dared not dream. I dared not imagine. I felt disempowered, disaffected and defeated. I looked around me and I resigned myself to the fact that I would never amount to much. And there was an underlying anger which poisoned my life. My parents, who struggled to feed and cloth nine children, could not support my interest in art. "Boy don't be wastin' your time. . . . Boy, go out there and get a real job and stop this foolishness. . . . Stop your dreamin' ways and get back to earth." I never felt I had the right to ask my parents for art lessons or art supplies. And besides, there was no space for artistic activity. There were eleven of us living in a five-room basement apartment. I remember climbing on top of boxes in the closet used to store our winter clothes just to have a private space in which to draw. In a neighbourhood where most people were unemployed or on welfare, a career in the fine arts was just a fairy tale. Where I grew up most kids aspired to be pimps and con men because that seemed the only way to escape from poverty. I watched my parents come home from their service jobs—my father was a railway porter, my mother was a domestic and later on a factory worker—with very little to show for their hard work, very little money and very little self esteem.

We lived on Barclay Street in the Cote des Neiges area of Montreal, which at the time was a smorgasbord of nationalities—French, English, Italian, Jewish, German, Hungarian, Romanian. In a predominantly white neighbourhood, ours was one of the few Black families on the street. It was therefore almost impossible to develop a Black identity. In fact, in the late fifties, when I was nine years old, Black "identity" as we think of it now was not articulated.

The Barclay Street Development was built for the veterans who had come home after the Second World War. The apartment afforded my family the opportunity to get cheap but relatively decent housing. Because we were such a large family, it was a welcome relief from the St. Henri dwellings that they occupied when they first arrived in Montreal from their native Nova Scotia.

Room was scarce but we managed. Lineups at the bathroom were horrendous and fueled a lot of tensions in the house. Dinner was usually served in three sittings and if you missed the third sitting you simply did not eat that evening. The food was gone and you went to bed hungry. Saturday morning laundry was a major event in which all family members participated, and it was not uncommon to see our clothes hanging from the lines of all our neighbours. Because of my father's ingenuity we became the proud possessors of the longest clothesline on the block; it stretched from the cement foundation of our back balcony straight across the once grassy but now dusty play area to the next series of lots. I've seen a lot of clotheslines in my time, but never one that long.

When you entered the hallway of that apartment on Barclay, the smell of exotic foreign foods wafted through the air mingling with the smell of our own black-eyed peas and rice. Because there were so many nationalities, the children I played with and whose houses I visited were of many different cultural backgrounds. Because of the times and because the complex was a community unto itself, adults helped each other and the kids became very close. To this day I am still in contact with many of the friends I made during my childhood and teen years. One of them, of French-Canadian heritage, is one of my biggest supporters and follows my articles religiously. After an article appears, it is not uncommon for my old buddy, Gerald Fournier, to phone and give me feedback. Those bonds forged in childhood and the support of those children from working-class families were an important part of my formative experiences.

One day when some of my friends and I, the Barclay Street Gang, as we became known, were sitting on the front steps of one of those apartment buildings, a gang of French-speaking youths approached and began to hurl racial insults at me. When I heard the word "nigger" my body shuddered with rage. Angry, hurt and feeling humiliated, I got up ready to "kick ass" in response to their degrading comments, only to find several of my white friends standing in front of me ready to fight these racists on my behalf. It was a profound experience for me and I was proud of the fact that our bonds of friendship held together despite our differences.

I cannot remember exactly when I became conscious of the significance or stigma that was attached to the complexion of my colour. I was five years old when I had my first experience of being called "nigger black, nigger black." Ironically this taunt was used by one of the mixed-race children who had moved in next door. I suppose that expression was common in their old Eastend neighbourhood. As I grew older I became aware of the fact that my brothers and sisters and I did not look like most of the people in the neighbourhood. Our skins were black and our hair was nappy.

My brothers and sisters spent countless hours trying to straighten their hair. Hair grooming became a constant daily expression of the struggle to hide our Blackness. In some distorted way we rationalized the appropriation of this white aesthetic as a necessary part of the daily ritual. I remember watching in fascination the monthly ritual of the heavy, black, hot, iron comb with a rounded wooden handle worn smooth by the years of use slice through layered naps of hair leaving them smoking, lifeless and straight. And I remember vividly the smell of burning in the kitchen of our basement flat as the hot comb singed its way crackling through the hair. Why my sisters subjected themselves to this tortuous ordeal and the risk of becoming a human brushfire I could only wonder. My brothers' hair-straightening ordeal took a different form. I watched them in the bathroom put a chemical called "conk" in their hair in preparation for the Saturday night dances. Timing was very important in this endeavour—if you didn't get it right, the powerful chemicals in the conk would take your scalp off. A cap was then fashioned from a nylon stocking and tightly knotted around the head so the hair wouldn't become mussed up while one was sleeping. Sometimes the stocking cap was so tight that it left a visible indentation on my brothers' foreheads when they took it off in the mornings. I was fortunate enough to escape these white-makeover rituals. I was younger than my brothers and sisters and by the time I was "of age" Afros were "in" and the motto "Black is beautiful" was in fashion.

One of my most powerful memories is of hearing about a Black child who, upon being teased by his classmates about his skin being "dirty," went home, filled the bathtub with an assortment of cleaning agents and proceeded to scrub himself "clean" until his skin became raw. When that failed, he took a razor to his flesh and tried to scrape off his Blackness. This event dramatically demonstrated to me the devastating effects of institutionalized racism and its impact on the formation of one's identity. The negative stereotypes of Black people in mainstream media establish the criteria for how we are seen and how we see ourselves. Because these images are collectively held and conditioned in all of us they can spawn racial devaluation in all of us, Black people included. Studies have indicated that Black children tested said they preferred to play with white rather than Black dolls. When asked to colour themselves according to their skin colour, in almost all instances, Black children coloured themselves lighter than they actually were. When given images of Black and white storybook children and asked which one they thought was the most beautiful, in almost all cases, Black children chose the white characters.

In school we experienced a system skewed against the interests of Black students, a system which systematically stripped me and other Black students of our dignity, our self-esteem and our identity. One incident forever embedded in my memory is that of my first and last experience at the school guidance office, where I went to seek career counselling. I remember telling the guidance counsellor that I wanted to go to university, to which he replied, "Very few of your kind go to university. They can't afford it and they're not bright enough to make it." Secure in the knowledge that he was steering me in the "right" direction, he produced a booklet on a vocational school he thought I might be interested in attending.

Our futures were in the hands of a small army of teachers and other professionals who unquestioningly fulfilled their functions, unaware of other options for us and unaware of the devastating impact of their advice. More often than not, the curriculum negated the existence of Black people or presented us as non-entities, as caricatures or stereotypes. These images, fed to us under the guise of knowledge, served to reinforce our feelings of alienation and inferiority.

I watched in heartfelt agony as members of my family acquiesced to institutional racism. I watched my brothers and sisters and other Black students being streamed into "special classes" and later into low-paying, dead-end jobs because of an educational system that would not, could not understand their needs, hopes, desires or dreams. The school system only served to intensify the feelings of inadequacy and, for this reason, many of these youths took to the streets in search of alternative routes to fulfill their ambitions for recognition.

During the late sixties, the Cote des Neiges Black community experienced a major transformation, caused in part by the large influx of Black immigrants from the West Indies and in part by events in the United States—the Civil Rights Movement, the formation of the Black Panther party and the protests over the war in Vietnam. A new awareness was in the making, and with it, Black consciousness and Black pride. Expressions like "Black is beautiful" and "power to the people" were the popular slogans of the day and these were used to express an awakening Black identity.

Our interpretation of the world was changing and the new heroes were Martin Luther King, Malcolm X, Stokley Carmichael and Angela Davis. Here in Montreal, the champions of Black power were Carl Whittaker, Rosie Douglas, Leroi Butcher and Anne Cools (who is now a Senator). It was a time when dashikis and Afro hair cuts were a part of our emerging identity. The funky rhythms of James Brown singing "Say it loud, I'm Black and I'm proud" pulsated in the air. Black people held up their fists in salute to their new awareness. To be "baaad" was to be "good." We were subverting the language of the dominant white culture and offering an alternative mode of communication and an alternative sense of aesthetic.

Soul music was "in" and at the school dances Black and white students together swayed to rhythms of the pop sounds. B.B. King sang, "What is Soul," and the school officials looked the other way in hopes that "soul" was just another passing fad. Curtis Mayfied sang, "We're a winner," yet the hidden curriculum continued to turn us into losers.

A new Black intelligentsia was being created. This generation of young people had tasted the fruit of the tree of knowledge and they wanted it too. The only problem was that the tree itself was poisoned and the nutritional value of the fruit was rather dubious. The chains of bondage were no longer ones of cold steel but of white ideology. The challenge was one of breaking the chains of this ideological enslavement—of casting off the internalized images of ourselves as lesser beings and of our history as less significant. We needed to find new ways to reaffirm our cultural identity.

The Sir George Williams University computer riots that began on February 11, 1969 were to have a great affect on our thinking. The "Sir George Williams Affair," as it was referred to, witnessed the escalation of a conflict from a small internal charge of racism by six Black students against a professor at the university to a full-scale rebellion. When the students' protest was ignored, the situation escalated, resulting in the destruction of the computer centre. The events surrounding that incident exposed the racism that existed in Quebec society and helped to fuel the local Black power movement.

Black activism was proliferating rapidly, fed by the social and political upheaval in the United States and Great Britain. Our models were based on the rhetoric of the Black Panther Party and the Black Muslim Movement, who promoted Black essentials in the form of a reaffirmation of our African roots. In the highly charged racial atmosphere of Montreal during the seventies, dating a white woman was not the wisest choice a Black man could make. In fact it was tantamount to political suicide and ensured complete ostracization from Black essentialist groups. The Black student groups preached that message consistently. However I chose to set my own path. I started dating Olivia Rovinescu, the other contributor to this book, who is now my wife.

I was torn between contradictory forces pulling at me. Although I had encountered a lot of racism in my life, I had also encountered some white people who had helped and encouraged me along the way. I wasn't about to live my life according to other people's expectations. I hadn't been swept up in the Black essentialist mind-set. I believed very deeply that we must fight racism and oppression wherever we encounter it, but I also believed that it wasn't a solitary struggle, that oppression takes many different forms and that we would have to build bridges with other cultural communities and other individuals. I moved chameleon-like through different cultural terrains.

The most challenging terrain I had to negotiate was university life. Here I was, an angry young Black man with a chip on his shoulder and a very short fuse, suddenly immersed in an environment that was anathema to me. I had been fortunate enough to receive a scholarship to attend McGill University. As a result of a study that concluded that there were very few (less than 1 percent) Black Canadians studying at McGill, a group of Black educators encouraged McGill to set up a scholarship program for students whose ancestry was African Canadian.

Talk about feeling academically unprepared. As the professors made references to people I had never heard of, it was as if they were speaking in a foreign tongue. I stood there transfixed, afraid to open my mouth. It was like being in an insane asylum; nothing made any sense. It was as if the terrain had suddenly shifted precariously and I had lost my bearings and reference points. I had been stripped of whatever voice I had. As I sat there trying to decode this unfamiliar gibberish I hesitated to contribute my ideas because I felt I would not be understood. I had this wonderful opportunity to go to university and I did not want to blow it; I did not want to embarrass myself for fear that it would reflect badly on my race. When I did speak, the other students looked at me blankly. I felt that they did not hear my words, they only saw my Blackness. It seemed they could not comprehend the significance of my presence there. As a result of these experiences in white academia I became mute and invisible. However, this time my exclusion was self-imposed. Invisibility can take many forms. This phenomenon was not unique to me. From elementary school to graduate school there is something that depresses Black achievement. Claude Steele (1992) refers to this condition as "disidentification" caused by racial devaluation.

My working and personal relationship with Olivia, a white Romania Jew, elicited many negative reactions, from both white people and Black people. Our willingness to challenge these negative perceptions brought us closer together.

Even though we were from two completely different backgrounds we were able to forge a relationship that crossed cultural boundaries. An important part of our work had to do with developing materials and giving talks that spoke to these issues. Little did we know at the time that this relationship would be strong enough to last over twenty years and that we would marry, have children and continue our working partnership. Critical examination of racial issues continues to be the focus of much of our work—our writing, our teaching and the workshops we give to teachers and other professional groups.

Through the course of our work it was infinitely easier for Olivia than for me to raise the subject of racism. Whites seem to feel more comfortable when another white person raises this issue. They find it less threatening than when they come face to face with the victim of racism. Coming from me, it arouses anger, guilt, frustration and other uncomfortable feelings. Even when I try to discuss racism in a neutral manner, they feel I am accusing them of being racist and they withdraw.

Living with me for over twenty years and experiencing the way the world treated me and our children, by extension, Olivia began to live the Black experience too. However, hers is an experience of choice, whereas mine and that of our children is not. Her identification did not happen all at once. The first time I noticed the change in her was at a supermarket when a customer insulted a Black cashier by calling her racially derogatory names. Olivia reacted with such outrage it shocked even me. I realized that her immersion was complete one day as she was relaying a story about an event at which she participated. She unconsciously reported that, "there were no other Blacks there." The comment was revealing because it exposed the extent of her identification. It said that she saw with Black eyes, heard with Black ears. It said, "I may look white but I see the world with a Black perspective." At first I thought hers was a unique perspective due to the fact that we write and design anti-racist workshops together, but when I later interviewed other white women involved in interracial relationships, especially those who have raised Black children, they echoed the same feeling. They saw themselves as "Black" by virtue of being a part of a Black family. As one woman put it, "You can't raise Black sons in this society without identifying very strongly with the Black experience because whether you like it or not, it becomes your experience." This confirmed what I somehow always suspected, that "Black" is more than just a racial category, it's a way of viewing the world.

Black comes in many shades and many hair textures. My eight brothers and sisters looked very different from one other. I came out the darkest. My sister Joan came out the lightest. And there were variations in between. In fact Joan looked so light that when she worked in the southern United States her employers felt at ease making racist remarks in front of her. One day she had had it. When they made the comment, "No nigger would ever work here," she announced very matter of factly that one had been working there for all these years, and she walked out. One time I was driving to New York with my brother Monty and my sister Linda and a group of friends. The border guard saw that we both had the same last name and he hauled us out for questioning. He did not believe that Monty who looked more Chicano than Black could possibly be my brother. We were at the border for two hours until they established his identity.

The issue of colour has always ripped apart the Black community. When I was young the lighter you were the higher up in the colour hierarchy—lightness had to do with being better and having more opportunities. In recent times, that has changed. Light-skinned and mixed-race people are made to feel like they are on the "out" because they've got "too much of the man in them." This issue continues to fragment the already fragmented Black community.

Even those of us who think we have escaped racism because of our class or educational level, find ourselves victimized by racism's subtle and insidious ways—ways that subvert and undermine us and render us invisible. Maybe it's because we feel invisible that we shout louder at and are more aggressive with each other. James Baldwin (1990: 25) talked about this rage in "Notes to a Native Son," referring to it as a "dread, a chronic disease, a pounding in the skull and a fire in the bowels. And the danger lies not from anything other people might do but from the hatred you carry in your own heart"—oppression turned inward. We internalize racism's deadly poison and consequently undermine ourselves and our own community. Racism's deadly poison has sabotaged the Black psyche.

The Black male in North America is forever treated as a suspect. Border guards suspect us, police suspect us, store owners suspect us, school officials suspect us. In this society Black males become visible only when we become suspects. The rest of the time, we are "invisible." In every facet of our lives we're seen as unworthy of the same rights and privileges as our white counterparts. There isn't a Black man who hasn't experienced continuous assaults on his intelligence and on his character.

The Black experience in North America is very different from that of any other ethnic group. No other group has been brought here against its will and enslaved. The after-effects of slavery and segregation take a long time to overcome. As a result of lack of opportunity, long periods of unemployment and racial discrimination, Blacks in general have made relatively few gains, compared to other ethnic groups who have made great economic strides. Having virtually nothing to bequeath to future generations prevents Blacks from the possibility of empowerment across generations. People feel empowered only when they believe they have the capacity to shape and execute life plans. Without that belief, nihilism and defeatism set in—another of racism's soul-destroying side effects.

As I stated before, fragmentation is a real problem in the Black community, based partly on the fact that we come from many different places in the world and do not share a common culture or even a common language. The fact that there are so many Black community organizations in Montreal attests to this phenomenon. And there are class differences that further divide us.

Lack of access to the media prevents Black people from being in touch with other Black communities across Canada. The fact that there are very few Black journalists working in the mainstream media means that the concerns of the Black community are seldom part of that media's agenda. When they give attention to Blacks, we are more apt to be portrayed as villains and victims than as newsmakers, experts or citizens reacting to contemporary events. Although media depictions of Blacks are for the most part negative, in recent years there have been some efforts to change those images.

Stories that are relevant to the Black community—everyday life experiences, non-stereotypical role models, contributions to culture, politics and so on—are often either ignored or underplayed. Although individual acts of discrimination are certainly reported, they all too often appear as the transgression of a single person or company and not as examples of a systemic problem plaguing our society.

When we are "given" the chance to voice our opinions, an "intellectual apartheid" seems to prevail—in other words, we are deemed credible only when we are speaking on issues involving race and ethnicity. I have experienced this disconcerting phenomenon on a number of occasions. For example, a radio interviewer who did not deem my views on violent behaviour to be as newsworthy as my views on violent behaviour in Black children kept steering me away from discussing anything other than what pertained to the "Black agenda."

My life and the lives of my ancestors wind their way through three hundred years of Canadian history—yet they have been only marginally recorded; I still live in the shadows; I am not a part of mainstream history; I remain a foreigner in my own country. As a Black Canadian with an Amerindian heritage, I go back many generations in the history of North America—I am still made to feel that I do not belong. I cannot remember the number of times I have been told during the course of my life "to go back to Africa." I keep having to remind those that would have me return to whence I came that I wouldn't know where to go if I tried. "Non-recognition or mis-recognition," writes Charles Taylor (1992: 25), "can inflict harm, can be a form of oppression, imprisoning someone in a false, distorted and reduced mode of being. Since identity is shaped by recognition or its absence, by the mis-recognition of others, a person or a group can suffer real damage, real distortion if the people or society around them mirror back to them a conflicting or demeaning or contemptible picture of themselves." This is why it is important for me to make visible and give recognition to those people who inhabit the shadowlands, those individuals whose contributions have remained unrecognized, those who have remained invisible for too long.

## Overview of the book

The first chapter attempts to surface lost narratives, stories of people whose stories have never been told, whose importance has never been recognized. It also contains a photo essay which gives substance to the people who inhabit the shadowlands. It documents the incredible strength and perseverance of Black people in the face of tremendous adversity. The personal biographical photoessay represents the contexual background where memory merges with shadow, giving substance to my writings. Chapter Two is about encounters with racism and includes letters to the editors written in response to a column I wrote about a racial incident that happened to me in November 1991. This chapter also includes a critical deconstruction by Olivia Rovinescu which provides readers with an example of how text can be subjected to critical analysis—how worldviews are shaped by cultural assumptions, language and lived experience.

Chapter Three looks at ways in which education can be instrumental in combatting racism; what are the tools with which to fight racism; what programs are most effective. Chapter Four continues the themes of education—but this time focuses on the experiences of Blacks within the educational system—including my experiences as a student and as a teacher. Chapter Five includes stories about inter-cultural and cross-cultural issues, including my own marriage and the raising of bi-racial children. Chapter Six focuses on artistic concerns and examines the exclusion of Blacks from the Canadian art world and such issues as stereotyping, cultural appropriation and political correctness. In conclusion, Chapter Seven looks at some of the social problems that confront our society and some of the individuals and groups who are attempting to address these problems.

## Acknowledgements

I wish to thank Greta Hofman Nemiroff, Carolyn Knowles and Judy Kyle for their valuable input, support and encouragement. Also I'd like to thank the editors with whom I've worked over the years at the *Montreal Gazette*: Sandy Senyk, Doug Sweet and George Kalakerakis as well as Ray Bassard, the Managing Editor who gave me the opportunity to write the column. I'd also like to thank the publishing team at Fernwood who have helped to make this book a reality. And finally I'd like to thank our daughters Amy and Ali who have been a source of inspiration for several of the articles contained in this book.

My deepest gratitude is to Olivia Rovinescu, my wife, who worked on this book with me and who served as my initial editor providing me with constant criticism and encouragement. For many years she has been my best friend and the wisest counsel a writer could have.

## References

Baldwin, James. 1990. *Notes of a Native Son*. Boston: Beacon Press.

Brown, Claude. 1966. *Manchild in the Promised Land*. New York: Signet.

Claude, Steele. 1992. "Race and the Schooling of Black Americans." *Atlantic Monthly*, April.

Ellison, Ralph. 1947. *Invisible Man*. New York: Modern Library.

hooks, bell. 1990. *Yearning: Race, Gender and Cultural Politics*. Boston: Southend Press.

Taylor, Charles. 1992. *Multiculturalism and the Politics of Recognition*. Princeton, N.J.: Princeton University Press.

# The Shadow

To be nothing more than a figure-head
A shadow of something concrete
But the shadow is concrete too
Existing in the background
Its hopes, fears, aspirations
Swallowed up by the foreground
Opaque but striving to be noticed
By whom?
For what?

The moon grows smaller
But the shadow grows taller
Reaching for the moon
Slowly the moon disintegrates
The shadow is no more

The shadow's plight remains the same
Bent and twisted on the walls of pain

A shadow will always be a shadow
Nothing more.

# Shadowlands

# Personal

my mother's house on Lois Lane, in Yarmouth, Nova Scotia

my father, Harold Ruggles, as a porter

chopping wood with my father, at grandmoth
house in Annapolis Valley, Nova Scotia

# Biography

my father Harold Ruggles in second World War

with my father during second World War

family photo

Coronation School in the 1960s

father and I visiting grandmother's farm

growing up on Barclay Street

my grandmother's house in Yarmouth, Nova Scotia

my family at Christmas
(I am in my father's arms)

backyard on Barclay Street

my mother, Mary Eskins talking to neighbour Rose and her daughter Cindy

my sister Marilyn

my mother on Barclay Street with neighbours

my mother working in a factory
assembling parts for water heaters

my parents

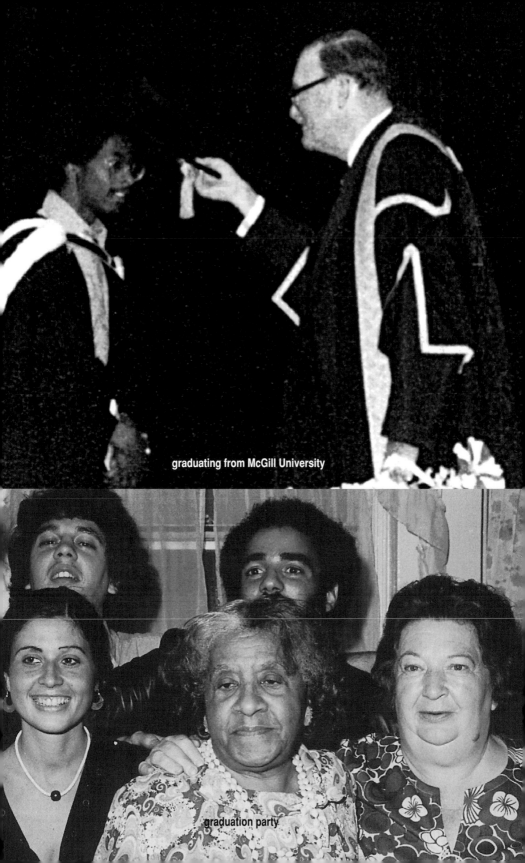

graduating from McGill University

graduation party

life on Barclay Street...

# History, Identity and the Politics of Exclusion

# African Canadian or black?
## Perspectives have changed

May 1, 1993

It was multicultural day at my daughter's school a few weeks ago and I agreed to set up a display depicting my cultural background. Her teacher called the night before, wondering what to label the display.

Would calling it "Africa" be all right?

"No, not exactly," I said, after mulling it over. "I'll be representing the African Canadian experience. I'm 300 years removed from my African roots. My ancestors were among the first blacks to settle in Nova Scotia. From a cultural point of view, I am Canadian."

She insisted that calling the display "African Canadian" would be confusing to the children since they would not readily associate someone like myself—a black as being a Canadian.

### Aboriginal roots, too

She, like many others, seems to think that because I'm black, I'm not a real Canadian. I argued that the students should know Canadians come in different colours. They are not all white, of European descent.

I wondered how long you have to be here to be a "real" Canadian. After 300 years, blacks are still invisible. It's a good thing I didn't get into my aboriginal roots, or we might have been at it all night.

After some lengthy deliberation, we finally agreed to call the display "Africa-African Canadian," even though she was still somewhat disturbed that the sign would not be consistent with the others, which referred to specific countries.

I pointed out that Africa is a continent, not a country, so there was no need to worry about consistency. I explained that the reason the people of African descent don't know which country they're from is because they were forcibly brought here, against their wishes, in the most degrading and demeaning of ways, herded like cattle onto slave ships.

We lost our names, our countries and our histories.

All the teacher wanted was a simple label for a display, not a lesson about the African diaspora. But explaining where you come from is a complicated matter when your history has been lost.

What to call ourselves? The issue seems to surface again and again. On April 5, The Gazette ran a front-page story about the question, reporting that some members of the black community now object to being called black because of negative connotations associated with the word.

They pointed out that dictionaries equate black with "dismal, gloomy, sullen, evil, wicked, atrocious and lacking in moral light or goodness." These people prefer instead to be called African Canadian.

They also object to the term black on the grounds that black is not an ethnic origin, but simply a reference to their darker pigmentation.

I still think of myself as black, although I have absolutely no objection to being referred to as African Canadian and often use the term myself. Times change. Language changes.

I'm a product of the 1960s, when expressions like "Black is beautiful," "I'm black and I'm proud," changed It represented that intellectual space where we could defend ourselves. We were now in control of the word. We infused it with new meanings. It no longer defined us. And we rejoiced in our freedom to reclaim the word and

Multicultural Display at my daughter's school

the way a whole generation of people, myself included, looked at themselves.

We took the dehumanizing aspects of the language with which we had been labelled and gave it new meaning. We took the language used to degrade us and make us feel inferior and we imbued it with our own significance.

Black became an affirmation of our strength and solidarity. "Black" with a capital B encapsulated an entire philosophy of resistance.

### Rejoiced in freedom

Black was a call to arms. It was the voice of the black liberation struggle.

redefine it.

In using the term "black" to identify ourselves, we confronted our discrimination head-on and wouldn't let ourselves forget the legacy of slavery. It was also an affirmation of our beauty. It said to the world, we are here, we are not invisible. We exist.

When I first starting calling myself black back in the 1960s, my grandmother tried to disown me. No grandson of mine is black," she bellowed menacingly. "There are no black people in my family."

She insisted on being called coloured, Negro, brown—anything but

35

black. She was enraged by the word black because for her it implied that she was darker than she actually was. She had been conditioned to believe the myth that "when you're light, you're all right; when you're black, step back." She lived her life according to that motto, an example of internalized oppression at its most insidious.

She was devoured by it. It distorted her ability to think clearly. She didn't know who or what she was. Such internalized oppression caused many black people to accept the negative stereotypes created about them, ashamed because their skin was "too dark" or their hair was "too kinky."

Sadly, they accepted the myth that "lighter is better" and thus perpetuated a colour hierarchy which has kept blacks apart for generations.

The move towards stressing one's ethnicity as opposed to one's race takes away from the real issues, dividing already-fragmented people of colour who should be seeing themselves as one—united by their experiences with a racist society.

Blackness, as I have come to know it, is an ideological position that simultaneously challenges the dominant society as well as celebrates our beauty as a people. The notion of blackness encompasses all people of colour, not just those of African descent.

It is a shared struggle and we are each other's fate. No matter what we call ourselves, our goal should be the same—the elimination of racism in all its forms.

Amy with Romanian Display on Multicultural Day

# Keeping the spirit alive
## Marcus Garvey Jr. carries on work of his father

June 22, 1994

On Saturday night, I felt like I had been transported back in time to the early 1900s.

When Marcus Garvey Jr. delivered a speech to a crowd of about 150 people at Le Manoir in Notre Dame de Grace [N.D.G.], there were times when I could feel the presence of his father, Marcus Garvey, founder of the Universal Negro Improvement Association [UNIA].

The audience response was as charged as Garvey Jr.'s speech. They clapped, they pounded on tables and gave him two standing ovations. He had succeeded in keeping the memory of Marcus Garvey alive, 54 years after his father's death on June 10, 1940.

The speech was part of the Union United Church's 12th Heritage Week celebrations.

Marcus Garvey founded the UNIA in Jamaica in 1914. The goal of the organization was to promote racial pride and encourage independent black economic and political development.

The UNIA transferred its headquarters to Harlem in 1916 and grew into the largest black movement ever, with chapters in cities across the United States, Canada, Central and South America, the Caribbean and in Africa. It had 6 million registered members in 34 countries.

An eloquent and charismatic leader who was fond of wearing a helmet of feathers "tall as Guinea grass" and a uniform of purple and gold, Marcus Garvey told people of African descent to "know thyself and do for thyself."

What he envisioned was united people of African descent all over the world.

The UNIA operated a steamship line that promoted trade between Africans of West Africa, the Caribbean and Central America. It created a nurses' corps; a manufacturing corporation; an unarmed African Legion; and a newspaper, which was published in French, English and Spanish. Given the economic and social conditions of blacks at the time, these initiatives represented monumental achievements.

According to Garvey Jr., it was when his father tried to organize the African Political Party that he met with opposition, which landed him in an Alabama jail and eventually had him deported back to Jamaica.

Some critics complained that Garvey's approach was too individualistic to address the problems faced by blacks. Others say he encouraged racism. Garvey supporters, however, argue that promoting pride and love of race does not make Garvey a racist.

And Garvey Jr. maintains his father meant to address the powerlessness of blacks worldwide "by advocating African identity, pride, self-reliance and economic and military empowerment."

Garvey Jr., who is the 7th president of the UNIA and a practicing engineer in New York, said he believes his father's message is as relevant today as it ever was and he feels compelled to carry on his work.

The first contact I had with the UNIA was 20 years ago when I interviewed and took photographs of Henry Langdon, president of the Montreal chapter of the UNIA, for a black history project I was working on. I remember being impressed by his level of commitment to African unity.

The photograph I took of him, poised thoughtfully beneath a picture of Marcus Garvey, left a lasting impression on me.

The Montreal chapter of the UNIA is one of its oldest divisions. It was started in 1919, three years after the UNIA was established in Harlem.

In 1982, the city expropriated the UNIA building for urban renewal, leaving the UNIA homeless. Ever-committed to the cause, Henry Langdon, now 83, pressed the government for com-

Henry Langdon in front of portrait of Marcus Garvey

pensation and succeeded in 1992 in getting a new home for the UNIA on Notre Dame St.

With the acquisition of the new building, the UNIA is rapidly getting back on its feet. Right now the upstairs is being used for low-income housing.

Various study groups meet there. The UNIA offers a black history course on Wednesday nights. Tap-dance classes are held Wednesdays and Saturdays. First-aid courses were offered last spring and will continue in the fall.

And the UNIA is once again planning to offer scholarships.

Listening to Marcus Garvey Jr.'s speech on Saturday reminded me of the depth of spirit and commitment within the black community.

I walked away feeling a part of something special—that being the richness of Montreal's black community's proud heritage and a bond with the struggles of people of African descent all over the world.

# Malcolm X
## Decades after his murder, blacks turn to enigmatic civil-rights leader. Why?

November 21, 1992

Twenty seven years after his assassination the legacy of Malcolm X lives on, in part due to Spike Lee's movie about his life, which opened this week in theatres across North America. But the movie is perhaps the crest of what has been a growing wave of interest in the enigmatic black leader. In recent months, Malcolm X books, magazine articles, baseball caps, T-shirts, rap records and even air freshener and potato chips have appeared in stores.

Why does Malcolm X have such popular appeal?

Branded 30 years ago by the mainstream media as "American's worst nightmare," Malcolm's lifelong mission was the empowerment of the disenfranchised, to, as he said, "expose any meaningful truth that will help to destroy the racist cancer that is malignant in the body of America."

He challenged blacks to change their social reality and redefine how they saw themselves, culturally and politically.

As a young boy, Malcolm watched as his father was killed by white supremacists and his family dispersed. He came of age at a time when black people in the U.S. were fiercely discriminated against and brutally treated.

The metaphor of the X—the self-sustaining symbol of perpetual strength—stands in opposition to and as a negation of the dominant culture. It replaces the name blacks were given by the slave masters. It speaks of our lack of identity, of African diaspora—the forceful dispersion of people of African descent, the cutting off of our history, our culture, our land. It represents the denial of our existence, our exclusion from history and the denial of our fundamental human rights.

One young black woman I spoke to, Joanne Hall put it this way: "For me, the X symbolizes the fact that we are branded by our colour. Young black men especially, are walking targets being shot down in the prime of their lives. It is saying to the world that 'we're not going to take it anymore.'"

Some people believe current interest in Malcolm X is nothing more than a fad, a cultural revival of the 1960s that lacks genuine historical or political understanding.

Another black woman, Marilyn Josephs, explained the phenomenon this way: "It's just another manifestation of popular culture churning out heroes for profit. It's consumerism, absorbing and assimilating opposition. I never thought I'd see the day that Malcolm X would become a commodity to be bought and sold in department stores."

Carl Wittaker, a political science professor at Concordia University, said many young people today have not actually read Malcolm X's autobiography, but have merely adopted the symbol of militancy and revolution.

"Wearing a cap with an X is not necessarily a recognition of the historical significance of the ideological commitment of Malcolm X and the many others of that period who have dedicated their lives to social change," he said.

Outside the theatre where the film premiered Wednesday night, perspectives varied. Some admitted to not knowing much about Malcolm X and had come to the movie to learn more about the man and the times.

One young man said he was there "merely to be entertained." One white woman, whose daughter was black was there "to learn more about my daughter's culture so that I can teach her about her own history."

Another young man said what most impresses him about Malcolm X was "his street life background and the obstacles he had to overcome in order to become such an inspirational figure."

Edina Bayne, director of the Black Community Council of Quebec, believes that the revival of Malcolm X is coming from black youths who are searching for an identity. It is not, she said, a "product" created for them by the media.

"The renewed interest in Malcolm X is part of our struggle as a people to redefine ourselves. It represents a bonding born out of separation, providing us with a unifying voice. This is a generation that has a voice and if the Ku Klux Klan raises its ugly head, this generation will not be silenced, they will take on the onslaught of racism."

Clarence Bayne, director of the Black Studies Centre, sees the revival of Malcolm X as a form of "popular rebellion"—a reaction to massive black unemployment, to continued discriminatory practices and to violence against the oppressed.

"People from all walks of life have embraced the X symbol. I have seen conservatives and radicals alike wearing Malcolm X T-shirts. It is a recognition of the integrated man, not a statement about violence as some people may think.

"It is a visual statement. You react to it viscerally. There are two types of knowing—one that is literal and one that is intuitive and comes from lived experience. The nature of a symbol is that it transcends literal interpretations and enters into the spiritual domain of the collective unconscious, the collective soul and the collective history."

The Montreal black community has been deeply affected by recent racial tension here and elsewhere in North America, said Pat Dillon, director of CKUT Radio. "Last week marked the fifth anniversary of the death of Anthony Griffith by the Montreal Urban Community police. The community is looking for a symbol of hope and they're looking into the past, as people often do, to find direction. In Malcolm X they found a symbol of hope, the spirit of revolution, of black pride."

But some hope that the movie and interest in Malcolm X do more than stimulate interest in militancy. Carl Wittaker hopes that the movie transmits to young people the importance of commitment to social change, to community service, to leadership and a continued struggle for black liberation.

That kind of thing, however, cannot come from cinema alone. It has to come from structures within the black community that address the practical problems, while at the same time nourish a core of young people who will provide the new generation of leadership.

Malcolm X has endured because the outrage he articulated about the condition of blacks in North America still persists today. He has come to be the symbol of uncompromising moral and political leadership, someone who conveys the aspirations of people of African descent.

He continues to challenge us to resist oppression and join together in solidarity. It is a challenge as appropriate today as it was 30 years ago, perhaps more so.

Embodied in the spirit of Malcolm X is the potential for individual change and it is the human being's capacity for change that will help prepare us for a multiracial society.

When I emerged from the theatre on Wednesday night, I found a flyer from the KKK slapped against the windshield of my car. It described Malcolm X as a hate-monger and claimed that people wearing the X symbol are promoters of racism.

None of the police officers in the five or six cruisers parked strategically outside the Imperial Theatre had noticed who had put these flyers on cars lining Bleury St.

As I sped away into the night, I was overcome by outrage and sadness. That racism should still be so prevalent in our society today, so many years later.

# Two looks at the man called X
## An inspiration to a whole generation of young black youths to throw off old feelings of inferiority

November 26, 1992

Malcolm X had a powerful effect on my life, as it had on the lives of many other young black youth.

Malcolm gave us a framework within which to understand the world. He articulated the rage that burned within us and that we had never been able to express. He gave us a strong sense of identity and a fierce desire to become educated so that we too could be involved in the struggle for black liberation.

I remember being profoundly affected by the story of how he educated himself while in prison, copying out virtually every page of a dictionary in the wee hours of the morning.

What really inspired me was his saying that becoming literate is becoming free. I wanted to experience this freedom, too.

Malcolm X is probably the reason I completed my education and became a teacher.

Malcolm X, along with other black radicals of his day, was responsible for creating a new generation of black youth who were searching for ways of casting off the internalized images of ourselves as lesser beings and our history as less significant.

Being at the premiere of the movie Malcolm X was a rare experience. It gave me the chance to recapture some of my youthful rebelliousness and offered me the opportunity to reflect on the development of my black consciousness.

The film portrays the many dimensions of Malcolm as he evolved from street hustler to separationist Black Muslim to a man who came to believe in the possibility of "people of all races coming together as one."

Members of the audience responded to the movie depending on their own preconceived notions, either about Malcolm or about race relations in general.

Those who liked Malcolm's unbending black nationalism cheered when Malcolm indicted the white race for its crimes against the black race. The crowd applauded enthusiastically, for example, when Malcolm bluntly told a white college student who wanted to know what she could do to help the black cause, that she could do "nothing."

In his autobiography, Malcolm said he later regretted having responded as he did, wishing he could contact this young woman to tell her that whites who are sincere can be involved in the battle against racism. But those who had applauded so overwhelmingly probably wouldn't have wanted to hear those words. They took what they wanted of Malcolm and discarded the rest.

Those who shared Malcolm's revised message about the brotherhood of all races were undoubtedly pleased that the movie did present the changes that he underwent in the last years of his life when he began to embrace a more universal perspective.

43

Ku Klux Klan flyers that had been placed on the windshield of the cars parked outside the Imperial Theatre presented yet another perception of Malcolm, albeit a one-dimensional one—Malcolm the hate monger who advocated violence against the white race. No evidence to the contrary would have convinced them otherwise. They took from Malcolm what they could use to justify their own racism.

I was among the last to leave the theatre and hadn't yet seen the flyers when I was approached by an individual who had already found one and had angrily ripped it up. Apparently someone had told him that I wrote for The Gazette. He gathered each one of those pieces from the wet ground and handed them to me saying, "You got to write about this."

Under the dim lights of the street, chilled by the night air, a group of blacks and whites, from different backgrounds and with different experiences huddled over a car and pieced the flyer back together like a puzzle.

The puzzle was like a metaphor for what Malcolm X had tried to do. And we were left to puzzle over the man, his message and the complex problems of racism.

When we had pieced it together and were able to read its message, we were outraged. We looked at each other, wondering what action to take. I noticed two police cars in the parking lot facing the Imperial Theatre.

Jamming the pieces of the flyer in my pocket, I marched over to the cars and asked whether any of the officers had seen who had distributed these flyers. No one had seen anything and they didn't seem too interested.

I counted at least six police cars parked around the theatre—an intimidating presence for a departing black movie-goer—and yet the flyers were distributed right under their noses.

For me, the film was successful. It portrayed Malcolm as a person of great integrity, a person with a tremendous capacity to evolve. It portrayed Malcolm as a seeker of truth and not a demagogue. The movie expresses Malcolm's view that an open mind is the path to truth. As Malcolm said in his autobiography, "I have always kept an open mind which is necessary to the flexibility that must go hand in hand with every form of intelligent search for truth."

I think most people who saw the film were moved by it in some way. I left the theatre with a sense of solidarity and with the feeling that each one of us, like Malcolm X, could make a difference.

# Black . . . and invisible

## Blacks have been part of Montreal for hundreds of years. Why weren't they included in a major exhibit marking the city's 350th anniversary?

October 17, 1992

Ambivalence is the word that best described my reaction to the 350th celebrations—a direct result I suppose of my feelings of disenfranchisement in a society that has systematically negated my presence—despite the fact that my ancestors were among Canada's first settlers.

On the eve of the dismantling of the Ainsi Va La Ville exhibit at Bonsecours Market, which depicted Montreal's history, I decided to overcome my ambivalence and see the exhibit. I was not surprised to see the black presence—my presence—was non-existent.

The exhibit paid tribute to the founding fathers—men like Redpath,

Molson and Van Horne and even to the workers who carried out the dreams of these great industrialists. White faces one and all.

According to information provided at the exhibit, blacks did not arrive until the wave of Haitian immigration in the 1960s. There was no mention of an indigenous black community. Apparently, as far as organizers of the exhibit were concerned, we did not exist.

The only images of blacks were photos of two children, identified as being Haitian, a radio announcer also identified as being Haitian and an unidentified trumpeter (most likely American) playing at the Montreal Jazz Festival. These photos were dis-

played in a section intended to play tribute to the ethnic diversity of Montreal.

Among other items, this section included a cappuccino machine to mark the Italian presence and photos of Jewish people working in the clothing industry. Selections from Zorba the Greek and Hava Nagilah provided the background music.

In the area of the exhibit that paid

the time the first known slaves arrived in New France but despite this, it is often assumed that they are Montreal's newest immigrants," she wrote.

This is due to what she calls "cultural invisibility," caused in part by the lack of emphasis on blacks within Canadian historiography and a lack of visibility due to a relatively small population of francophone blacks in Montreal until the arrival of the Haitians.

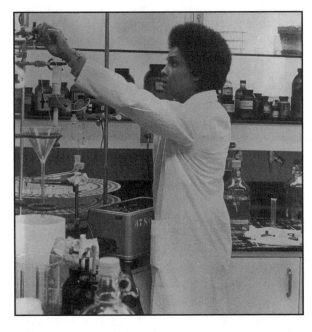

tribute to art and culture, there was no mention of such world-renowned black Montrealers as Percy Rodriguez or Oliver Jones. However, Oliver Jones was invited to attend the closing of the exhibit and did.

Dorothy Williams, author of Blacks in Montreal 1628–1986: An Urban Demography" explained why blacks are often overlooked in history.

"Blacks have been in Montreal from

There has been an obvious and systematic obfuscation of the historical black presence in this country," Williams writes. "Systematic racism . . . maintains this illusion that they (blacks) are foreigners to this soil, while it clearly sets up the assumption that Canada was, and is, a white country."

There was, as Williams's book makes clear, a vibrant black community in Montreal which grew significantly between 1897 and 1930, marked by the establishment of the Coloured Women's Club in 1902, the Negro Community Centre in 1927 and the Universal Negro Improvement Association in 1919. Montreal's black community grew from a meagre 300 blacks in 1897 to an estimated 5,000 by 1930, with 90 per cent of all working men employed by the railways.

Interestingly enough, a significant part of the Bonsecours exhibit was dedicated to the railway industry and to railway paraphernalia. Yet there was no word, photo or artifact depicting the presence of the black porters who worked the railways.

Porter paraphernalia—a shoeshine box and brush, porter's coat and hat, along with paintings, photographs and transcripts of interviews with porters, was on display this summer at the Black Studies Centre on de Maisonneuve Blvd., along with other historical works depicting the black presence here.

The 350th celebrations did help sponsor this event, and others representing other cultural communities.

Their sponsorship of this event however, does not exonerate them. The message that was sent out from the Bonsecours exhibit was loud and clear: the black presence was not deemed significant enough to be included in the main exhibit that tourists and Montrealers alike were most likely to see.

I asked Denis Jean, director of communications for the Musée de la Civilization which organized the exhibit, why the indigenous black population

was not represented in the main exhibit.

Jean replied that "we didn't make decisions on a racial basis. We had to make choices. Why we made the choices that we made, I don't know."

Jean emphasized again that the decision was not a racially oriented one.

"I'd have to speak to my psychiatrist to know if my choices were unconscious."

Clarence Bayne, director of the Black Studies Centre was outraged by the lack of representation of blacks in the 350th celebrations. "To hell with the 350th," he said in an interview. Early in the planning stages of the celebrations, he wrote to 350th organizers expressing the need to include the black presence in the mainstream exhibits. Bayne said he made it a point not to attend any of the 350th events as a sign of his profound disappointment.

What goes into the making of history and what gets left out, depends on the point of view of the teller. The facts of history never come to us in "pure" form. They are always refracted through the mind of the recorder, or in this case, the curator of the exhibit. History does not tell us what happened, but only what people want to convey to us about what happened. The process of history is inherently a process of selection and exclusion.

What is not said is sometimes just as significant as what is. The fact that there was virtually no mention of the presence of black Montrealers—a community that dates back at least 300 years—"speaks" in a way that is just as significant as having a state-

47

ment of racial policies and practices.

Montreal has a Declaration Against Racial Discrimination permanently displayed for all to see, but the exhibit at Bonsecours told another story—a story of exclusion and omission and, ultimately, of discrimination.

The seminal question here is not why the black presence was absent from this exhibit, but, to paraphrase black feminist author Toni Morrison, what intellectual feats had to be performed in order to erase the black presence so effectively?

The exhibit was an example of the hidden ways in which the dominant culture succeeds in rendering certain groups invisible by minimizing their presence and marginalizing their contributions.

Fighting racism involves recovering the "narratives" that have traditionally been left out of Western accounts of history.

As educational author Henry Giroux points out in his latest book, "Border Crossings," the dominant culture secures its dominance by presenting its narrative as the only narrative, its version of history as the only version, its version of reality, as the only reality. It is time to challenge this "master narrative" with "counter narratives" that navigate across borders to embrace differences.

Locating ourselves in history is fundamental to self-empowerment. In the future, public exhibits of this kind should be prepared in consultation with the cultural communities so that their voices can be heard and their presence felt.

Such was the case of the Kanienkehland exhibit also on display at the Bonsecours Market, which was a sensitive portrayal of the history, culture and aspirations of the Mohawk nation by the Mohawk people.

Gazette columnist John Griffin's July 11 article about the Bonsecours exhibit begins with the sentence: "If the 350th proves nothing else it will prove that history can be interesting."

I'd like to change the last word of his sentence to read as follows: "If the 350th proves nothing else it will prove that history can be erased."

48

# Remembering the other forgotten soldier

November 5, 1992

Remembrance Day always brings me back to rainy Novembers when my father would take us down to Dominion Square to commemorate the lost lives of his comrades-in-arms.

When he donned his poppy and veteran's pin, he seemed to stand taller than I ever remembered him.

Shivering from the cold, I would move closer to him for warmth. He put his strong hands firmly on my shoulder, pressing me closer to him. His pride was my pride.

I remember the preparations for that day. Each of us would have to shine our shoes, to have what he referred to as a "spit-polish shine." When you look at that shoe, you should be able to see the reflection of your face. And if you didn't, he'd make you do it again. He'd take a quarter out of his pocket and drop it on one of our beds. If it bounced, we passed inspection.

Everyone understood the importance of these ceremonial proceedings. When the final preparations ware concluded, when every shirt was tucked in, every button done up and ties so tight you felt as if you were about to choke, we were ready to embark on our trip to Dominion Square.

Beaming with pride, I'd ask him, "Dad, how do I look?" And he'd reply, "Sharp as a tack and twice as dangerous." Then, like soldiers on parade, he'd march all nine of us children out the door.

My father's wartime experiences

My father, Harold Ruggles in Annapolis Valley, Nova Scotia (March 17, 1953)

were very positive. He was very proud of being part of the liberation forces. He felt it was among the few times he, as a black man, was regarded as a human being and I guess that's why he wanted to remember it.

Most of my dad's life was spent experiencing rejection and discrimination. Suddenly, for the first time in his life, thousands of white faces welcomed him as he marched through towns in Europe as part of the liberation troops.

Blacks were very much divided over participation in the war: for some it was a white man's struggle. Other blacks, however, saw the war as a

"God-sent blessing," in the words of one black newspaper at the time, "to earn white regard and advance the standing of the race by valiant wartime service."

Even then, the debate over military service by blacks wasn't new.

Robin Winks, in his book Blacks in Canada, reports that during World War I, blacks were not allowed to enlist. The commander of the 104th Overseas Battalion wrote that he rejected 19 black volunteers from Saint John: "I have been fortunate to have secured a very fine class of recruits, and I did not think it was fair to these men that they should have to mingle with negroes."

The commander of the 106th Battalion, on the other hand believed that "coloured men should do their share in the Empire's defense" and was willing to accept them. However, since several whites who were on the verge of enlisting refused to do so if black men were allowed to enlist, he decided not to accept them.

Here is how he expressed it in a letter found in the General Headquarters papers: "Neither my men nor myself would care to sleep along-side Negroes, or to eat with them, especially in warm weather."

The commander of the military came up with a compromise. He suggested that "Negroes might be welcomed into some French-Canadian units and because of their great capacity for manual work, they could be taken into a construction battalion."

And thus, the No. 2 Negro Construction Battalion was formed on July 5, 1916.

During World War II, the Canadian army initially rejected black volunteers, although seldom openly on grounds of race, and the Royal Canadian Air Force was reported to have refused to accept qualified black applicants. Army officers had to be British subjects and when West Indian students applied for the university officers' training plan, they found "British subjects" meant "white subjects."

In 1941, the black community, under the leadership of Rev. Este of the Union United Church in Montreal, protested against the racist policy of the military. As the war accelerated and the protest within the black community mounted, blacks in Montreal were finally permitted to serve.

As a gesture of his profound belief in democracy, Owen Rowe left his homeland in Barbados and came to Canada to join the armed forces in 1942. To his dismay, he discovered that he would not be sent to serve in the Pacific.

Rowe recalled in a recent interview: "I was supposed to go to the Pacific front but then the Canadian commander called me to his office and said, 'Sorry Rowe, it's not our fault. The Canadian troops in the Pacific are under the indirect command of the American forces and they don't want blacks.'" Frustrated and disgusted, he transferred into the air force and eventually became a flying officer.

Being in the air force was not without some racial tensions.

He remembered a serviceman in his barracks kept eying him. "Eventually he approached me and said: 'You don't smell. You wear clean clothes. You don't talk about women all the time. I can't figure it out. You're not at all what I expected.'"

"At least he had the guts to confront his prejudices. Many others didn't. What I can't figure is, when you're down there in the dirt, when you're on that battlefield, you're all the same."

"Colour doesn't matter."

Oct. 24 marked the 50th anniversary of Owen Rowe's arrival to Canada, as it did the arrival of other West Indians who came to fight in World War II.

In 1962, on the 20th anniversary, Rowe convened a reunion of those West Indian war veterans in the Montreal area. Twenty years later, in 1982, they convened again and it was at this gathering that an association was formed and a decision was made to have an annual get-together.

"Tears still come to our eyes when we talk about our comrades lost in arms. It's important for us to remember. That's why we still get together after all these years. We have a responsibility to remember. . . that our history—black history—will be recorded for all time."

These men had fought for democracy, lived through a war, paid their dues and they had greater expectations than before. For some, it was the first time in their lives when they had experienced a kind of equality—the equality of the battlefield.

The war experience gave these black men a sense of self-worth, the belief that they too could play a role in shaping history. They came back with a sense of honour and dignity and the hope that their contribution would be acknowledged.

Dorothy Williams, author of Blacks in Montreal 1628–1986, reports that World War II helped to improve conditions for blacks. It increased employment and lessened their marginal status after the war.

The war years are remembered as the first time when blacks were able to demonstrate and exercise their level of proficiency and education.

Another key aspect was the acquisition of war veterans' benefits. The black veteran returned to the community able to benefit from university training, grants of land, loans for houses.

But some of the gains made against discrimination in the military were lost after the war. Montreal's white veterans did not want to associate with their black comrades, so the Canadian Legion segregated its members and established coloured war veterans' branches.

Well-known black historian W.E.B. Dubois once wrote of the black soldiers who fought in the wars: "Perhaps their greatest credit is the fact that they withstood so bravely and uncomplainingly the barrage of hatred and offensive prejudice aimed against them."

My father believed in the ideals of liberty, justice and equality for all, regardless of skin colour.

Ironically, he fought for these ideals halfway across the world, only to return home to face an old, familiar enemy—systemic racism.

And that battle rages on.

# Black History Month: Does it really help?

February 4, 1993

February is Black History Month and schools will be putting us on the educational agenda. A month is better than nothing, I suppose.

I must confess I have always been a little leery of approaches that designate a particular day or month for the study of a group of people.

Although this approach may have its merits, it is based on the premise that exposure to other cultures will decrease prejudice. This "tourist approach," as it has been called, often amounts to nothing more than putting up bulletins on specified cultural days or hosting once-a-year assemblies to celebrate minority historical figures.

I am not cynical about the concept of Black History Month, only its scope and implementation. I strongly believe it is important for us to articulate our cultural identity—an identity that, for the most part, has been rendered invisible.

It is important for young black youth to know whence they came, to know the struggles of their ancestors and to derive strength from this knowledge.

Studying black history is as important for white students as it is for black ones, not only because it would give them more knowledge about black culture, but because it would give them knowledge about their own privileged position within history.

As the late African-American author James Baldwin put it, such knowledge would be "liberating to white people who know nothing of their own true history. If you have to lie about my real role here, if you have to pretend that I hoed all that cotton just because I loved you, then you've done something to yourself."

Eric Mansfield, of the multicultural department at the Protestant School Board of Greater Montreal, said he believes black history is important for students because they should know that "our history goes back more than 400 years. History is taught as if ancient Egypt were not a part of Africa. Yet it was. The ancestry of the Egyptians can be traced to Ethiopia and to the colonization and development of the ancient Greek civilization.

"Black kids are made to feel that they are not part of that history. We should not be allowing the dominant culture to define who we are."

Dorothy Williams, author of Blacks in Montreal, says it is important to examine how blacks figured in Quebec's exploration, settlement and development and why most historians have ignored, denied or suppressed black history.

"Blacks must be included not because we are new to Quebec but rather because we are old," Williams said. "The denial of slavery in Quebec over the past 156 years has only served to confuse. So many people believe that blacks are a recent addition to the fabric of Quebec. . . . The historical ignorance makes it easy to assume the problems faced by blacks today are part of their own cultural baggage transplanted from different cultures."

Williams went on to explain that when information was made public that Marguerite d'Youville owned slaves, callers to radio shows de-

Carifête Parade

nounced the black community for perpetrating lies, so strong was their unwillingness to believe that slavery had existed in Quebec.

Leon Jacobs, who teaches black studies at Dawson College, said what he finds particularly disturbing is "hearing official bodies like the police or government agencies who are unaware of just how long blacks have been in this country."

"When talking about black people they immediately refer to us as immigrants. Blacks have remained perpetual immigrants. In parts of southwest Ontario and Nova Scotia, black history goes back at least 10 generations."

The other reason for Black History Month is to teach people that racism still exists. The stories of Donald Marshall and Marcellus Francois must be told because these things go on. There is a smugness as Canadians compare themselves with Americans: we are better, we shielded people. That myth has to be exploded. Racism happens in this country, at this time and we have to face up to it.

Black History Month should go beyond a mere recovery of the past, but rather should give us insight into the different ways in which we are shaped by the telling of history.

For students, a cross-cultural perspective is essential because histories are written by humans and as such are biased. There is a need to open dialogue among different cultural groups about history. This would lead to a better understanding of the tensions among different ethnic groups.

Celebrating black history represents the struggle of memory against forgetting. It means reclaiming the legacies of pain and triumph that is our past, so that it may inform and transform the present.

# Black newspaper plays important role

April 7, 1994

If you've ever gone into Mom's Caribbean Haven on Sherbrooke St. in Notre Dame de Grace [N.D.G.] to buy Jamaican patties, you might have seen an issue of Community Contact, the black community newspaper, and you might even have leafed through it while your order was being filled.

Community Contact, published and edited by Egbert Gaye, surfaced two years ago and can be found in many West End stores, especially those that serve the black community.

The newspaper is published monthly out of Gaye's Girouard Ave. apartment and is distributed free. It receives no government subsidies and survives strictly by the selling of ad space. Besides writing, editing and selling ads, Gaye, 37, also delivers the 5,000 to 10,000 copies to various sites around the city.

### 'Labour of love'

All those who contribute to the newspaper are volunteers, including Gaye, who draws no salary and makes no profit. In fact, sometimes Gaye has had to use his own funds to get an edition out when the advertising dollars just weren't there.

Why does he do it? Because he believes it's important, because he believes he's making a contribution to his community, Gaye said. "It's a labour of love.

"You play a dual role," he said. "On the one hand, you're highlighting the black community, showing the rest of society what blacks are accomplishing. On the other hand, you're acting like a watchdog: keeping the community honest, being critical of any wrongdoing."

Gaye has a degree in journalism and political science from Concordia University and is no stranger to managing community news, having worked for Afro-Can, a competing black community newspaper with a more Afro-centric slant.

Gaye said he wanted to create a paper that didn't advocate one particular viewpoint, but presented information from many sources and perspectives. His goal was to bridge journalistic principles and advocacy.

"Doing this kind of journalism is very different from managing mainstream news," Gaye said. "You can't apply all those principles you learned in journalism school. Objectivity and impartiality simply don't exist in community news because it's not about managing news, it's about building community, it's about social change.

"You walk a fine line," he said. "You don't want to misinform people or give them partial information or start unsubstantiated rumours. You go for accuracy and reliability, but you're also aware that you can't be impartial or objective. You're part of the story and you have a stake in it."

For Gaye, the hardest thing is reporting on the negative elements within the community. Recently, Community Contact ran an article about sexual harassment in the black community. Gaye said he tried to stay away from the issue as long as he could, hoping it would somehow go away. But it didn't,

54

and he went ahead and published an article on it.

"Sexual harassment is something the black community never talks about. It's such a touchy issue," Gaye said. "I'm glad we opened it up because we're finding that people really want to talk about it."

On the whole, Gaye said, the community has been very supportive. And he said the paper simply wouldn't exist without the help of volunteer writers and the support that comes in the form of paid ads from the community.

According to Gaye, alternative community newspapers are necessary because "there's an inherent bias that mainstream media have when it comes to reporting on the black community."

Gaye said he believes that the answer lies in having more black students going into journalism and eventually occupying more positions in mainstream media. When he graduated from Concordia in 1988, there were few black students in journalism and he said the numbers haven't changed significantly.

Although there have not been many blacks involved in journalism in Canada, there have been some notable ones. Between 1854 and 1859, Mary Ann Shadd edited the weekly Provincial Freeman in Windsor, Toronto and Chatham, Ont. (Shadd Academy in Cote des Neiges is named after her.)

According to Robin Winks, author of Blacks in Canada, Shadd was worried by the constant quarrelling within the black leadership and by the un-

willingness of different black groups to work together.

The same issues that plagued the black community then still do so today.

In Nova Scotia, Carrie Best founded the Clarion in 1946. What started as a church bulletin became a four-page bimonthly publication. By 1949, Best began nationwide circulation of her newspaper under the name Negro Citizen.

## Politically conservative

According to Winks, there had been, up to the time of the publication of his book in 1971, 23 black newspapers in Canadian history.

Many of them were politically conservative, shying away from issues of racial discrimination, choosing instead to focus on racial pride, which often took the form of reporting on local social events and highlighting local black businesses.

However, short-lived and myopic these newspapers were, they did contribute to the black community's sense of pride and from that perspective they can be seen as having been a source of strength.

Today's black community newspapers must have a wider mandate and a greater vision. They need to provide accurate information and thought-provoking critiques that help develop a greater understanding of issues of concern to the black community. They should create dialogue with the hope of spurring action to unify an otherwise fragmented community.

# Black Church's roots in Montreal go back to 1907

October 5, 1995

When I was growing up, going to church Sunday morning was one ritual in our family that I will never forget. In order for all nine of us to get ready for church we had to get up at the ungodly hour of 6 a.m. Once the jockeying for the bathroom was over, the tedious task of hair grooming began with older children fighting with the younger ones until every little nap of hair was perfectly in place. Even God up in heaven would have to take notice of our neatly groomed hair and our freshly scrubbed angelic faces.

When every bow tie was snapped into place and every pigtail had a brightly coloured ribbon attached to it, my father would come out to inspect us. Once we passed inspection,

Rev. Gabourel in front of Union United Church

he'd give each of us ten cents for the collection plate.

At church we were told the money would be used to feed and educate the poor. We were struck by the irony of giving money to the poor since we were "the poor". That being the case, we devised a system—half of us gave in the dime and the other half pocketed the money to be used later to buy ice cream. So long as nothing dripped on

attendance, we certainly would have been in first place.

Going to church certainly kept us off the streets. Although I found it difficult to stay awake through some of the fire and brimstone sermons, (especially when I came home late the night before), I did manage to walk away with a sense of right and wrong. And to this day I can still quote some of the books and verses from the bible.

Rev. and Mrs. Bigby at Marcus Garvey Jr. Dinner

our clothes, no one would be the wiser. Being the god fearing children that we were, we hoped God would forgive us for our minor indiscretion.

Like many children, we tried to played hooky from church and especially from Sunday school, whenever we could. We used every imaginable excuse from stomach aches to malaria—but to no avail. The parade to church occurred no matter what. It was my father's finest moment—to enter church with all nine of use in tow—for all the congregation to see. Rain or shine, sick or healthy, in the worst snowstorms in Montreal's history, the Ruggles children were in church. If God gave out awards for

The most significant part of going to church was being part of a community and participating in the activities of the church.

Like many black families, my parents believed that "church-going" and the values it promoted were the essential cornerstones to healthy, well adjusted lives.

Religion has been important to people of African descent. It represented one of the few outlets available to African slaves on the plantations. In some areas blacks were not allowed to gather in groups of more than five except in church. There they were allowed to meet, with the owners permission, provided that their services were strictly religious and musical. Out of the slave interpretation of Christianity and its practices emerged what has come to be known as the Black Church—an institution which has played a pivotal role in the survival of people of African descent. Prayer meetings and other church services were used as opportunities to plan attacks on the slave system.

In time the Black Church performed a variety of roles in the fields of education, social welfare, employment, civil rights and immigration and served as a unifying centre for blacks. Some of the most prominent black leaders have emerged from the ranks of the church.

"In the late 1800s blacks were not welcomed in white churches or if we were permitted to attend, we were relegated to the galleries" says Rev. Bigby, of the Union United Church, Montreal's oldest black congregation which was founded in 1907 by a group of Canadian Pacific Railway porters.

One of its first ministers was Reverend Charles Este, under whose 43 year leadership the Union United Church became a pioneer in helping blacks find employment. Rev. Este was instrumental in getting black soldiers admitted into the army, helping black nurses find positions in city hospitals which up to that point had not been hiring black nurses. The Union United Church spawned many other organizations which became the backbone of the black community in Montreal—the Negro Community Centre, the Coloured Women's Club, the Negro Theatre Guild where Percy Rodriguez started his career. The first black library was started in the early 40s in the basement of the church.

Thelma Weeks, who received an honorary doctorate from Concordia University for her work with children at the N.D.G. YMCA, spoke about the Union United Church and her memories of Rev. Este during an interview: "Rev. Este held the community together. He was so commanding. When he was aroused about an injustice he was not afraid to stand up and speak out."

Historically the black church has played a fundamental role in emphasizing black self affirmation and awareness and pressing for necessary social changes. However, practicing Christianity for many blacks has also meant "turning the other cheek", walking in humility and enduring cruel and debasing treatment. Since the days of slavery black folks have learned to sublimate their anger in order to increase their chances for survival. Unfortunately these practices have also obscured the struggle for freedom and has led to the loss of credibility of the church in the black community.

To maintain its leadership role, the black church must continue to address issues of poverty, discrimination, education, underemployment as well as the celebration of African heritage. It has to challenge the religious icons that contradict black experience and consciousness. And it must work to counteract the despair and powerlessness that many black people feel in today's society by continuing to emphasize self affirmation and self esteem.

# It's not a black Christmas
## Kwanzaa is a holiday that we can call our own

December 8, 1994

From the day after Christmas until the first day of the new year, many African-Americans and African-Canadians celebrate Kwanzaa.

The name comes from the East African Swahili phrase "matunda ya kwanza," meaning "the first fruits," and refers to a harvest celebration similar in some ways to Thanksgiving. It's not the black version of Christmas, as some people may think, although it does take place around the same time.

According to the creator of Kwanzaa, Maulana Karenga, professor and chairman of black studies at California State University at Long Beach, "first fruit" celebrations are recorded in African history as far back as Egypt and Nubia and appear in ancient and modern times in Ashanti, Yoruba and Zulu cultures.

The African-American origins of Kwanzaa go back to the 1960s Black Movement which stressed the reconstruction of African history and culture.

For Karenga, Kwanzaa is a product of creative cultural synthesis, including both continental African and diaspora African cultural elements. He said it was important for black people all over the world to have one holiday that is truly their own.

According to Karenga, there are five common values and practices central to African "first fruit" celebrations: ingathering, reverence, commemoration, recommitment and celebration.

Olivia Rovinescu

Kwanzaa celebration at my daughter's school

"Ingathering" refers not only to crops but also to people, a bringing together of the most valuable fruits or products of the nation, its living human harvests.

"Reverence" refers to respect for creation and a concern about living in harmony with nature.

"Commemoration" of the past is particularly important to Kwanzaa. To commemorate the past is a also to commemorate people's struggles to shape their world in their own image and interest.

"Recommitment" to cultural ideals refers to reaffirmation and dedication to co-operation, reciprocity, collective responsibility, sharing and mutual caring as the grounding and social glue for the community.

"Celebration," the fifth aspect of Kwanzaa, is about renewing acquaintances, dialogue, narrative, poetry, dancing, singing, drumming and feasting.

## Building on the past

The celebrations begin on the first of seven days of Kwanzaa, when a hand-woven mat is placed on a table top, which is meant to represent the past. On the mat is placed the "kinara" or candle holder, symbolizing all black people past and present. Also placed on the mat is a basket filled with "mazao" or crops. One ear of corn is included for every child in the home.

The seven candles in the "kinara" stand for unity, self-determination, collective work and responsibility, co-operative economics, community development, creativity and belief on our people.

When the candles are lit, family members, including the children, say how they plan to honour those principles in the year to come.

Children are encouraged to participate in Kwanzaa as fully as they are able.

My first experience with Kwanzaa was in the late 1960s in Roxbury, in the heart of Boston. I was fascinated by the array of African costumes and the sense of ceremony. I had never before been exposed to the richness of African life and culture and I was suddenly filled with a sense of pride that I had never experienced before.

I attended my second Kwanzaa celebration at Le Manoir in Notre Dame de Grace last year with my family and it was just as memorable as the first.

I marvelled at the atmosphere of festivity and the richness of heritage passed on from one generation to the next through these ceremonies.

I have participated in both Hanukkah and Christmas celebrations over the years but never felt that these celebrations had much to do with me. I have enjoyed them, but much like a cultural voyeur experiencing somebody else's customs and rituals.

My daughters' reactions were as interesting as they were different. The 4-year-old got right into it, readily participating with the rest of the children dressed in their African regalia. From the proud expression on her face, you could see that she felt that she fit right in.

The 9-year-old however, was more reticent, less willing to embrace yet another cultural celebration at this time of year. Handling both Hanukkah and Christmas is a lot. Where did this new holiday suddenly come in?

## Questions of identity

For her, Kwanzaa brought with it questions about her identity as a multiracial person. Can she legitimately participate in all these cultural celebrations without being disloyal to some?

Our answer was an emphatic "yes." In this case, "more is better."

Far those who are interested in knowing more about Kwanzaa, the display window of Ethnic Origins Book Store on Notre Dame St. W. and Atwater Ave. shows various objects relating to the Kwanzaa celebration. The store carries a wide selection of books on the subject for both young and old.

# Black history: Racism on the railway
## Porters who fought back were fired

February 11, 1995

Trains have always had a certain significance in my life—hardly surprising since my father spent most of his working life on trains. Back and forth he'd go between Montreal and Vancouver; 10 days on, four days off. His job: to carry travellers' suitcases, make their beds, make sure they got off at the right destination.

As a boy, I thought there wasn't a more exciting job on earth than being a railway porter. Then I worked as a porter myself—partly because I needed the money and partly to learn more about my father's life.

For many years, being a porter was the best job a black man could get, and those who worked on the railroad were considered among the fortunate few. It was steady work. They met different people and got to see this country. And in the early part of the century, black men who worked as porters were able to provide for their families in ways that other black men were not.

My father never talked to us about his work on the railroad.

Maybe it was his way of protecting us, and maybe it was this reluctance that made me want to know more about it. It was only after his death, when I was in my early 20s and a McGill student that I dared apply for a porter's job.

The old-timers who knew my father were glad to have me on board. "Kenny's boy," they called me. They made it clear that by the time I came along in the early 1970s, working conditions had improved dramatically. The hours used to be much longer and the racism more pronounced.

In 1930, 90 per cent of all working

Winnipeg Station

black men in Montreal were employed by the railways, Dorothy Williams says in her book, Blacks in Montreal 1628–1986.

"It's important to remember that in those days there were no black bus-drivers, no black taxi-drivers, no black policemen, no black store clerks," film-maker Selwyn Jacobs, who is planning a new film tentatively called

Sleeping Car Porter, wrote in a brief summary about the film.

"Blacks could not rent or build in certain parts of the country and blacks could not even get a haircut in some barbershops.

"Within this context, the job of porter was not only the best job available, it was the only job."

Jacobs hopes the film will give viewers insights into how the porters coped with their abhorrent working conditions and will look at the emergence of black community organizations that helped these men.

While they were fortunate to have the job, it was not easy being a black sleeping-car porter. The harassment came both from management and from passengers.

Retired sleeping-car conductor and ex-porter Ernie Husband recalls that one of the racial insults frequently levelled at porters was being called "George," a generic name given to slaves in the southern U.S., which came to be as demeaning as being called "nigger." Some porters couldn't take the abuse, fought back, and were fired.

"To work as a porter meant you had to be diplomatic in dealing with prejudice," Husband said in an interview. "The guys who lost their jobs were the ones who didn't know how to handle the passengers.

"The worst was working the bar car because you had to be an entertainer. People would get drunk and make racist jokes and you had to continue being Mr. Personality.

"Many of the guys just couldn't handle that kind of job. Sometimes my nose would just start bleeding. I think it was the stress of constantly dealing with people."

"Racism was always there," retired porter and sleeping-car conductor Carl Simmons said, "but there was very little you could do about it. You (had to) fight it with your mind."

"We were treated like 5-year-olds," another porter told me. "We couldn't talk back. If you did, they'd punish you, put you out on the street and make your wife come down and beg for your job.

"The passengers would insult us, humiliate us, and no matter what insult was hurled at us, the conductors were always reprimanding us, apologizing to them, promising them that we would be disciplined."

Several porters I interviewed years ago when I worked on the trains spoke to me on condition they'd never be named. Many were reluctant to be frank, and it was clear they still worried about losing their jobs.

"Most of these men had families and they wanted their kids to get a good education and they tried to do their work and stay out of trouble," one porter said. "They'd have died if someone had taken their jobs away from them for no reason. I've seen men cry like babies and shake."

One retired porter told me that some of his colleagues had such disdain for the uniforms that symbolized their degradation that they burned them on retiring.

False accusations frequently arose from personality clashes with white conductors, who filed reports that resulted in demerit marks or firings. Sometimes they claimed porters had become familiar with female passengers—an accusation often levelled against someone close to retirement as an excuse to deny him a pension.

The first black sleeping-car porters were hired in the U.S. in the 1860s by George Pullman, president of the Pullman Railway Co. Black workers provided cheap labour. Also, it was considered natural, and actually prestigious, for white passengers to accept services from black porters.

Wages were low and porters were expected to supplement them through tips. But sometimes, even with a smile and cheerful service, they still didn't make the tips necessary to earn a decent living.

"Yes sir, Mr. Charley, no sir, Mr. Charley," is how one porter characterized it. "From the minute you get on that train, you wear a mask, and you don't take it off until you get off that train."

Gradually, things changed. Younger porters were less willing to put up with insults and abuse. But as late as the 1970s when I worked the trains, some inspectors still demanded porters shine passengers' shoes. One inspector actually smelled the shoes to see if they were freshly shined. Some of us put some smelly cheese into a shoe once to teach him a lesson.

"I always tried to satisfy the customer," said one retired porter who was over 90 when I interviewed him. "If someone bawled me out, well, I never paid him no mind. One fellow come out of his compartment one morning and I says, 'Good morning, sir,' like I usually do. He started cussing me out, 'Goddammit boy, don't be saying nothing to nobody lest they be saying something to you first.'

"I didn't say nothing except, 'Yes sir.' And that's how it went. No use in getting mad. Someone'd bawl me out, I just paid him no mind. You're a servant, see, no matter what they say, you've got to be polite, that's your job."

Not everyone endured the harassment quietly. In the summer of 1918, the black porters of the Canadian National Railway's transcontinental run organized the Order of Sleeping Car Porters. When they applied to the Brotherhood of Railway Workers, they were told its constitution restricted membership to whites. As a compromise, the brotherhood agreed to charter the proposed order as an auxiliary organization.

From 1955 to 1961, Lee Williams, chairman of the Winnipeg local, lodged repeated protests against the discriminatory clause in the collective agreement that prevented porters from being promoted to sleeping-car conductors. Finally, the Canadian Labour Congress launched a human-rights inquiry and reported that the CN as well other railways had indeed practiced a policy of racial discrimination.

The story goes that while Williams worked on the trains he met John Diefenbaker, who sent him a copy of the Canadian Fair Employment Practice Act to help him in his fight.

As Williams tells it, "Diefenbaker was a good man, because when he would get on the train, instead of talking to other people he would come back and talk to the porter. It was he who advised me to lay a complaint."

# Women of great achievement
## Perhaps unrecognized, they're not remote but in our homes and communities

March 9, 1995

When I first started to write today's column in honour of International Women's Day, marked yesterday, I planned to write only about black women who have made great achievements.

Then it occurred to me that so many black women have made contributions—women like my mother and all the others who helped build our community. The black community could not have survived without their efforts.

"Men write history, women are history," newspaper publisher and broadcaster Carrie Best wrote in her autobiography. "Long before there was a women's liberation movement, the black female was involved in a death struggle for physical and mental survival, both for herself and her family."

This quote exemplifies my mother's existence. One of eight children,

Annie Stucker, one of the oldest members of the Montreal Black community

she grew up in a shack beside railway tracks not far from the docks in Yarmouth, N.S. Like many other women of her day, she had few opportunities. As in Langston Hughes's poem, she watched her dreams dry up like a "raisin in the sun."

She came to Montreal in the hope of making a better life, but soon discovered there were very few jobs, other than working as a domestic, open to black women.

### Household servants

Peggy Bristow, in a book titled Recovering Women's History, describes what times were like for blacks after the economic crash of 1929: "Young black men could not move around the country in search of work. Nor had industrialization benefited black woman wage-earners. The only work to be had for most, in the best of times, was as a hired hand or a household servant.

"For the women, the scarcity of work and wage made them reach even deeper for ways of stretching their limited resources."

In his study on blacks in Canada, James Walker points out that, in 1941, 80 per cent of black adult females in Montreal were employed as servants. Whereas women from other ethnic groups saw maid's work as a stepping stone to other occupations, black

Betty Reilly, founder of "Black Is" community television station

65

Jane Kuehaganga, Esmarelda Thornhill, Emily Clyke
at Celebration of Coloured Women's Club.
Mrs. Clyke receives award for outstanding contributions to the black community.

women were trapped in domestic service. Racism denied black women access to factory jobs until World War II.

## Resisting racism

Despite the hardships, black women all over the country continued a long tradition of activity in community organizing.

In the mid-19th century, black women organized the first True Band Society in Amherstburg, Ont., to improve black schools and arbitrate disputes, giving assistance to those in need and resisting racism. By 1856 there were 13 True Band Societies in Ontario.

In 1882, black women established the Women's Home Missionary Society. According to the account of Dorothy Shadd Shreve, the women "travelled about on horseback, through the bush and over roads almost impassable at times, ministering to the sick, collecting and delivering food and clothing to the needy and preaching the Gospel."

In Montreal, the Coloured Women's Club was established in 1902 and has a long list of humanitarian and social-service credits.

Since there were virtually no social services in those days, the club's initiatives were extraordinarily important. It operated soup kitchens and maintained a bed at the local hospital. Its members volunteered as nurses and mothers' aides. The club also provided bursaries for black students and helped establish a black-studies library at the Negro Community Centre.

Women in the United Negro Improvement Association organized a branch of the Universal Black Cross nurses. Black women also played a role in organizing the Brotherhood of Sleeping Car Porters. They also organized Negro History Week, the predecessor of Black History Month.

There are several exceptional black Canadian women everyone should know about. These are some: Mary Ann Shadd, teacher, author, lecturer, school principal, lawyer, wife and mother, became the first woman editor of a weekly newspaper in North America. The paper, the Provincial Freeman, was published between 1854 and 1859 in Ontario. Among other things, she enrolled in the law faculty at Howard University and established a successful law practice at the age of 60. Shadd Academy in Cote des Neiges is named after her.

Anne Packwood is a former president of the Coloured Women's Club and chairman of the Montreal Health Council of Women. In 1956, she undertook a program for the CBC on child care, with the focus on the multiracial child. In the 1930s and '40s, she took part in the Negro Theatre and performed with Percy Rodriguez in the prizewinning play The Emperor Jones. Her sister, Clara de Shield, was a founder of the Negro Community Centre.

Teacher Velma Weeks, of Notre Dame de Grace, is a pioneer in the organization of the Montreal Nursery School Association and in children's creative programs at the local YMCA. She received an honorary doctorate from Concordia University for her advocacy work for children.

Carrie Best, now in her 90s, probably has received the most recognition for her humanitarian work. Best was honoured with the Order of Canada and an honorary doctorate of law from St. Francis Xavier University in Nova Scotia, for her long involvement in community affairs and civil rights. She was a newspaper editor and columnist from 1946–56.

Maisie Dickensen-Dash.
Active in the Montreal Black community

Black women today bear the same burden as their predecessors. They are asking a lot of questions about their role in this society, however.

During a recent interview, Sherrie Elder, a social worker from Notre Dame de Grace, described their problems:

"Everybody is standing on our shoulders. The black man is standing on our shoulders. The white woman is standing on his shoulders and the white man is on top.

"We have done too much, as far as I'm concerned, too much for others. We have to start doing more for ourselves.

"We've had to be strong. But are we buying our strength by weakening our men? I'm hoping to see more young women asking these sorts of questions. And I'm hoping that standing next to them are the young black men who are listening and asking the same sorts of questions."

# Black History Month is better than ever

February 23, 1995

I guess practice does make perfect. Every year it seems that Black History Month gets better.

This year is no exception. Performances celebrating black historical and cultural contributions ranged from lectures, art exhibits, music, theatre, dance, film, poetry and even a demonstration on caring for black hair.

Black History Month evolved out of African-American educator Carter G. Woodsen's 1926 Negro History Week. It has a dual purpose: celebrate the experiences and achievements of blacks and educate blacks as well as non-blacks about that history.

The West End had its share of Black History Month events. "Free Your Mind Return to the Source" at the Loyola Concert Hall featured more than two dozen musicians. It showcased the evolution of black music from the chants and drumbeats from the heart of Africa, to the Americas, from slavery to hip hop.

In the middle of one of the worst winter storms this year, blacks and whites came together to hear the sounds and the stories of the African diaspora.

One of the most impressive performers was South African vocalist Lorraine Klaasen.

She sang songs that spoke of the black struggle for liberation in South Africa as well as a song based on a traditional cry of joy. And she reminded parents of the importance of teaching children about their ancestors and culture.

Maison de la Culture Notre Dame de Grace and Maison de la Culture Cote des Neiges had a full array of

Bust of Tommy Simmons at National Gallery in Ottawa Black History Month Celebrations, February 1995

activities to celebrate Black History month. I was particularly taken with Pat Dillon's portrayal of a black domestic talking about life, politics and the condition of black women in "Clemmie is M'friend."

The one-woman play gives historical significance to all the black women who have worked as domestics, my mother included, and who in some ways have been the backbone of the black community.

During the play, she reads aloud a letter she to her mother and children in Jamaica. She tells of the police shootings of black men and recounts the bitter irony of how these black men were killed. She concludes her letter by telling her mother not to send her teenage son for fear that he might become one of the police statistics.

Even the National Gallery of Canada got involved in Black History Month this year by having a series of talks on such topics as African art and aesthetics and the image of blacks in art.

I attended one of these talks given by art educator Maureen Flynn-Burhoe called "The Positive Presence of Absence: A History of African Canadians through Works in the Permanent Collection of the National Gallery of Canada." Even though there weren't many works either by or about blacks, Flynn-Burhoe managed to use certain paintings in the permanent collection to discuss the social and historical significance of these images to the black Canadian experience.

What wasn't there became as relevant as what was there. One fascinating story was about the portrait of a naval officer, painted for his bravery. However, what was not hanging there, Flynn-Burhoe noted, was a painting of an equally brave soldier who was on another ship at the same time, and who was awarded the Victoria Cross. His name was William Hall and he was black. The omission speaks volumes.

But the most fascinating thing about the art tour was coming face-to-face with a bronze bust of one of my relatives—Tommy Simmons, who worked as a railway porter and coached an all-black girls' baseball team.

It is one of the few existing sculptures of a black Canadian person. The bust, by Orsen Wheeler, was found in 1975 in a studio at Sir George Williams University.

Bud Jones, also a relative of Simmons, was on hand at the National Gallery to give some historical information about the bust.

The talk reminded me how the contributions of black Canadians have gone missing from the pages of Canadian history. Black History Month came to life for me when these untold stories began to surface.

Reactions to Black History Month vary within the black community. Most of the people I spoke to were very positive about its scope and impact.

One view was that besides giving blacks an opportunity to celebrate themselves, Black History Month forces the involvement of societal institutions like governments, schools, art galleries and various media.

Other people, however, were skeptical of the benefits of dedicating just one month to this agenda.

One person I spoke to expressed concern that there were not enough young people at the events; another that there weren't enough people of other cultural groups.

One view was that Black History Month should work toward incorporating into the programs events that have a focus on the future.

Black History Month showed the diversity, richness, and talent that can be found in the black communities. It was a testimony to the pain, joy and difficulties of the black experience.

# Montreal fans went wild over Robinson

March 19, 1995

"The crowd surged around the black man. Men and women of all ages threw their arms around him, pulled and tore at his clothes."

Hold on—this isn't what you think. It's not a lynch mob out of the U.S. Deep South.

The year is 1946. The place: Montreal. The black man in question: baseball hall-of-famer Jackie Robinson.

The article by Sam Maltin, sports columnist for the Montreal Herald, continues:

"His stalkers are shouting, 'Jackie Jackie Jackie!' One wields a baseball bat, not to club the black man but to have him autograph the bat. It was probably the only day in history that a black man ran from a white mob with love instead of lynching on its mind."

Robinson had just played his last game for the Montreal Royals before moving to the Brooklyn Dodgers, and the fans were wild. Robinson had led the Royals to a stunning comeback victory over Louisville in the Little World Series. The fans sang, "Il a gagne ses epaulettes" (he won his bars, or spurs), and carried him around on their shoulders; they wouldn't let him go.

Tears streaming down his face, Robinson told the crowd he would never forget. Even though he had played for the Royals for only one year, Montrealers had come to love Jackie Robinson.

The signing of Jackie Robinson to the Montreal Royals, the Brooklyn Dodgers' Triple-A farm team, was considered the most controversial sports development of the century, according to A.S. Doc Young, author of Negro Firsts in Sports. Baseball history and race relations in North America were irrevocably changed.

On Tuesday, the United Nations' International Day for the Elimination of Racial Discrimination, we will commemorate the breaking of the colour barrier in major league baseball by the legendary Jackie Robinson. Representatives of the federal and provincial governments, the city of Montreal and the Montreal Urban Community plan to unveil a commemorative plaque in a ceremony at the YMCA on Park Ave. (This is also the UN's Year of Tolerance.)

It is fitting that the event be held at the YMCA, given its long tradition of fighting discrimination. As early as 1853, the Montreal organization withdrew from the North American Association of YMCAS to protest against the segregation policy of separate Ys for blacks in the Southern United States.

When Dodgers president and general manager Branch Rickey signed Jackie Robinson, he exploded the baseball world's most sacred and vicious policy—the unwritten ban against black players. Maltin quoted Rickey as saying in an interview that he believed Robinson to be a good prospect, and his conscience would not allow him to turn Robinson down because he was black.

"I knew I was right, and when a man is right he can do no wrong," Rickey said in the interview. "Those who are against it can shout to the hilltops and protest, but it won't matter. This is a movement that cannot be stopped by anyone. The world is moving on and they will move with it, whether they like it or not."

Robinson was willing to be a racial pioneer, but he did not want to be considered a crusader: "My conduct and my ability as a baseball player will win over more people who think the Negro has no place in organized baseball than a lot of preaching about constitutional rights. I'm going to take a cut at the ball every time a good one comes over the plate, try to connect, run like hell for first base and play the game hard and clean. That way, lots of them will soon forget my colour, I hope."

As anticipated, Robinson ran into a lot of opposition. In an article in Ebony magazine, writer Walter Leavy quotes Joe Black, a former teammate on the Brooklyn Dodgers: "Many times Jackie would slide into a base and jump up wiping his face. Fans thought he was wiping perspiration, but in actuality an opposition player had spit in his face."

"It was so hard for him," former Royals teammate Jean Pierre Roy recalled in a recent interview with me. "When we played in the Little World Series in Louisville, Ky., they didn't want to let Jackie play. The Royals as a team stood behind him. If Jackie didn't play, neither would we. We were on Jackie's side.

"One time in Syracuse someone threw a black cat on the field when Jackie came up to bat. Players on the opposing team would shout racial in-sults at him when he passed their dugouts. Montreal fans heard about Jackie's treatment through the media and when those teams got here, they returned the jeering.

"The pressure and the constant tension on him almost caused him to have a nervous breakdown. He ran into all kinds of adversities on and off the field. He was such a unique individual, though. One of a kind. He was somehow able to transform the situations presented to him. He behaved so proudly, people had to accept that not only was he a great ballplayer, but a man of integrity, a man of character."

And Montreal fans loved him.

"Jack and I always attributed a great deal of our eventual success to the love and respect we received in Montreal," Rachel Robinson, Jackie's widow, said in a recent interview from New York. She recalled living that summer at 823 Gaspe St. in Montreal's east end.

"I was pregnant and Jack was on the road a lot of the time, and the neighbours did everything they could to help me out. Even though I didn't speak French and they didn't speak English, we still got along. "It was a big contrast to what we had experienced in the South where everything was segregated. Toilets and drinking fountains were marked Whites Only or Coloured. I had to sit in the Coloured sections of the ball parks just to watch Jackie play."

Today, Rachel Robinson manages the Jackie Robinson Foundation, which was incorporated after his death in 1972 to perpetuate his memory and his achievements. The foundation's mission is to award scholarships to minority youngsters to go to university in the United States.

The city of Montreal, the MUC, the Quebec Department of International Affairs, Immigration and Cultural Communities as well as Heritage Canada have each committed $5,000 this year to the Jackie Robinson Scholarship Fund overseen by the Montreal Association of Black Businesspersons and Professionals.

For my parents' generation, Jackie Robinson represented hope. He represented the struggle for human rights. He had dared to dream the impossible, so why shouldn't they? The expression "Quicker than you can say Jackie Robinson" became part of their lingo and ours, too.

Black kids of my generation knew the name Jackie Robinson, we knew he was a good ballplayer, we knew he was black and that he was some kind of hero, but we didn't really understand the significance. By the time we came along there were lots of other blacks in sports. We didn't realize Jackie Robinson had paved the way.

As for black youths of today, I did a quick survey and found, to my surprise, most had not heard of Jackie Robinson.

Nowadays, many of us could not imagine that any sport—or any endeavour, for that matter—would bar someone simply on the basis of race.

But we still have a long way to go. We have Jackie Robinson and other pioneers like him to thank for getting the ball rolling. The rest is up to us.

As Rachel Robinson put it: "We need to stop talking about how far we've come, and concentrate on our efforts and action on reaching new goals."

# 'Black to the Future' call to action
## Roll up your sleeves and join community-centre cleanup

June 4, 1994

The Negro Community Centre [NCC] in Little Burgundy is issuing a call to the community: it needs your support and it needs it now.

"Black to the Future," a symbolic resurrection of the NCC, will take place next Saturday. People are being asked to roll up their sleeves and get to work, reclaiming in spirit—and in deed—an institution that has played a significant role in the life of Montreal's black community.

Volunteers will be sweeping out the three-storey building on Coursol St., washing windows, taking an inventory—on a ceremonial day that is meant to help the community get in touch with its roots.

"In the past, people used to get together and help one another build a new barn or help bring in a harvest," says Linton Garner, chairman of a task force working to revitalize the centre.

"We've lost that spirit. It's time the community reclaimed its past. You can't know where you're going unless you know where you've been. It's important for young people, especially, to know where they've been. That's what Black to the Future is all about."

The NCC was established in 1927 at a time when there was a great deal of discrimination in Montreal and the black community was looking for an institution that would provide services to its members.

The centre was founded by Rev. Dr. Charles Este, pastor of the Union Church on Delisle St. Originally attached to the church, it moved in 1955 to the former Iverley Community Centre on Coursol St.

For a time the NCC was the only institution with the resources to attend to the needs of the black community. It filled a void in Montreal's black community. It was the glue that held the community together.

When I was growing up, the centre was the hub of our activities. I remember going down there on Saturday mornings to get help with my homework. In the background you could hear Daisy Sweeney, Oscar Peterson's sister, giving piano lessons. In another room you could hear the clacking of shoes as kids—including my sister—practiced their tap-dance steps with Olga Spence.

It was at the centre that I had the opportunity to act in my first play. Friday nights, it became the rendezvous spot, where we'd meet our dates and dance to the funky rhythms of James Brown, Aretha Franklin and the Temptations. In the summers we went to the camp organized by the centre.

The NCC was like a second home for many of us. It was a welcoming space, where everyone knew everyone else.

Sylvia Warner, 73, remembers going there on Saturday nights as a teenager and doing the jitterbug. It was at the NCC that she learned how to embroider, as did many of her friends.

She still cherishes the brass pin she received as a member of the Little Mothers' League, a group that taught young girls how to look after children. Like many of us, she says her whole childhood revolved around the NCC.

"The centre used to be very active," says Owen Rowe, a long-time NCC board member and one of its program directors during the 1950s.

"We had an impressive array of activities for people of all ages: the Teenage Club, Sepia Girls' Club, Co-op Club and the Pioneers' Club, which was formed to facilitate the adjustment of West Indian domestics into Canada.

"We had a school-meal program and the kids would come over from neighbouring schools for their lunch. The centre was also involved in things like Brotherhood Week, where people from various ethnic and racial groups took part in activities together."

In recent times, however, the centre has been hauntingly inactive, with no source of revenue, no staff to speak of, and no real programs.

The deterioration began slowly. Part of the problem was that large parts of the community were displaced by the advent of the Ville Marie Expressway and the gentrification of the neighbourhood. Centraide stopped funding the centre about five years ago, and it fell on hard times.

A few services and activities survived—a daycare service, an after-school program, a French course. Community groups still met there on rare occasions.

Because of what the NCC once was, because of what it still represents to many people in the black community, the board brought in a task force to work on a plan to revitalize the centre.

Task-force members Garner, Candyce Follette, Marlene Jennings, Keith Lawrence and Roland Wills evaluated the present state of the centre and met with more than 100 individuals and community organizations to get a sense of what the NCC meant to them in the past and what future role, if any, it might play.

What came out, Garner said, is that "the community wanted its centre back."

Many of the people interviewed lamented the fact that their kids could not experience what they had at the centre, he says. They longed for a centre that cared, a centre that knew them and their families, a centre that was like a second home. They said they missed the feeling of security the NCC used to inspire in people, the feeling that if they had a problem—at home, at school or with city hall—the NCC would take care of it.

Some blamed the neighbourhood's deterioration on the demise of the NCC. One example given was that of kids who now have nowhere to go and are subjected to all kinds of bad influences in the streets.

Historically, Garner said, the centre was open to everyone in the community, not just blacks.

"We interviewed white francophones who had lived in the area for the last 50 or 60 years who said they used to go to the NCC for a hot meal for 5 cents and to participate in sports activities. If they needed clothing, the NCC gave it to them. If they needed to go to camp, the NCC arranged it.

"The NCC was a vital and integral part of the community for them, and they said that when the NCC is ready to reopen, they will be there to help out."

Garner said he wants to see this cross-cultural aspect of the centre continue. "The centre will retain its emphasis on helping the black community, but it will be open to the community at large and will address issues that affect the Little Burgundy community as a whole."

(During the 1970s, there were some discussions about changing the name of the NCC to the Black Community Centre. Some members felt it was no longer appropriate to leave the word "negro" in the name because they thought it was important to change with the times. However, other members said keeping the centre's name intact was important from a historical point of view—the NCC was a household name and changing it would cut the link to the church and the past.)

The centre's role and programs will evolve once the community identifies its needs. Garner says the task force has targeted five areas—youth, seniors, culture, information dissemination and community development.

The centre would also develop a fundraising foundation. Last year, renowned jazz pianist Oliver Jones helped raise funds for the centre in a benefit concert called For the Love of Burgundy. Jones hung out at the centre as a youth and took piano lessons there with Daisy Sweeney.

The NCC has also applied to the federal, provincial and municipal governments for funds under the infrastructure program set up by the Liberals in Ottawa.

But the first step is the Black to the Future cleanup next Saturday.

"I am looking forward to the centre's doors swinging open and closed, children coming in and going out with smiles on their faces and sparkles in their eyes," says long-time member Rowe. "I want to see people who are committed and who will give their hearts to the revitalization of the centre."

# A well-worn path
## Montreal blacks are drawn to march's offer of hope

October 14, 1995

That it is the right time to address the condition of the black male in America, there is no doubt.

The black male is in a state of profound crisis. The life expectancy of a black man in the United States is less than that of a man in Bangladesh. One-quarter of all black men in their 20s are in jail. Black men consistently lead the unemployment and high-school-dropout statistics. The homicide rate for black men is seven times higher than that for white men. Black men have become the personification of drugs, crime and spousal abuse.

Staging the Million Man March to Washington, D.C., on Monday is one way of capturing public attention and creating discourse about the problems, their antecedents and possible solutions.

Marches can be effective in bringing important issues into the public forum. Black trade union leader A. Philip Randolph used this strategy in 1941 in mobilizing the Negro March on Washington that demanded the abolition of discriminatory hiring practices and the abolition of racially segregated units in the armed forces. In the 1960s, civil-rights activists used marches to bring the world's attention to the plight of black Americans, bringing about important and long-lasting social changes.

The problem, however, is that this march is being organized in part by the controversial group the Nation of Islam, headed by Louis Farrakhan, whose anti-Semitic comments have strained relations between the black and Jewish communities, communities that have a history of combatting racial discrimination.

Some agree that the march has the potential to advance the influence of Nation of Islam and should be boycotted because any association with hatred and bigotry should not be tolerated. As Martin Luther King once wrote, "You cannot substitute one tyranny for the other, and for the black man to be struggling for justice and then turn around and be anti-Semitic is not only a very irrational course, but it is a very immoral course."

Others feel that since the march is being supported by a coalition of black groups and individuals, who do not share the same sentiments as Farrakhan, that his views should not be at issue.

Does participating in the march mean that one is inadvertently supporting the Nation of Islam? Members of Montreal black communities have conflicting views.

Even though the Nation of Islam has not gained much credibility in Montreal, the idea of participating in this march has some people very excited about its possibilities. Saida Bruneau, a mother of four who lives in Little Burgundy, said she wishes she could send her 10-year-old son to the march.

"Even though I don't believe in the Nation's politics, I think the march itself is very important. Nothing like this has happened since the civil-rights movement. It's symbolic of our struggle. It's important for black men to take to the streets in this way. It's self-affirming. Black men need this kind of experience. I would want my son to be a part of that, to be with other black men who are talking about the issues that affect their lives. I hope it can be a foundation for other kinds of actions that will impact positively on the black community."

Although interest in Montreal is not nearly as great as it is in the U.S. or even Toronto, there are a few busloads of black men going to Washington to participate in the march.

Jamal Johnson, owner of Intelligence Books, became affiliated with the Nation of Islam because he considers Farrakhan to be the most outspoken voice in the black community. "He has that up-in-your-face approach that I like and he's much closer to every-day folk than other black leaders.

"Although I don't agree with some of the Nation's politics, I think that what they're doing in terms of cleaning up young black men and keeping them out of jail and making them more responsible is remarkable. I've seen the effects on black men who were going nowhere. They now have respect for themselves." Johnson adds that any person with a good head on his shoulders will be able to separate the sense from the nonsense.

But some black women express concern about the exclusion of women from the march. "It's not simply a black male problem, it's a community problem and everyone should be welcome to participate," said community worker Saada Branker. "The Nation of Islam has a reputation for being patriarchal and anti-Semitic and I really have a problem with that."

This march is a culmination of the racial crisis plaguing North America and the narrow scope that black leadership has used to approach the problem. In the future, marches such as this need to be more inclusive, involving all oppressed groups as well as individuals committed to working against racial injustice.

If people can put aside their differences and see the problems of others as affecting them, marches such as this can have a positive impact.

King once wrote, "If we don't learn to live together as brothers, we will surely perish together as fools."

# Transcription of an Interview conducted with Danny Houser, A Civil Rights Worker

Interview conducted by Clifton Ruggles and Olivia Rovinescu

If you was Black you had to know your place. We'd work from sunrise to sunset. We'd do all the work and the white man took all the money. No matter how hard you worked, you couldn't get nowhere. Most of the Blacks working on the plantations were illiterate. We was treated like animals. We had to ask the white man for everything. Today it seems unbelievable. How did we live through it all? I remember when I was growin' up there was a girl living with us. I remember when she turned 16 a man come to take her away. How did my parents let him do it? And do you know what it's like to be told by some little white kid where you supposed to go to the bathroom and you have to take it, 'cause you can't talk back to white folks no matter how old they are, 'cause they're supposed to be better than you. Or, you be workin' in the fields, side by side with a white feller and then you can't even eat together with him.

It was very hard to see your children growin' up just as poor as you come up. You want something more for your children and you get real discouraged when you see that ain't nothin' change all them years. You get real anxious like for somethin' to happen.

I didn't want my children sayin' "Yes, Sir, No, Sir" like I did and like my father 'fore me. When the civil rights movement got goin'...that was my time, yes siree. I'd been waitin' for it all of my life. I was ready to accept the persecution that was coming.

Always did know somethin' was wrong. People not suppose to treat other people like that. Growing up on assistance like I did I always known somethin' was wrong with livin' like that.

When the war come along and they wanted me to join the army I outright refused. Why should I fight for a country that wasn't doin' nothin' for me, a country that denied me an' my children a good education, a country that allowed the white children to ride to school in buses that my tax money done paid for, while I be walking 5 miles to school. That wasn't fair. Now they tell me that I have to fight this man's war when this country wasn't doing nothin' for me or for my people.

I was on the run for a year before they caught up with me and inducted me. I was in there for about 5 months before they shipped me back home. They kept trying to tell us that the enemy was the Japanese and then they'd ask you just to make sure you remembered. When they asked me if I knew who the enemy was I said, "You, you and you and pointed to everyone in the room. The next thing I knew I was goin' home. Can you beat that? Guess they didn't like my answer. As far as I was concerned, the Japanese didn't enslave my people, the white man had whipped me all of my life.

White soldiers be allowed to eat on the inside of the canteen, and they put a bench out back for the Black soldiers. That was the most hurtful thing. Here we were all going to fightin' the same war, gonna get killed together, but they had to separate us all the same. Doesn't that beat all? It was right then and there when I was eatin' on that bench that I decided I wasn't about to fight this man's war for nothin' in the world, 'cause this man done nothin' for me.

I'll never forget the day I knew I couldn't take no more. I was laying bricks for this white man. He came in and said to me, "You hear about what that Martin Luther King plannin' to do tomorrow, he plannin' to march through the streets here. You better hope it rain, cause if I catch one of my niggers there. . ." and he slapped his hands together. When he said this, I put my stuff down, and walked away, and I never came back no more. It was when he spoke, I realized then and there that I couldn't take no more of that kinda talk. I've been talkin' it all my life. When you got children you've got to take that stuff. And I've been talking it for too long. It was enough garbage. If I die, let me go. My children will survive. They're all grow'd up. I didn't care what happen to me. That's when I went public. Before that, I was working underground–like, doing a little here, a little there. "Gotta raise my children," I'd be saying to myself. Can't be gettin' into trouble. Can't let raising my children make me like my Daddy before me, destroyed by white folks. I thought maybe if I do something, my children and their children might do something more. If my Daddy had done something earlier, maybe we woulda got somewhere faster.

What I did I had to do. There was no other way for me. I had been working up to it all my life. I saw my chance to do something good. I knew that there was the possibility I wouldn't survive it. I knew what the consequences were. We all did.

My job was educating people, organizing them, talking to them about their problems. My main thing was to motivate the folks to do something. Most people wanted to leave it to God. All's they wanted to know was how to get to heaven. I showed them that they had to live on this earth that maybe there was no heaven to go to after all. Let me live here. Why should the white folks get their share while I have to wait to die to get mine. "Pie in the sky when you die." Not for me. "Walk the milky white way." I want to walk through these streets out here, right now.

How many times my first wife would say, "Them white folks ain't gonna give you nothin', they gonna do what they want to do." What she didn't understand was that I wasn't waiting no more for what they were going to give me, I was taking what was rightfully mine. It's been coming for some 400 years. Black people been defeated a long time. Remember, we was stolen from our homeland and sold like cattle. Until recently Blacks had nothin' to be proud of. We didn't know nothin' about ourselves. I always knew what an education could do for me. It would make me strong. I had to sneak around just to learn my trade. Black folk weren't allowed to look at a blueprint. Every time we started a new construction project I'd steal the blueprints and make copies of them. I'd work all day laying bricks and I'd study the blueprints at night. I still have the blueprints in my attic today.

I was a damn good organizer. My strategy was to get to the kids. Best way of getting parents into the movement, you get a bunch of their children in jail. Their mamma gonna be there for sure. I remember one time I got three hundred children in jail. There wasn't a parent that stayed at home. Not in the whole community. The jail wasn't big enough to keep them all, so they had them in a big pen outside. Then it started raining and the kids started singin' and clappin'. It was a sight to behold. I'll tell you. A sight to behold. That's how you organize. And I was a great organizer. I worked very well with the kids. On account of them kids that we was able to do the work that we done. The kids done more for this country than anybody else. Dr. King couldn't have done a thing without the kids.

I remember one time I was working with Dr. King in Preville, Alabama when one day we invited Stokley Carmichael to come to one of our meetings. That riled up the white folks somethin' fierce. They broke up the meeting at my office so I suggested that we go over to my house. Next thing we know, the KKK was there, the police was there. . . nearly every white person in town was there, in front of my house. We had a five hour gun battle. I was wounded all over but I wasn't really hurt badly. When it was all over the police decided to carry me over to the jail. But before I ever got to the jail they started brutalizing me right there in the street, broke three or four ribs, broke my nose, crushed my chest, I had a hole in my head the size of a tea cup.

In fact I lost my hearing on that side of my head on account of the injury. I never thought I could suffer all that and still live to talk about it. Then they decided to take me to the Alabama River and drop me in. I remember lying there in the car thinkin' I was about to meet my maker. I was ready though, 'cause I'd made up my mind long time ago that I was willin' to die for freedom. But they never did throw me in the river. Before they was gettin' ready to do it, one of the state troopers changed his mind. He told the other that he got a wife and children to live for and he can't be takin' no part in killin' me 'cause I was too well known. He said he wasn't about to destroy his family on account of the likes of me. So they brought me to where the KKK were havin' a rally. They dumped me there hoping that the KKK would finish me off so that they wouldn't have to do it themselves.

Somehow I managed to get away 'fore the KKK could get to me. Don't ask me how I done it 'cause I still don't know—wounded and beaten as I was. A friend carried me to a reporter's house who took me to the hospital in Montgomery. From there they had to transfer me to a hospital in Tuskeeke, Alabama where the police was ordered to protect me. They had to do that on account of they woulda killed me for sure, right there in the hospital. The police were told that if anything happened to me they would be held responsible.

After that I turned around and sued the city and I won the case. I didn't get nothin' materially speakin', but I did get an injunction for Black people to be treated as citizens. That still exists today. Before this injunction a white man could whoop a Black child with chains and nobody would do nothin' 'bout it.

Nothin' changed after that. It didn't scare me off. It's not somethin' I would want to relive. But it didn't stop me from organizin'. I was determined to continue doin' the work I'd been waitin' all my life to do. It got easier 'cause I got to the point where I really didn't care what happened to me. The work I was doin' was more important than I was. That's how Dr. King felt, he knew he was goin' to die, but he didn't care. It was the work that mattered. If we thought about ourselves we never would have done what we done.

Black people been scared into keepin' quiet for too long. To survive we had to keep silent. White folks in the north thought we was happy with things being like they was 'cause we wasn't saying nothin'. Now was the time for us to express ourselves. If anything, the beating made me realize how much work needed to be done. So I went around the country speaking to people, telling them what was going on in the south.

Around the same time I met my present wife, Bertha. I think I must have been the only Black man ever to dare live in the south with a white woman in those days. Bertha was down there working as a civil rights lawyer when I met her. We had to get two houses because she was trying to get into the bar and they wouldn't let her in on account of me. By having two addresses we thought we'd fool them. But we didn't fool anyone, especially not the KKK. For two and a half years we were trailed by the KKK. They painted crosses all over our house, our lawn, everywhere.

My kids were very angry I married Bertha. My nephew broke her arm in three places. Lots o' Black folks resented me. They resented me because they thought I was climbing beyond where they were. They thought I was marryin' a white woman to get away from them, to get up in the world. They thought I was leaving them behind. Wasn't no truth in that though. Bertha did more for my children than I woulda ever been able to do for them. She paid the hospital bills for my paralyzed daughter. You gotta understand that my kids were all grown up when I left my first wife. The youngest was 17. I didn't abandon my babies. I didn't owe them nothin' no more. They were grown up with kids of their own.

I stayed with my first wife for 24 years. There was no future for me with her. I have nothin' bad to say 'bout her. She was a good person but it wasn't possible for me to amount to anything stayin' with her. She never wanted me to be involved in the civil rights. She'd always be asking me, "What you'll want now, git yourself killed. . . you know the white man ain't never gonna give you nothin'." She thought she had nothin' to offer and she thought I had nothin' neither. But I did. I surely did. She never saw that. She wasn't what I needed. I loved her. She was a fine woman. But she wasn't thinkin' o' nothin' but survivin'. She had no dreams. She was illiterate and education wasn't important to her. She didn't know what education can do for you. It never bothered her that we wasn't able to educate our children proper. But it sure bothered me. So long as they wasn't dead or starvin', they was fine, that's how she thought. She didn't care where that food come from, so long as it come. She didn't care if it came from public assistance so long as she had it. See, I cared. I wanted to do it on my own but they weren't lettin' me. She didn't know no better. She was a victim, see. I ain't against public assistance. But what I can't understand is why in this world of plenty someone's gotta go to someone for somethin'. I don't wanna be asking no one for nothin'. I have a right to earn my own keep. I don't want nothin' except the opportunity to get what the next guy has, no more, no less.

My kids never did appreciated the work I did. Not one of them ever give me credit for what I done for Black people. When they were young I took them to demonstrations with me. They done got arrested with the other kids. I made them go. "Let's all get out there with them other kids," I'd say. They never did want to go. But I had to get them out there 'cause you know what people be sayin' next, "look a' him, he keepin' his kids at home while he be expectin' us to send our kids out to get arrested. How could I be tellin' other people to take part in demonstrations when my own kids weren't there. People always be tryin' to find somethin' on you. That's how people is. It was on account o' me tryin' to keep the thing going that I had to force my kids to go.

Other kids wanted to go, they were proud to go. But not my kids. Strangers kids used to come around and talk to me with real respect like, but never my children. To this day, my children never want to talk about them days. It's like they want to forget they ever existed. I keep tellin' 'em that whatever they have today is because of them days. Don't rightly know why they don't see that. They should feel proud that they were there, not ashamed.

They were real bitter on account of my marryin' Bertha. They never could accept that. They say to me once, "That what the movement all about, to get yourself a white woman? That's how close-minded they were. They thought I did what I did, just to git myself a white woman. That hurt me. That hurt me real deep. I didn't plan to marry a white woman. It just happened. I just wanted someone to love and someone to be happy with. Darn the colour. Colour didn't mean a thing. Isn't that what all this was about?

So long as we make each other happy. That's what life is all about being happy. And Bertha made me feel like a somebody. All my life I felt like a nobody ....a nobody. I never been called a bad word by Bertha in the 25 years we been married. She made me feel real good about myself. All my life I been pushed down by Blacks and whites.

With Bertha I could dream. What's a man without a dream? Nothin'. When I met Bertha I didn't have no job. I couldn't help myself. I couldn't help my children. What good was I? She pushed me on. She believed in me. My life really started when I met her.

I don't believe in violence, but I believe in self-defence. If defending myself causes violence, then that's the way it has to be. When they come shooting at my house that night, I took out my gun and shot back. I wasn't looking for no violence but when they come to my house, they invading my property, they tramplin' on my rights. If they come into our church and kill four children, then things have gone too far. I have to protect myself. You gotta do something. It's your obligation to do somethin'. How can you live with yourself if you don't? Dr. King's non-violent methods were good at the beginning. But the time had come to do more.

I think I was more angry than most people . . . more angry than I even knew I was. So when Dr. King come around that sort of stirred things up. It brought back all the anger, anger about not being able to go to school, anger at the mobs actin' like judge, jury and executioner. I remember one time a Black man go in a hotel with a white woman. No time at all a mob had formed ready to lynch him. What business is it of anyone's if a man goes into a hotel with a woman? Nobody's business but their own. That kind of stuff stayed with me. It just kind of piled up and made me explode.

I was mighty sad when so many of the people I worked with in the civil rights got killed. But you know, if you acceptin' death for yourself then you've got to accept it for somebody else. Dr. King knew he was gonna get killed. He was prepared. When you know you're right you don't give a damn about death. When you get to the point that you can shoot at another individual because you know that you're right, then you don't mind dying yourself. You don't give a darn when you know you can accomplish just this one thing, especially if someone done you wrong, your whole life they been doing you wrong. All your life you been stomped on and tramped on and you ain't never had the courage to say nothin' and then suddenly you get the courage to say it then you ready to die for it.

I want to be who I am. I don't want to be more than I am. Give me the opportunity to be what I am. That's all I was fighting for—to get what was mine, what was rightfully mine. If I want to be a nobody, give me the opportunity to be nobody, but if I want to be somebody don't stand in my way, no, don't stand in my way. I been deprived all of my life of being a human being. All I wanted was to be treated like a human being. If I die today, at least I know I accomplished what I wanted to accomplish.

photographer unknown

Black youth being burned in Southern U.S.

# Struggle for equality
# has both a past and a future

March 7, 1996

This year's Black History month may have come to an end but the racism in Canadian society continues to thrive. There have been numerous attempts to ease tensions but most people are generally unaware of them. The battle for equal rights has been a long one, with some gains made as well as disappointments.

Each year in February, the focus on black history gives blacks and whites alike the opportunity to ponder the black experience and understand some of the issues confronting black people. It gives a chance to celebrate both our struggles and our accomplishments.

Canadians are often under the misapprehension that racism was never as rampant here as it was in the United States and that we never engaged in the slave trade or outwardly discriminated against blacks.

The struggle for human rights in Canada has an interesting history that few know about. We tend to be much more knowledgeable about the human rights struggle in the United States and know little about our own history.

A recent study by the Centre for Research Action on Race Relations (CRARR) gives specific examples of human-rights violations and the ways our legal system dealt with them.

The year 1793 saw the first bill introduced in the Parliament of Lower Canada to abolish slavery here. However, it was defeated and it was not until 1833 that slavery officially ended with the Act for the Abolition of Slavery Throughout the British Colonies passed by the British Parliament.

The abolition of slavery, though, did not mean fair treatment for blacks. In 1899 a black Montrealer, Frederick Johnson, and a black female companion bought tickets for the orchestra section of the Montreal Academy of Music but were refused permission to occupy their seats. "The theatre's usher offered them seats elsewhere since orchestra chairs could not be accessible to 'colored persons,'" the CRARR report informs us.

Superior Court awarded Johnson damages on the basis that a publicly licensed theatre is not so strictly a public enterprise as to justify the owner to admit one and exclude another member of the public at his will.

Last year CRARR held an awards banquet in the honour of Johnson. The Frederick Johnson Award recognizes actions undertaken by an individual or an organization to combat discrimination based on race, colour, ethnic or religious origin.

At the banquet, former CRARR president Helene Wavrock (who was herself refused access to a bar in the early 1970s because of her race) re-enacted the story.

Another important case, also cited in the CRARR study is Loew's Montreal Theatres Ltd. vs. Reynolds (1919). Mr. Reynolds, a black man, was denied a seat of his choice after purchasing a ticket of general admission at a Loew's theatre. Reynolds decided for breach of contract. Superior Court ruled in his favour and granted him $10 in damages.

The Court of King's Bench (now the Court of Appeal), however, reversed the ruling upholding once again the principle of freedom of commerce over that of non-discrimination.

In that court's opinion "while it may be unlawful to exclude persons of colour from the actual enjoyment of all rights and privileges in all places of public amusement, the management has the right to assign particular seats to different races and classes of men and women as it sees fit."

Another case cited, that of Christie vs. York Corp. (1939) involved two black men, Fred Christie and Emil King, who were refused service by the York Tavern in the Montreal Forum building because the tavern had a policy of not serving "colored persons."

Christie filed suite before Superior Court, claiming $200 for breach of civil contract and public humiliation. The court ruled in his favour, awarding Christie $25 and court costs.

Once again, however, the Court of King's Bench, reversed the decision of the principle of freedom of commerce, ruling that "a merchant was free to carry on his business in the manner he conceived to best for his business."

The Supreme Court of Canada upheld the decision on the basis that in refusing to serve beer to "coloured people" the tavern did not commit any act "contrary to good morals and public order."

These three cases reflect the extent of racial discrimination, and more specific racial segregation, in Montreal before World War II, when the Canadian judicial system considered freedom of commerce to be more important that the principles of racial equality and human rights. Anti-discrimination legislation, as we know it today, started to be adopted by several provinces only in the 1940s.

The first modern provincial anti-racism law (the Racial Discrimination Act) was adopted by Ontario in 1944 but was limited to the display of racist signs. The first comprehension human-rights law was a Saskatchewan Bill of Rights. Quebec enacted anti-discrimination laws in the early 1960s, such as the Fair Accommodation Practices Legislation in 1963 and the Fair Employment Law in 1964.

In 1975 the National Assembly of Quebec adopted the Charter of Rights and Liberties of the people of Quebec to combat racism in all its forms.

In 1983 the government of Quebec created a commission to investigate allegations of racism in the taxi industry in Montreal. This is the first time in Quebec history a commission was set up to investigate racism.

After the tragic death of Anthony Griffin in 1987, the government of Quebec established a human-rights commission committee, headed by Jacques Bellemare, to investigate the relations between the police and ethnic minorities.

After the shooting by police in 1991 of another young black man, Marcellus Francois, coroner Harvey Yarosky's scathing report led to an investigations into relations between the black community and the MUC police, by a committee headed by university rector Claude Corbo, and a probe by retired judge Albert Malouf of the administration of the police force.

These inquiries as well as the most recent on the Ontario justice system, have shown that racism exists in Canadian society and in the justice system. One has to question whether or not the legal system can ever be impartial when judging a person of colour.

All these events suggest that Quebec society has been and continues to be in a state of evolution with regard to its treatment of minorities. There is no doubt that we have made great progress, yet despite these efforts, the daily reality of racism and discrimination continues to plague blacks and other people of colour.

CRARR's recognition of the contributions of the three black Montrealers—Johnson, Reynolds and Christie—who first tested Montreal courts with their allegations of racism has unearthed a largely forgotten part of Montreal's legal and social history. It is a history that must be remembered, because it reminds Montrealers and Quebecers of the deep roots of racism; more importantly, it documents the progress of human-rights initiatives in Quebec and Canada.

# Racism
# and Everyday Life

# Growing up black:
## The differences aren't always subtle

September 5, 1991

Premier Robert Bourassa recently made the claim that there is no systematic racism in the Quebec justice system. Like most other Quebecers, I would probably tend to believe him— that is, if my own experience of growing up black did not tell me otherwise.

I remember vividly my first encounter with the police as a youth growing up in Cote des Neiges.

There had been some trouble in the neighbourhood involving some black youths. I was on my way home from work when suddenly a police cruiser almost knocked me over while swerving on to the curb to block my path.

Two policemen jumped out of the car, demanding to know what I was carrying.

"Work clothes," I explained politely.

One cop threw me against the car. The other wrestled the bag from my arms, emptying the contents on the sidewalk.

Seeing there was indeed nothing incriminating in the bag, they shoved it back into my arms, got back in their car and sped off.

No apologies were made.

No effort was made to help me retrieve the contents of my bag.

It made no difference to them that I was innocent. By virtue of my blackness, I was guilty.

On another occasion, I was on a bus when a skirmish occurred between a black youth and a white youth. When the police arrived, they herded all the black youths off the bus and took them to the station.

No questions were asked to determine who was actually involved. Not one of the white youths was detained.

Surely a few properly addressed questions would have solved the mystery as to who was indeed guilty. How necessary was it to arrest all the black youths?

What had inspired the decision to detain only the black youths? Was this a conscious or unconscious act of racism?

Whatever the motivation, the result was the same. We were turned into suspects. We were guilty by virtue of our blackness.

It is difficult to have faith in the justice system when that system does not have faith in you, when it takes away your dignity and your self-esteem and renders you "invisible."

It seems that in this society, visible minorities become visible only when we become suspects. The rest of the time, we are, to use author Ralph Ellison's term, "invisible."

This invisibility can be forced upon you or can be of your own making.

I recall vacationing near Cowansville one summer when word of an escaped black convict hit the news. Coincidentally, sightings of this convict occurred exactly in places I had been.

I had my own newsflash—it was me they were after. Reports that local farmers were arming themselves made me exceedingly paranoid. In an at-

88

tempt to keep my black face out of circulation, I spent most of my vacation shut up indoors, a prisoner of my own making.

In response to the fear that some would-be hero might blow my head off (claiming afterwards that he was sorry, an error had been made, a case of mistaken identity) I made myself invisible.

The most significant recollection I have occurred when I was in CEGEP.

Prime Minister Pierre Elliot Trudeau was to speak at St. Kevin's Church in Cote des Neiges about issues of concern to the community. Having a newly acquired sense of civic responsibility because of my recent involvement in the black community, I decided to attend.

Upon arrival, I was stopped by the RCMP and refused entry. I was told it was "security reasons."

When I probed a little further, he told me that foreigners were not permitted to attend. Temporarily discouraged, I stood back and observed which people were allowed to enter.

They were all white.

I finally made the connection and challenged the RCMP with my realization. I told him that I was probably more Canadian than he was, that my mother is a native North American Indian and my father's ancestors were among the first slaves that arrived here in the 1860s.

Here in my own country, in my own neighbourhood, I became disenfranchised because of my blackness, prevented from participating in the democratic process guaranteed today in our Charter of Human Rights.

## Another humiliation

A white person grows up taking for granted that one has certain fundamental rights—freedom of speech and of assembly, that one is innocent until proven guilty.

As a black person, the reverse is true, you live your life as a suspect.

The police suspect you, store owners suspect you, school officials suspect you.

In every facet of your life you are seen as an undesirable, unworthy of the same rights and privileges as white counterparts. Colour sets the criteria for your interactions in the world. And it is the colour of your skin that sometimes condemns you.

Such was the case of Marcelus Francois, 24, who was unarmed when he was shot in the head by a Montreal Urban Community police officer on July 3.

Such was the case of Anthony Griffin, who was unarmed when he was shot and killed in a police parking lot in N.D.G. [Notre Dame de Grace] in 1987. These are the extreme instances, but there are countless others that occur on a daily basis that no one hears about.

For Bourassa to make the statement that there is no systematic racism in our justice system shows very little understanding of the nature and complexity of this phenomenon.

No, Mr. Bourassa, racism in this society may not be systematic, but it is definitely there, embedded in the complex framework by which our society functions and how the people of that society interact with each other.

I have tasted it.

# Incidents of racism too frequent to be dismissed as paranoia

October 7, 1993

There's a line in one of Woody Allen's films when he describes the heights to which his paranoia of anti-Semitism has taken him—hearing innocent phrases like "How are you?" transformed into pejorative "How are Jew?"

My own paranoia of racism reached near-similar heights this summer when I visited the United States.

Did I experience real or imagined cases of racism? I'll let you decide.

• • •

After an exhausting day of sightseeing, I sat down at an outdoor restaurant in a well-to-do district of San Francisco. Instead of being approached by an eager waiter anxious to rattle off the specials of the day, I was rudely warned that unless I planned to order something, I was not to sit down. On what basis did he decide that I was not going to eat?

As soon as my wife and children appeared from the washroom, his attitude changed dramatically. I wondered, is a black man with a family less suspect?

One of the more memorable experiences of the trip was my aborted attempt to do laundry at a Holiday Inn. No sooner did I reach the door of the Laundromat than I was approached by a security guard who demanded to know where I was going.

My wife had jokingly warned me not to "go out there alone." One would think I was going into the streets of South Central L.A. and not the base-

ment of the Holiday Inn.

I never did get to do the laundry that night. My wife had taken the kids to the swimming pool and had taken the key with her. The only way to prove I was staying at the hotel was to find her and produce the key.

Imagine how I felt retrieving her from the pool.

painting by Clifton Ruggles

Imagine how I felt exposing my children to the vulnerability that race carries in this society.

Even the airplane ride was not exempt from racism—or at least that's what we concluded.

We were seated in our assigned seats when the flight attendant informed us that we had been improperly placed and that we would have to move—something about people travelling with children not being permitted to sit near the emergency exit.

Understandable. Would we mind changing seats with the people behind us? No, not at all. We're all for safety.

We climbed out of our seats, trailing all our baby paraphernalia, baby screaming all the while.

Once settled, we overheard the flight attendant profusely thanking the people who changed seats with us for their co-operation.

Then I heard her offer them complimentary drinks. I wondered if she would extend the same offer to us.

I knew the answer. But I wanted to give her the benefit of the doubt.

Unfortunately, my first hunch was right. No thank-yous were forthcoming, no offer of complimentary drinks.

It was when she brought the other people their drinks and once again thanked them for their good will that I demanded my complimentary drink.

She seemed genuinely puzzled, but honoured the request nonetheless. I don't think that it even dawned on her that we were just as entitled to it as the other people, that we were just as inconvenienced as they were.

As I sat there sipping the screwdriver that I didn't really want, but which I felt obliged to consume, I thought about the incident.

Was it racially motivated? Maybe there was something else that could account for her differential treatment.

Maybe it was our youthful appearance, or maybe it was our casual dress. Maybe she just didn't like kids.

The people we switched places with certainly looked a lot more respectable than we did, sporting attache cases, laptop computers and cellular phones.

Maybe it was a class thing, not a race thing at all.

• • •

None of these incidents is very significant. But when you have so many disturbing experiences in such a short time, you begin to suspect that you are not being excessively paranoid, but that your perceptions of how people treat you are, in fact, correct—that you are being victimized because of your colour.

The most disheartening part of the story about my trip to the States is that the security guard at the Holiday Inn was black. The waiter who gave me a hard time was Asian. The flight attendant was Latin American.

We felt discriminated against by people who are themselves the victims of discrimination in North America.

Racism in Canada is certainly much more subtle, much more veiled than it is in the States, but it is just as poisonous and the results just as damaging.

A 1988 Canadian Recruiters Guild survey found that all job-agency recruiters and 80 per cent of corporate headhunters received requests to discriminate against minorities.

A total of 94 per cent said they rejected job-seekers on the basis of colour.

A 1988 study by the Quebec Human Rights Commission found that more than twice as many blacks as whites were turned down when looking for rental accommodation.

A 1984 Toronto study by the Urban Alliance on Race Relations and Social Planning Council of Metropolitan Toronto showed that white job applicants received three job offers to every one for blacks who had similar qualifications.

Racism is part and parcel of our standard operating practice. Racism pervades our lives in myriad ways, ways we may not even be conscious of.

# Shattering the myths
## Experience as tourist provides
## new insights into Cuba

June 4, 1992

No one who visits Cuba can remain untouched by its beauty, its history and its people.

Cuba is rich in images and myths—images of a bygone era when Cuba was the Monte Carlo of the Caribbean; images of earnest young revolutionaries taking on the government of the United States and winning.

My myth was in believing that in the Cuba fashioned by Che Guevara and Fidel Castro, there would be no discrimination. I am, after all, a child of the '60s who grew up on the youthful ideals sparked by the Cuban revolution and protests of the war in Vietnam.

When I got off the plane at Varadero Airport, I was awed by the number of black faces. I felt instantly comfortable in a country with such a large black population. Except for the language barrier, I felt quite at home.

But my sense of comfort was short-lived. No sooner did I put the key in the door of my hotel room, than I was stopped by a security guard who demanded to see my passport.

I tried to explain to him that the hotel had kept it, as was procedure. I produced my airline ticket, which under other circumstances, might have been sufficient proof of my identity.

But clearly I was too dark to make a credible Canadian. Canadians are white. Canadians do not look like them.

He studied the ticket closely then handed it back and walked away.

Early the following morning, there was a pounding at my door. The same security guard was at the door, shouting something in Spanish. Once again, he demanded to see my passport, which, once again, I could not produce. Again, he just walked away.

I figured that since Cuba is a militaristic state, this is the way they "welcome" all their foreign visitors.

But I found myself stopped everywhere I went—be it walking into a restaurant, a store or even strolling on the beach.

What I came to discover from the Cubans I met is that they are not allowed in the hotels, in the restaurants, nor in the stores designated for tourists.

They are eyed with suspicion if they are found lingering on the beach or hanging around anywhere where tourists might be found.

My biggest liability, apparently, was being there with my wife, who is white. The authorities automatically assumed I was a Cuban looking for a one-way ticket out of the country.

An English-speaking policeman actually told me that he thought I was a gigolo. "An honest mistake," he explained, "for we don't see any black tourists here."

Cuba is the largest, most racially mixed and culturally diversified country in the Caribbean.

Blacks first arrived as slaves from Africa in the 16th century.

By 1825, the black population outnumbered the white. Greater numbers, however, did not give them any more rights. Slaves were brutally treated and their families were systematically broken up.

Cuba was the last country to abolish slavery. Officially, blacks and whites are considered equals in today's Cuba, which boasts a commitment to human rights and racial equality.

But the unofficial story is that even in this land of youthful ideals, blacks are still looked upon as second-class citizens.

I discovered in speaking to black Cubans that even though there is no official discrimination in Cuba, employment practices still favour whites. One tour guide told me that he is a mechanical engineer, although he has not been given the chance to work in his profession.

Many of his white classmates have been more fortunate. Several black Cubans I spoke to confirmed these kinds of discriminatory practices have

happened to them as well.

What struck me was their lack of bitterness. They appeared very supportive of their government. They were quick to point out all that has been done for them: their streets are clean, they have food, they are literate, they have jobs, they have housing.

The streets were safe to walk through at any time. It seems that every street corner has either a school, a daycare, a library, a community centre or an art gallery.

Education is free. Anyone who wants to go to university can. Literacy is 98 per cent—the highest in any Latin American country.

The air is clean, as most people travel by bike.

Despite the constant harassment, I fell in love with Cuba. Like many North Americans I had all kinds of preconceived notions. Each day brought new experiences and with the experiences, new insights that shattered the myths.

# Clashing Cultures (Kafe's story)

September, 1993

William Kafe, a 53 year old teacher from Ghana endured 15 long years of vicious racial harassment at the hands of his students at the Commission Scholaire Deux Montagnes. The result he says, was depression and anxiety so severe that it incapacitated him and prevented him from working. Kafe took his complaint to the Quebec Human Rights Commission which in April of this year, ordered the school board to pay $10,000 in moral damages for failing to protect him.

On February 18, 1993, two months before the Human Rights Tribunal reached its decision, Kafe was arrested for sending a letter to the Mayor of Verdun in which he made reference to a "shooting rampage". Kafe was arrested and charged with uttering a death threat. He was denied bail and was detained at Parthenais Jail since then. Last month, a jury found William Kafe guilty as charged. Although the charge carries a maximum 5 year jail term Judge Jean Guy Boilard suspended Kafe's sentence with the condition that Kafe see a psychiatrist regularly.

Kafe's story is fascinating. It is a human drama which raises important questions about what happens when Western thinking finds itself face to face with Third World cultures whose reference points may be markedly different; it explores how psychiatry and the legal system deal with issues of race, culture and ethnicity—and whether our standards of objectivity and sanity should be seen as the criteria to which all other cultures must adhere. The case also raises interesting questions about what constitutes a threat—should a threat be judged in terms of how it was intended or how it was perceived; and finally, the question of what toll years of racial harassment can take on an individual, how this toll can be measured and by what means should it be compensated?

At his trial Kafe testified that over the years students had brought excrement to throw at him; twice the students set fire to his classroom and shouted "we're going to burn down the nigger"; they flooded his classroom and shouted "we're going to drown the nigger". They kicked him and held him down by his tie, pulling him around like a dog. They told him he was dirty and brought soap and a face cloth to "wash the dirty nigger." They did mocked African dances chanting "Zulu, go back to Africa".

Kafe has countless documents supporting his claims—letters from students that illustrate the hostility of the classroom atmosphere in which he had to work: " My mother is a racist" reads one letter, "here is her phone number. She's going to tell you all about racism. She's going to sock you." Another says: "You're supposed to be my slave not my teacher, haven't you seen Roots?" And another simply says, "Tu pus"—you stink.

Marie Michelle Renaud, interim principal at Polyvalent Ste Eustache in 1984 testified in court that the students were taking bets on how long it would take to drive Kafe away. "I could not have endured what Mr. Kafe went through", she told the court.

Kafe alleges that some of the school officials supported the students and consequently helped to make his life unbearable. Kafe claims that one principal invited students to come to his office to complain if they had a problem with Kafe's teaching—of course the students complained.

When asked if there was any truth to Kafe's allegations Pierre Leduc, Director of Commission Scholaire Deux Montagne said: " Absolutely not, the problem was Kafe's. We have other black teachers in the same school, working with the same students and they don't have any racial problems. Problem students give problems to both their white and to their black teachers." Alain Gascon, lawyer for the school board echoed Leduc's position. According to Gascon, "Disciplinary measures were taken against the students responsible. The Human Rights Tribunal found that the school board did act appropriately in 1990, but did say that it could have done more to protect Kafe in 1988."

After Kafe had been on sick leave for two years, the school board initiated measures to have Kafe disengaged. Kafe was assessed by a board appointed psychiatrist, Dr. Marc Guerin who concluded that Kafe was suffering from paranoia and delusions. On the basis of this assessment the board fired Kafe. Kafe distrusted Dr. Guerin and suspected that there was a conspiracy to prevent him from returning to work. It was at this point that Kafe wrote the letter that brought him the attention that he was so desperately seeking.

On December 25, 1992, before the ruling of the Human Rights Tribunal

had been made public, Kafe wrote the impassioned seven page letter which he sent to the office of the Mayor of Verdun, to the Ministry of Education, to the Quebec Human Rights Commission and to the Ministry of Cultural Communities and Immigration. In this letter Kafe makes references to a shooting rampage taking place in Verdun—at the office of Dr. Marc Guerin, the board psychiatrist who had evaluated him. "Those who commit suicide or go on shooting rampage, etc." writes Kafe, "usually try to do their best to avoid it by trying to have the society listen and/or help but society refuses to listen". He continues by saying that he "is not anticipating any shooting rampage in Verdun but everybody knows what provocation and injustice of this magnitude can do".

Dr. Leon Phipps, the psychiatrist who had been following Kafe since 1985 testified at Kafe's bail hearing that Kafe was not dangerous and that circumstances turned him into "a desperate, lonely man who wanted to reach out." He explained that Kafe was "sad, depressed, anxious, scared, hadn't been sleeping, was afraid he was going to lose his job and the human rights case was lingering."

Dr. Maria Alice Sanchez, of the Philippe Pinel Institute was asked to assess Kafe in order to determine his dangerosity. In her report which was subsequently submitted as evidence at Kafe's trial, Sanchez wrote: " We found no personality disorder of any importance, however, we did find that Mr. Kafe does have a defensive attitude with respect to the state of suffering that he has experienced. Even

William Kafe

to the jury Judge Boilard said that it is irrelevant whether Kafe intended to carry out the threats he made. "Whether the person doing the threatening intended to threaten is irrelevant", said Judge Boilard, "what is relevant is how the words were received". He also instructed the jury that Kafe's psychological state at the time he wrote the letter was immaterial as was the fact that Kafe had been the victim of harassment.

Kafe's lawyer, Theresa Kennedy argued that a threat has to occur in a context. Her defense rested on attempting to prove that Kafe's reference to a shooting rampage was merely an attempt to get attention and was not intended as a threat to any one particular person. The defense called to the stand Mike Mensah-bonsu, a social anthropologist specializing in African cultures, who testified that, as a rule, Africans tend not to threaten, in the sense in which North Americans understand the word, but rather they call upon the spirit of their ancestors to correct an injustice perpetrated against them. If they mean to kill someone they simply do it, said Mensah-bonsu, they don't talk about it.

In her closing remarks Kennedy said that one cannot ignore the fact that

though he tends to intensify certain things, nevertheless his perceptions were founded on certain concrete facts." Sanchez explained that Kafe's way of mediating conflict appears to be through his writing since he seems to have no other means for appeasing his anxiety.

The arresting officer, detective Raymond Poirier testified that he found boxes and boxes of Kafe's writings as well as piles of other documents pertaining to the case stacked in Kafe's apartment.

The case was tried on the basis of whether or not Kafe knowingly uttered a death threat. In his instructions

Kafe is culturally different, that he understands the meaning of things differently and that his points of reference are different from our own. She reminded the court that Detective Raymond Poirier, the arresting officer testified that Kafe was genuinely surprised that he was being charged with uttering a death threat.

The crown prosecutor, Lucy Duffresne, on the other hand argued that "the letter should speak for itself" and that objectively speaking, Kafe did utter a death threat, as the word is used and understood by this society.

Kafe's early life as described in Dr. Sanchez's report provides some insight into the man. Kafe was one of nine children and grew up in a very religious household. His father was a professor and Kafe tried to emulate his father by studying to become a minister. In 1969 he went to Chicago to study theology but eventually decided to go into teaching. Sanchez believes that it was because Kafe had led an extremely sheltered life both at home and in the ministry that he was unable to deal with life's painful realities. He had never before experienced discrimination and it completely overwhelmed him, leaving him "vulnerable and hypersensitive".

Why did Kafe stay and subject himself to years of racial harassment. Why didn't he just leave? Kafe says that he stayed out of principle. He didn't want to be forced out of his job and says he wanted to see justice prevail. On April 10, 1993 the day he read the Human Rights Tribunal's judgment awarding him the $10,000 in moral damages, he wrote the following words while he was in jail awaiting his trial: " A wonderful day for humanity and for lovers of justice, because injustice permitted anywhere can affect justice everywhere".

This case also raises questions about whether years of persistent racial harassment on the job can lead to mental illness. The Quebec Human Rights Tribunal awarded Kafe the $10,000 for "moral damages" only—but did not award him the $86,000 for "material damages" because there was no proof that the racial harassment was responsible for Kafe's sickness. Can it ever be proven that racial harassment can be the cause of mental illness—and if so, what should an employer's responsibilities be?

Kafe is not the only teacher to face racism in Canadian schools in recent months. The Ottawa Citizen reported that last May Solo Di Mavindi, a native of Zaire working for the Ottawa Carlton French Language School Board was fired. He too had been racially harassed by his students and he too was dismissed under conditions similar to Kafe's.

This case raises important questions about how our institutions deal with issues of race, culture and ethnicity. It is important for our institutions to acknowledge the changing face of Canadian society and adapt themselves to this new multicultural reality. These institutions have to look for ways of dealing with the problems of cultural bias and racism so that all citizens of all colours will receive fair and equitable treatment in accordance with the Canadian Charter of Rights and Freedoms.

# Time to act
## Problem of racism must be addressed

May 7, 1992

There it was, vividly displayed on national television for all of black America to watch—Rodney King brutally beaten in Los Angeles by four white policemen while 20 or so of their peers stood watching.

Those policemen didn't just violate King, they violated every black person who has lived that and similar experiences.

King's screams of pain became the amplification of the silent screams of the oppression of hundreds of thousands of black people in America.

What has the U.S. judicial system revealed about itself after the King affair? At the very least, it has revealed that if you're black, the judicial system does not protect your rights.

How, in the face of overwhelming evidence of police brutality—recorded on video—a jury could render a non-guilty verdict defies reason.

But reason is not the enterprise here. If it were, surely one of the jurors chosen would have been black. In a trial with such racial import, for there not to be one black juror is scandalous.

### Seen as the accused

One juror was actually quoted as saying that "King got his just desserts."

It was King he was judging, not the accused—the policemen. In the minds of the jurors, by virtue of his colour, King always remained the accused.

Justice was never intended to prevail in this case. The trial was a pretense of justice that attempted to create the illusion that everyone is equal under

Gazette, July 14, 1991

98

the law and that the system is capable of policing itself.

One would think that based on what they saw, the jurors would have come to a unanimous conclusion that the police were guilty of assault, yet they did not.

Why not? Because the act of seeing is not a neutral act, it is an act imbued with prior meanings, ulterior motives, unconscious fears and hidden desires.

When people are confronted with such a blatant miscarriage of justice, they lose their faith in the system. The result as we have seen, was an anger so deep, so pervasive that it fuelled a riot of unsurpassed fury.

Rioters protesting against the injustice believed that it was time for the people to rise up and let the politicians know that the outcome of the trial was an insult and a travesty of justice.

Others, caught up in the windstorm of events, vented their anger and pent-up frustration at a system that has failed them, that has denied them opportunities and basic human rights.

They saw an opportunity to act out and exert a power they had never experienced. The material objects they had to do without were suddenly within arm's length and they reached out and took what they felt they had a right to.

### Lies in ashes

A third category comprised the criminal element who exploited the situation for personal gain or who used this incident merely as an opportunity to engage in acts of violence.

Whatever the motivation, the protesters and rioters made the point that blatant state-sanctioned racism will not be tolerated. Unfortunately, an entire community lies in ashes. Once again, it is the victims who are victimized.

We haven't experienced such extreme demonstrations of frustration in Canada, but we shouldn't be as smug as our politicians in believing ourselves to be beyond reproach.

As the recent shooting of a black man and the ensuing demonstration in Toronto show, we should pay more attention to combatting racism, rather than congratulating ourselves and feeling superior to the Americans.

If there is any cause to feel superior, it is not because of the behaviour of the police or because of the exemplary administration of justice, it's in the restraint shown by the black community in its reaction to police brutality.

Unarmed teenager Anthony Griffin was shot and killed in a police parking lot. Marcellus Francois, mistaken for a murder suspect, was shot and killed in a bungled police operation.

In both cases, the police were acquitted.

The trial raised fundamental questions about racism, questions that must be addressed.

Otherwise, there will be no hope in salvaging race relations in North America.

# Fear of the Police

## 'I have felt that terror every day of my life, even though I was guilty of no offence . . . by virtue of your colour, you are automatically perceived as a suspect.'

January 11, 1993

Another black man dead at the hands of police. Once again, the facts surrounding the death are contradictory.

The man, Trevor Kelly, was alleged to have lunged at police, yet the coroner's report tells us he was shot in the back.

Police say he had a knife. An eyewitness says he did not.

Why are there so many unexplained details when a black man is shot by police? Why is the response always the same—"no indication the officers acted improperly" says a Montreal Urban Community [MUC] police spokesman.

Linton Garner, a former member of Public Security Minister Claude Ryan's task force on relations between black communities and the MUC police force, says the shooting of Kelly is "yet another example of over-reaction by the police and an indication that they tend to perceive the black population as a threat to them."

"Not once," Garner notes, "has a Montreal police officer been actually shot by a black man."

For the black community, Garner says, "Kelly's death reinforces the perception that we are not as well protected by the MUC police as are members of the larger society."

In view of the contradictory information surrounding this case, Garner said, the black community has every right to demand a detailed report of the events that led up to the shooting, including information such as why Kelly was visited by police before he was shot; why officers then followed him; the production of the knife Kelly is alleged to have used, including fingerprints.

Since the police ethics committee was created in 1990, 1,697 complaints have been made. How many involve racial matters is not known.

People tend to think that police violence affects only those who have committed a crime. But the effect of unequal treatment of minorities has far-reaching implications. It denies people recourse under the law because of the unequal treatment by the justice system.

The fact that Trevor Kelly was said to have mental problems raises other disturbing issues about being black and mentally handicapped in our society. A friend of my family, who is black and whose 35-year-old, intellectually handicapped son suffers from epilepsy, says she's afraid to let her son walk the streets of Montreal for fear he will have a seizure and be shot by a police officer interpreting his actions as those of someone high on drugs.

This lack of faith in the police force's ability to make effective decisions when dealing with blacks was echoed by a white woman who told me about watching a black man trying to cross the median on Cote de Liesse Rd. Her first reaction was to call the police on her cellular phone because the man was endangering himself and others.

But she decided against it.

"I figured he probably had more chances getting across the busy highway than at the hands of the police. I never used to think this way. But I no longer have faith in the objectivity of the police when it comes to dealing with blacks."

Jack Todd put it best in his Jan. 4 column when he said blacks feel "sheer terror" when approached by the police.

I have felt that terror every day of my life, even though I was guilty of no offence and have never had any criminal record. As every black person in the city knows, innocence has nothing to do with it. By virtue of your colour, you are automatically perceived as a suspect.

It is interesting to note that in a recent document published by the MUC police force entitled "Learning to Cope with Diversity," the force spells out very clearly the manner in which it employs stereotypes: "Police work by its very nature requires the identification and classification of neighbourhoods, groups of streets or types of individuals: for the police, stereotypes are therefore to some extent a professional tool."

If stereotyping is standard operating procedure, then I venture to suggest that every black man walking the streets of Montreal is a potential target.

A year ago, I wrote a column in the West End edition of The Gazette in which I described an incident involving a disputed parking spot. A white woman grabbed me by my lapels, hurled racial insults at me and proceeded to call police, claiming I had assaulted her.

I was able to convince the police of my innocence and was not arrested or detained. In the column, however, I speculated about how this event might have turned out under different circumstances, suggesting that I would likely have ended up in jail or worse.

Denis Lauzon, director of police Station 31, interpreted the column as a criticism of the police and wrote a letter to the editor. He distorted the incident, left out crucial details and referred to me as the "suspect" (even though the police report refers to me as the "victim" and the woman the "suspect.") He chastized me for having "incited" the incident even though all evidence pointed to the contrary.

Lauzon could not understand the meaning and significance that I, as a black person, attached to this experience. "Alarming hypotheses," he

called my concern with what might have transpired had I been less articulate, less credible, had I been wearing Rastafarian braids, had a police record, become so irate I could not properly communicate my side of the story or been so intimidated as to remain silent.

Nor could Lauzon understand my insistence on pressing charges against the woman. But I did lay charges, and on Dec. 7 she pleaded guilty to simple assault.

It is high time we started learning how to co-operate and communicate across our differences, time we learned how to share our perceptions and become "border crossers" in order to understand each other's point of view.

It is time Mr. Lauzon and I sat down and helped each other understand the perspective that is the foundation for our positions.

The time for pointing accusatory fingers is over. It is time to initiate meaningful discourse.

The police need to understand how racism has affected the black psyche and how this in turn has affected the manner in which blacks perceive themselves—and, consequently, respond—when approached by police.

Multicultural training should help officers begin to understand the deeply held beliefs that structure their thinking and decision-making in respect to visible minorities. This would promote a greater degree of self-reflection and a predisposition to exploratory dialogue rather than the usual leaping to conclusions and unwarranted assumptions about people whom police often see only as "stereotypes."

The Corbo report, otherwise known as the task force on relations between the black communities and the MUC police, recommended training for every officer in professional ethics as well as mandatory courses on cultural diversity, racial discrimination and racism. It also recommends complete professional integration of police officers from the cultural communities, particularly the black communities. It recommends investigating the policies, procedures and practices of the MUC police to prevent any discriminatory exercise of discretionary police power.

The MUC police and black communities have worked on various task forces dealing with harmonizing relations. From these co-operative ventures, recommendations have been made to the minister of public security.

A major stumbling block to change is that few of these recommendations, which could begin to solve some of the problems, have been acted upon.

The black community is angry, and rightly so. The Yarosky report, the Belle Maire report, the Malouf report and now the Corbo report are all sitting on Claude Ryan's desk.

In the meantime, mistrust between police and the black community continues to escalate. We don't need any more reports. We need action. We know that serious problems exist within the police force; let's begin to act on some of these recommendations. Instead of shouting "racism" we should be saying, "Enough is enough, let's move on those recommendations now."

# A time of mourning—and a time for community to come together

## After the tears and anger over another fatal shooting, perhaps blacks can find a way to work collectively for rights

January 14, 1993

The monolithic church stood bleak against a fading horizon and the penetrating January cold sent shivers of dread through my entire being as I entered Trinity Church on Sherbrooke St. in N.D.G. [Notre Dame de Grace].

Inside was the funeral service for Trevor Kelly, who was shot by a police officer on Jan. 1.

There were no huge crowds of people as I expected. And I wondered if I was even in the right place. Friends, relatives, sympathizers and members of the various black community organizations gathered to share their grief and their outrage.

They came seeking solace and to lend their support to the Kelly family. Their presence here was also a political statement to demonstrate the solidarity of all the black communities in Montreal—the Jamaican, the Haitian, the African, the indigenous black.

### Putting aside differences

Not one culture, but many cultures. No one identity, but many identities. Bonded together by the colour of our skins. Putting aside differences in recognition of our common problems.

It was here that I came to know and understand another side of Trevor Kelly—the side that some of the media never gave us: a hard-working, decent person who became ill but nevertheless always retained a certain dignity.

He was not the knife-wielding desperado that police portrayed him to be.

Sharon Stanley, a relative of the dead man, was critical of what she considered to be the media's insensitive and sensationalized handling of the event. She felt that the media had totally misrepresented the family's account of the real Trevor Kelly and the reality that was his life.

She also expressed the family's sadness and concern that people will too soon forget about the senseless tragedy; that nothing will change. She felt that black community leaders have a responsibility to make this issue a priority and to continue to put pressure on the government and the police to remedy this situation.

Lorna Marriott, who delivered the eulogy, said that "it is not through individual effort that these problems will be solved. It must be a collective effort."

Noel Alexander of the Jamaica Association read an excerpt from Martin Luther King's famous speech, I Have a Dream, and talked about the need for all of us to work together to achieve a free and democratic society.

Marc Germain, from the Haitian community, spoke about the need for Quebec to recognize the changing racial composition of its society. He called for a society that is just, where the doors of opportunity are open to

Marcos Townsend

Funeral of Trevor Kelly

everyone regardless of their colour or ethnic background.

Dan Philip, of the Black Coalition of Quebec, also spoke eloquently about the need to create a society that is truly democratic and suggested it is time to take our grievances to the United Nations Human Rights Commission.

The funeral services were also attended by Claude Ryan's political attache, Geoffrey Kelley.

"I think it's a sad thing that happened," Kelley said. "I was impressed by the carefully chosen words that echoed the frustrations and pain that the black community is faced with."

Kelley said he "understood the message coming from the black community to be one where they are not going to abandon a peaceful approach to achieving the justice that they seek but would continue to forge partnerships in an on-going effort to find solutions to the problems of racism in our society."

When asked if Ryan's office will ask for an investigation of the shooting, Kelley said that there is no official statement yet. Ryan's office is waiting until it has the coroner's and police reports.

To the best of my knowledge, no one from the Montreal Urban Community [MUC] police department attended Kelly's funeral, although the chairman of the advisory committee on intercultural and interracial relations of the MUC was there.

## Unanswered questions

Others who attended the funeral expressed fear, anger and apprehension. The haunting questions on everyone's mind: "Was there no other way for the police to disarm Trevor Kelly other than to shoot him in the back? Are police officers taught no other ways of disarming a black man other than to shoot him down?"

Others expressed concern about how we make our streets safe: "We do not want to walk in fear of the police. Where do we turn and what do we have to do to protect our lives and the lives of our children? Women cannot walk the streets for fear of being raped, gays cannot jog through a park without having their heads bashed in by skinheads, and black men cannot walk the streets without the fear of being shot by the very people hired to protect them."

Through the songs we sang, we not only mourned Kelly's death, we mourned the deaths of Anthony Griffith and Marcellus Francois and the other black men who have been gunned down by police. We mourned Rodney King, who was brutally beaten by Los Angeles police, and we mourned every black person who has ever been subjected to the brutalities of racism.

We sang of the pain, of the frustration, of the rage. We sang because, as reknowned African-American writer James Baldwin said in The Fire Next Time, "there has been almost no language to describe the horrors of black life."

But a language and a voice we must find. Because unless we can name our pain, we cannot hope to eliminate it. I looked around me at faces of the African diaspora, faces of hope meshed with despair, faces both young and old searching for answers.

Montreal remains scarred by this tragedy. It's unfortunate that it takes something like Trevor Kelly's death to bring the fragmented black communities together. But it will take a continued effort to keep the channels of communication open between these communities.

In order to fight for justice and to fight effectively, the effort must be a collective one.

# Individual rights come first
## Justice system must protect important principles: Dignity, autonomy

November 4, 1993

After sitting through more than 100 hours of testimonies at the Police Ethics Committee that investigated the conduct of police Lt. Pablo Palacios and five other officers charged with carrying out two illegal searches in her Little Burgundy apartment two years ago, Julie Alleyne, the woman who laid the charges, was glad her ordeal has come to an end.

Palacios was found guilty of abusing his authority. The ethics committee hasn't yet rendered a decision on sentencing.

"The whole thing was a nightmare for me," Alleyne said. "Beside everything else, the hearings were all in French and I couldn't understand what was going on."

The fact that one of the incidents was videotaped by a CBC Newswatch crew and had been introduced as evidence in the case, meant that Alleyne had to experience over and over again the feeling of being violated in her own home by police as well as the reminder that her private life had been televised nationwide.

From the time she first decided to press charges, Alleyne said she has lived in fear. "I couldn't sleep at night. I developed a stress disorder. When I did sleep I'd wake up with nightmares. Many times I was sorry I ever started this thing."

Her fears were confirmed when on the weekend before one of the hearings, Palacios and his officers searched Alleyne's apartment, claimed to have found drugs on the premises, arrested her and charged her with possession.

"This was all out-and-out lie," Alleyne said. "They may have found drugs in my house but I am convinced that it is they who put them there," she said. "This was a tactic to try to discredit me."

The drug case is still pending.

What Alleyne did was test a system put into place three years ago to ensure that individual rights are protected under the law. It gives an individual the right to file a grievance with the Police Ethics Committee, which decides whether there is sufficient grounds for an investigation and for the police officers to receive a warning, a reprimand or a suspension.

The CBC tape used as evidence showed that Palacios didn't identify himself as a police officer, but pretended to be a pizza delivery man when he came to search Alleyne's apartment.

Using the CBC video, Alleyne's lawyer cited some blatant contradictions. If Palacios believed dangerous criminals were in Alleyne's apartment, why did he burst in the apartment carrying only a walkie talkie? And why was he followed by a camera crew and not by armed police officers?

And if this was the first time he'd ever been in Alleyne's apartment, as he'd claimed, then how did he know the layout of the apartment well enough to turn on a light switch in total darkness?

And what are we to make of the last scene of the video where we see Palacios shouting victoriously into the night, "I'm the lean, mean machine?"

Another interesting aspect of the case was how police lawyer Mario Letourneau tried to discredit organizations in the black community that supported Alleyne. As reported in *The Gazette* Feb. 20, Letourneau told the hearing he believed the complaints were filed as part of a conspiracy to have Palacios transferred out of Little Burgundy.

Leith Hamilton, former director of the Black Community Council of Quebec, said he was outraged by the suggestion that the black community had engineered the case to get rid of Palacios. "The real issue is whether Palacios entered Alleyne's house illegally," Hamilton said.

"The black community is not interested in protecting its criminals and is very concerned about eliminating the drug trade. We want Palacios out of the area because he did not follow proper police procedures."

Hamilton was also disturbed by suggestions that he personally encouraged Alleyne to file a complaint with the commission. Alleyne repeatedly said she contacted the council for advice, and not the other way around.

Hamilton was delighted by the finding of the ethics committee. "This case should give other people the confidence to go up against the system."

• • •

Palacios might have been effective in eliminating crime in Little Burgundy, but at what cost?

While Palacios' intentions might have been honourable, by using unorthodox methods he violated the rights of individuals.

In my view, the justice system should be weighted in favour of protecting the individual from intrusion by the state, at the cost of abandoning the more efficient crime control that would result if police could stop, question and search anyone without a warrant and without following due process.

In refusing to allow this to happen the justice system protects two important principles—dignity and autonomy.

It might appear that anytime police nab criminals, even in unlawful ways, it benefits the collective good.

These efforts might eliminate problems threatening the collective good, but ultimately the collective good is undermined because it depends on the protection of individual rights.

# When police and minorities meet, issues are not BLACK & WHITE

February 6, 1993

They came with mixed emotions. Some were apprehensive, others suspicious and cynical. There were those who were downright frustrated, but still willing to try new methods for dealing with old problems.

As a result, the air was electric.

For three days, from Jan. 26 to 28, representatives of the Montreal Urban Community [MUC] police force, the black community, three levels of government and other institutions attended a seminar on how to build bridges between groups. It was organized by the Trinidad and Tobago Association, the Quebec department of immigration and cultural communities and the Lacolle Centre for Educational Innovation of Concordia University.

Cherie Brown, director of the National Coalition Building Institute [NCBI] of Washington, D.C., and five of her colleagues from the Toronto chapter of NCBI conducted the seminar which tried to teach this diverse group of people how to communicate across their differences.

They came, young and old, of different backgrounds, different classes and different ethnic groups, seeking new ways to combat an old enemy—racism. The one thing we had in common was the hope that building these bridges across social, political and cultural borders would lead to social change.

Some younger members of the black community were angry, impatient and skeptical. They wanted change and they wanted it now. I saw myself 20 years ago and understood their anguish and their defiance. We, too, were determined to make change happen.

The older members of the black community came too—battle-worn, scarred by years of oppression, they were seeking to revitalize that fighting spirit and willing to learn new ways to communicate.

## Depth of our pain

Painstakingly, we groped to find the words that best expressed our point of view, hoping this would help transform others' perspectives. We expressed the depth of our pain and in so doing discovered that it was not dissimilar to the pain of others. We were all moved by the commonality of our humanity and it was this realization which bonded us and enabled us to work through some of the difficult issues.

Brown's approach was to teach people the bridge-building skills which pull them closer through listening and realizing that similarities exist even when conflicting views are expressed.

It was important that we examined discrimination in a larger context that included not only racism, but also anti-Semitism, sexism, homophobia, age and disability discrimination. By learning how different groups experience maltreatment, we began to understand in a profound way the personal effect of discrimination.

We learned that if one does not forgive, one continues to hate. And the hate poisons one's life. To end oppression, we must seek out the humanity in those who are hurting and in those who are causing the pain.

In personal narratives or "speakouts," as Brown referred to them, we heard an Oriental woman express her feelings of invisibility. A young black woman expressed the rage she felt in high school when she was told the reason she was never chosen for parts in plays was because she was black. She told us how this experience stripped her of her self-esteem and her confidence.

Another woman related what it was like being the child of Holocaust survivors and the fear with which she approached every day of her life, trusting nothing to remain the same, expecting her whole world to cave in at any time.

A gay man described the painful experience of being victimized and the feelings of powerlessness that evoked. One woman talked about her experiences of poverty, trying to raise her children as a single mother. She told of the insensitive treatment she received at the hands of social workers who made her feel inadequate because she was poor. Eyes filled with tears, she shouted: "I want to know who put a price tag on loving your children?"

The director of a police station related how as a young boy he had been beaten up by a group of black youths and how he had to overcome his prejudices through education.

One member of the group said she hadn't been conscious of the burden black leaders carry and the toll this hopelessness extracts.

You can't build bridges until you understand someone else's pain as well as our own. You have to personalize pain in order to activate the need for change.

We walked away with a renewed commitment to work together. We agreed that never again would we tolerate oppression in any form.

For three days we looked at issues confronting our community—harassment of blacks by police, black soli-

National Coalition Building conference

darity, black leadership and support, how to empower our youth to have hope, the importance of education, the fragmentation of the black family, violence and social change, hierarchies of oppression, understanding the effects of internalized oppression, how to engage the whole community to become involved in the process of social change.

When Yvon Labelle, director of MUC police Station 24 in Little Burgundy was asked how he felt walking into this workshop, where tensions between blacks and police were so prevalent, he said he knew what he was getting into. "As soon as we walked in, we knew that we were the agenda. These things have to be resolved."

"There is a common goal in the hearts of everyone," he said. "People may have opposing views, this is natural, but everyone wants to make it a better society.

"Dialogue helps to break barriers. My goal now is to help share this vision with the police officers at my station. We are going to be holding meetings with the community in order for the community to understand us and so that we can understand the community. Some of the techniques used here might be very effective in getting us to talk to each other."

Talking with Labelle, seeing him as a human being, struggling with an extremely difficult job, was informative. He ceased to be the faceless enemy and became a person.

As Russian philosopher Nikolai Berdyaev said, you can only make war on objects, not on subjects. Relating on this subjective level, in this informal setting, where we broke bread together and attempted to communicate our positions, was tremendously important in the understanding of each other's perspectives.

A powerful moment came when two individuals, with very polarized perspectives on how the black community should deal with the police,

National Coalition Building conference

enacted a discussion in front of the group. They each made an attempt to listen to the other, repeating many of the points the other had raised.

Despite their efforts to listen and be as accurate about what the other was saying as possible, each left out significant information that helped explain the other's point of view. This demonstrated the extent to which we tend to hear what we want to hear in an argument and leave out or minimize information that we don't agree with or are not comfortable with.

Breaking interpersonal barriers is important, but ultimately we've got to break institutional barriers. Racism is a systemic problem. What needs to be changed are the relations of power.

The reality of the matter is that we do not hold power equally. We may have been empowered by this experience, but it is important to keep in mind that empowerment is more than a psychological condition. It is also social, political and economic.

Individual police officers may be very open to change, but the force as a collective still retains all the power.

Negotiating implies that both sides have equal power, when in reality they do not. We have to find ways of altering these power relations.

## Singing seen as inappropriate

But the question remains: is it realistic to suppose we can use the master's tools to dismantle the master's house?

Some members of the black community felt it was inappropriate to be shown singing and holding hands with the police so soon after the incident in which a black man, Trevor Kelly, was shot and killed by a police officer.

Perhaps the sing-a-long was staged for the media in the hope it would convey a positive message to the public.

Yet for some it downplayed the pain and the outrage the black community is feeling and it gave the erroneous impression that relations between blacks and police are more amicable than they actually are.

Similarly, the police were not ready to be portrayed singing together as if the problems of racism have been resolved—because the problems have not been resolved.

The session, however, may be seen as a first step in a very long and difficult journey. And, as the adage goes, a journey of a thousand miles begins with a single step.

National Coalition Building conference

111

# Face to face
## Voices are sometimes raised in anger but at least the black community and police are talking to each other

July 8, 1993

They came in full police gear—uniforms, guns, billyclubs. Some even wore bulletproof vests.

However, these police officers were not on a SWAT team operation. They had come to eat Sunday breakfast and talk with members of the Cote des Neiges black community at the Jamaica Association on Jean Talon St.

The encounter last month was part of a program to make police officers more aware of issues confronting the black community, as well as help the black community understand police concerns.

Who knows what the long-term effects of the clash last Saturday between police and spectators at the Carifete parade will be on these talks. Even now, there are divisions shaping up between senior and younger leaders in the community about how to respond.

The sessions are one component of an elaborate plan developed by the Montreal Urban Community, community organizations and government agencies to improve relations between the police department and the black community. The plan has three major parts: developing relations between black residents and police officers; making young people aware of their rights and the role of police; and preventing crime and substance abuse.

Stations in N.D.G. [Notre Dame de Grace], Little Burgundy, Cote des Neiges, Montreal North and Riviere des Prairies are participating.

Since five previous sessions had gone so well, the organizers thought it was time to invite the media in.

Much to their chagrin, however, the session did not start well. Tempers flared and voices rose as a group of youth workers complained about how police officers had acted during a recent investigation at a youth centre.

Police officers had entered the youth centre at Mandela Park, took the animators outside and proceeded to interrogate youths inside without ever stating their purpose and without consulting centre organizers.

The youth animators were outraged, they told the police officers: The officers' behaviour would undermine the work the centre was doing because kids would avoid a centre where they know they might be harassed by cops. And they wouldn't trust the youth workers any more.

There was a question of respect, as well. As one youth animator expressed it, police officers don't normally walk into a school, bypass the principal and begin to question students, nor do they walk into a home and disregard a parent.

The police should have the same respect when they walk into a community organization, they argued. "If you have a reason to come in, come, but state your purpose and help us do our job, too. Don't undermine us.

"We both work the streets. We want our community cleaned up, too. We've got to work together."

Initially, police officers responded like this: "There had been some problem in the area and we had to take action.

"We followed proper procedure."

What that "problem" was, was never made clear, however.

But after a heated debate, the police officers finally saw the youth workers' point of view and assured them they would act differently in the future.

That debate pointed up the value of these face-to-face meetings.

The discussion moved from angry finger-pointing to a stage where possible solutions were discussed.

What was great about the session was that it allowed the community an immediate way of conveying concerns to the police.

The sessions are animated by Paulette Spence, a police/community liaison officer employed by the MUC [Montreal Urban Police] and working out of the Jamaica Association, and Nicolette de Smit, a social worker from Jewish Family Services.

Spence said the program is an attempt to bridge some of the gaps and misinformation between the police and local youth.

"A lot of the officers were very excited about the workshops because they got the opportunity to come face to face with the youth animators and with members of various black organizations," she said.

"For many of them, this was the first time they had made contact with the black community in an informal and non-threatening environment and not in a crisis situation."

One of the difficulties encountered during the sessions was the reluctance or inability of some police officers to speak English.

According to Spence, some know how to speak English but weren't comfortable about using it because they felt they would lose a sense of control. "As far as I'm concerned, police work should not be about control. It should be about communicating and understanding—and if you can't communicate in a common language it defeats the purpose of what you're trying to do."

When the sessions began, Spence said, many of the officers were not aware of the services available for black anglophone youth and as a result didn't use services that could have helped them do their job more effectively. An example would be making use of youth workers at various community organizations.

But police and members of the black community shared one concern: they believe the news media oversimplify issues and tend to polarize conflicts. And the media fail to give in-depth analysis of a situation.

For example, there is a tendency to portray the black community as crime-ridden and drug-infested, and the police as racists.

This tendency has made both groups very defensive, and the job of developing partnerships has become much more difficult.

Nicolette de Smit said the most significant session occurred at the Maison des Jeunes in Cote des Neiges with front-line police officers.

"The officer in charge was an incredibly enthusiastic, positive guy and saw this meeting as a great opportunity for himself and his police officers to get to know people from the black community.

"He got his men really pumped up to enjoy the session. They came marching out carrying the police flag. It was the biggest show de Courtrai St. has ever had."

The session was very upbeat and there were a lot of positive exchanges, de Smit said.

Noel Alexander, president of the Jamaica Association, sees the problem of crime prevention in Cote des Neiges not simply as a policing issue: "It is a social problem. It involves education, employment, housing, immigration. It's caused by the frustrations of black youths in dealing with all the institutional barriers they have to face. . . . And when they start to exhibit 'deviant behaviour,' society expects the police to handle it."

The Community Crime Prevention Project takes the viewpoint that the problem of delinquency can't be solved simply by improving police-youth relations. The aim is to help dismantle barriers that hamper black youngsters and their families, as well as help overcome deeply ingrained beliefs and stereotypes about visible minorities.

De Smit says the solutions initially were perceived in simplistic terms: "People thought that by getting a couple of cops out there to play basketball with the kids, that would solve all the problems. They thought that if the

kids saw the police as human beings, everybody would all get along better."

But the originators of the program soon realized the problems were much more complex.

They realized that one cannot look at crime prevention without addressing many other problems: why the dropout rate for black students is so high, why blacks are over-represented in the penal system, why the unemployment rate in the black community is so high.

It would take a great deal more than a few meetings to find solutions to these and other problems. But the fact that black people and police are talking is encouraging.

Linton Garner, MUC adviser on race relations, said the idea behind the action plan is to create some lasting and permanent partnerships so that black residents can feel as well-served and well-protected as residents of any other group.

"It is only through these partnerships that we will be able to realize institutionalized change—by working together diligently so solve common problems."

When asked whether the confrontation last weekend between police officers and blacks at the Carifete parade would have any impact on the action plan, Garner said: "It's important not to let one event erode the development of initiatives that already have produced concrete results." If anything, he added, the clash should point to the need to continue these dialogues.

But Lois Martineau of AKAX, a youth group that opposed dialogue with police, feels the police intervention shows the talks didn't achieve anything significant.

"Clearly ,the police reactions during Carifete once again demonstrate how police choose to use force instead of reason."

So it's going to be a while before we see the full impact of the police action.

A parting observation from one who was somewhat intimidated by so many weapons at the breakfast workshop: meaningful dialogue occurs where there is mutual trust. Guns and bulletproof vests are not exactly the best breakfast ingredients.

Next time, guys, leave your battle gear at home.

# Beauregard way off base
# in comments about immigrants
## Lineup incident more than 'cultural misunderstanding'

May 4, 1995

There's a sign at Westmount High School that reads "Just say NO to pizza." The reference, of course, is to the pizza police officers used on April 6 to lure nine black students from Westmount High to Station 24 where the students, aged 12 to 15, spent about 45 minutes in a police lineup. Police had already been denied permission by the school principal, Richard Meades, to take the students. The youths had their photographs taken, were put in a room with suspected criminals and placed in the lineup despite protests from some of them.

One of the young boys, a 13-year-old, has been traumatized by the experience. According to his mother he has been very withdrawn since the incident. "I'm very worried about him," his mother said. "He's very angry, very edgy, he's been having trouble sleeping but he won't talk about it."

The Little Burgundy black community was very disappointed in the actions of the police officers, especially in light of the recent bridge building that's been going on between the community and the police officers at Station 24.

Residents of the area say they are put off by the recent events and that even the apology by police chief Jacques Duchesneau does not take away the sting of what happened.

Participants at a meeting I attended in Little Burgundy argued that even if the police had a legal right to pick up the youths, they still exercised poor judgment and have lost whatever credibility they've gained. They say that what frustrates them most is that this kind of police treatment of black youths has been an on-going problem: promises of change have not materialized.

A cultural misunderstanding is how Kettly Beauregard, chairman of the committee that oversees MUC [Montreal Urban Community] police, characterized the incident in a quote published in The Montreal Gazette on May 1.

The reason the black community reacted so "virulently," Beauregard said, is because "we immigrants and cultural communities are not used to this type of thing."

Forever the perpetual immigrants. Not quite integrated, not quite assimilated. Don't quite understand. A stranger in a foreign land.

Like many of the people who attended the meetings pertaining to this case, I am a seventh generation black Canadian. Yet I am forever considered an immigrant. "What island are you from," is the inevitable question; to which I automatically respond, "the island of Montreal."

Many of the people who reacted so "virulently" were third-and fourth-generation black Canadians who are

116

quite used to dealing with the system. Many have been involved in community work in the Little Burgundy area for years.

Along with the assumption that all blacks in Montreal are immigrants is the belief that people in the Little Burgundy area are not knowledgeable about routine police procedures—like the one pertaining to the use of children in police lineups.

Another assumption is that community members were too vocal in registering their disapproval, that their responses were not justified but actually "virulent" as Beauregard put it.

(Incidentally, the Houghton Mifflin Dictionary defines virulent as: 1. extremely poisonous or pathogenic, said of a disease, toxin or microorganism; 2. bitterly hostile or antagonistic, venomously spiteful; full of hate; 3. intensely irritating, obnoxious or harsh.)

Another underlying sentiment that is being suggested here by Beauregard seems to reflect the all-too-common view that immigrants should be thankful that we've let them into this country, and that the least they can do is perform in their civic duty and stand and deliver—in a police lineup—without creating such a fuss. This lack of civic generosity, such reasoning implies, can only be attributed to their immigrant status, their non-affiliation with a society that has been so generous as to allow them into the fold. Not wanting to co-operate is tantamount to disobeying the law.

Principal Richard Meades was most outraged by this violation of the rights of these children. Meades is considering launching a complaint with the Quebec Police Ethics Commission, the Quebec body which investigates complaints against police.

Beauregard's reasoning also implies that rounding up of children during the school day is standard police operating practice in any community, regardless of colour. I wonder when the last time was that the police went to Selwyn House or Lower Canada College or Beaconsfield High School to pick up white youths to do their civic duty in a lineup? I would think their parents would have been quite "virulent" if they had.

As a parent I am asked my permission every time my child is taken out of school on field trips.

We take it for granted that as parents, we and we alone decide what activities and experiences our children are to have or participate in. We have become accustomed to the privileges and rights that this country extends. I do not know any parents who would consent to their child being taken from school and placed in a room with known felons, photographed and ordered to participate in a lineup against their wishes.

The use of the nine teenagers in the police lineup has to be viewed within the context of the police and black community relations in Montreal. Too much has happened, too much has been said, too many reports have been written for something like this to occur today.

Black male youths in this society live under tremendous pressure, as do their parents. The police seem to exhibit very little understanding of the significance that the Little Burgundy community attaches to this incident.

They seem incapable of putting themselves in the shoes of others and seeing reality from their vantage point.

From the perspective of a black youth living in Montreal, it is not at all unreasonable to feel terribly at risk when one is asked to stand in a police lineup. In the past few years, five black men have been shot to death by Montreal Urban Community police officers and relations between police and the black community have been particularly tenuous.

Independent investigations have shown that there is racism on the police force; the fear felt by black youths is legitimate.

As black people we have all internalized, at least to some extent, the image of Rodney King being pelted with innumerable blows by members of the Los Angeles Police Department. It has become a part of our collective historical memory. It influences our perceptions of the police; we see them not as our protectors but as our adversaries. In this context it is not unreasonable that the 13-year-old who was put in the lineup has nightmares. Perhaps a white youth would not have had such a strong a reaction because his experiences have led him to believe that the policeman is his friend.

If our society were not tainted with racism and if stereotypes about the worthiness of blacks were not prevalent, then perhaps we could presume that the police are acting in our best interests.

I may be overly suspicious, but I find it interesting that on the one hand the police department has apologized for the incident. Jacques Duchesneau said he has issued a new policy requiring officers to obtain the parents' permission before asking minors to stand in lineups or participate in any type of police work.

Yet on the other hand, Beauregard, herself black, transmits another message—that the black community was ultimately wrong to react so strongly in this simple matter of "cultural misunderstanding." Beauregard's comments echo some of the negative views about immigrants that have been expressed by people in mainstream society who believe that immigrants have not adapted to their host country, that many of society's woes are attributable to them.

Also, her comments negate the long history of brutal behaviour of police toward black youths and tries to give the impression that the police actions were rational.

# Deconstructing racism: A case study

## Olivia Rovinescu

This chapter examines two accounts of the same event: one by a person of colour, the other by the director of a police department who is white. Their accounts clearly embody different perceptions, because they are situated within relations of power that determine how information is understood, processed and communicated. They exemplify both a "master narrative," as Henry Giroux (1992) calls the voice of institutionalized reason and a "counter narrative," the voice of someone who has been marginalized by this institutionalized reason.

The question, "Who's account really counts?" prompts us to consider the extent to which knowledge is socially constructed, and thus how "objective events" are subject to multiple interpretations. These two conflicting accounts provide us with an opportunity to interrogate the language, ideas and relations inherent in the logic of prejudice.

Here I provide a concrete example of what Giroux (1992) calls "border pedagogy," and I will make suggestions for how "border pedagogy" might be translated into classroom practice. Much work has articulated the need for critical pedagogy, but not enough suggestions have been provided for how it might translate into classroom practice—what materials can be used and what kinds of questions best stimulate and engage critical inquiry of the type that critical pedagogy is interested in. This chapter presents a model of how the issue of racism can be explored in a classroom situation and demonstrates how this kind of case study can generate critical discourse.

Our case study looks at a letter to the editor written by Denis Lauzon (1991), a white Francophone male, and director of a police station, in response to a column written by Black male Anglophone columnist Clifton Ruggles (1991b) that described an incident involving a disputed parking spot. In his column, Ruggles alleges that a white Francophone woman grabbed him by the lapels of his jacket, hurled racial insults at him and then proceeded to falsely accuse him of assaulting her. The police were summoned and a complaint was made by the woman against Mr. Ruggles which was subsequently dropped. Ruggles, however, proceeded to lodge his own complaint against this woman on the grounds that it was she who had assaulted him both physically and mentally and had put at risk both his own life and that of his six-year-old daughter, who was with him at the time.

Lauzon interprets Ruggles' column as an attack on the police, and in his letter to the editor he endeavours to explain what he calls "the police point of view." In doing so, he presents an account of the incident which casts doubt on Ruggles report of the event.

Lauzon's letter became a *cause célèbre* in Montreal. The *Montreal Gazette* devoted three weeks to publishing letters to the editor that commented on Lauzon's letter. Among these letters was one from an eye-witness, Harold Spanier, who corroborated Ruggles' account of the events. Particularly disturbing was Spanier's claim that the police refused to allow him to make a statement at the scene; he eventually had to go to the police station on his own accord and overcome attempts to dissuade him before he was able to file his eye-witness report.

This article presents a close examination of Lauzon's response to the Ruggles column and examine what might have motivated and directed this response. It examines how personal prejudice and institutional power might have affected Lauzon's reading and understanding of Ruggles' column and influenced his response to it.

This case study provides a basis for students to analyze critically what Giroux (1992: 183) calls "the forms of intelligibility, interests, and moral and political considerations that different voices embody." Lauzon's account represents a set of underlying interests that shape how his narrative is told and situated within relations of power that determined how the information was understood, processed and communicated. An examination of Lauzon's account can help students uncover and demystify how claims to knowledge come into being and how they can distort reality. Ruggles' account can be viewed as an example of what Giroux (1992) would call "dangerous memory"—testimonials of oppression that "keep alive the memory of human suffering, along with forms of knowledge and struggles in which such suffering was shaped and contested." Giroux sees the presentation of these "dangerous" accounts as essential ingredients in a "pedagogy of possibility" which will help students to acquire their own "voice" and place the experiences that students bring to the classroom at the forefront of the educational agenda. This case study can be seen as a model of the kind of discourse that students can begin to initiate on their own.

I will also demonstrate how the skills and dispositions of critical thinking (Paul 1990) might be used in the service of border pedagogy. Critical thinking is the ability to reflect on the assumptions that underlie our customary, habitual ways of thinking and acting. It consists of identifying and challenging these assumptions that underlie ideas, beliefs and values we take for granted. It is an awareness of and reflection upon how context shapes what we consider "normal" and "natural" ways of thinking and living. It involves imagining and exploring alternatives to supposedly fixed belief systems. Identifying and challenging assumptions is central to critical thinking, as is challenging the taken-for-granted, common-sense notions about how we live in the world and should interact in relationships.

## Analysis of Lauzon's Response

Lauzon's letter leaves out important information that is relevant to a proper understanding of the event. Conspicuous by its absence is any mention of the racial incident that precipitated the affair. Lauzon does not applaud the woman's provocative racist remarks nor her physical attack on Ruggles; in fact, he seems to think they are not worth mentioning at all. Nor does he mention that she had falsely accused Ruggles of assaulting her. Lauzon merely tells us that:

> Ruggles admitted to taking the parking place of the victim and added she
> reacted very bitterly and adamantly.

Actually, Ruggles never admitted to "taking the parking spot of the victim."
What Ruggles says instead is that he

> hadn't noticed the dark car double parked up ahead. There were no
> flashing lights indicating the driver's intentions. As soon as I got out of
> my car, the female occupant of this vehicle approached me in a rage,
> insisting I had taken her spot. I explained that I wouldn't be very long,
> that I was merely picking up my daughter from her gymnastics class.
> The woman grabbed me by the lapels and proceeded to hurl racial
> insults at me: maudi negre, barbre, sauvage, chien sale.

Because Lauzon left out so much necessary information, it is difficult for a
reader to understand the framework within which this confrontation occurred. By
leaving out information necessary for a proper understanding of the events that
led up to Ruggles lodging formal charges, he makes Ruggles' account appear
incredible. Is it that Lauzon doesn't consider the woman's racist remarks
important to the case, or is he choosing not to focus on them because he can then
proceed to portray Ruggles as the troublemaker? Note how twice in the letter
Lauzon chastises Ruggles for having instigated the incident. First:

> It is to be noted that Mr. Ruggles is himself responsible concerning this
> incident and the judicial procedures occurred when he insisted that legal
> actions be taken.

And at the conclusion of the letter he says:

> I would appreciate it if you would publish this letter so that the
> population may be made aware of the police view regarding the incident
> incited by Mr. Ruggles.

For those who did not read the initial column, it would indeed seem odd that
Ruggles would be pressing charges against someone who merely "reacted
bitterly and adamantly" after having her parking spot taken. By leaving out the
woman's verbal and physical attacks and her attempt to have Ruggles arrested,
Ruggles' motives for pressing charges against her are obscured. Lauzon does not
address the fact that the woman had attempted to use the judicial system for racist
ends. He is much more interested in seeing Ruggles as the instigator of the
incident, even in the face of overwhelming evidence—the eye-witness report and
the report from his own police officers, who vindicated Ruggles of any wrong-

doing. Lauzon himself wrote that his police officers told Ruggles that "his story was not only plausible but most probably what had happened and wrote it in the report." Yet, despite this information, Lauzon continues to pursue the idea that Ruggles was the instigator. Lauzon tells us nothing of the racism that precipitated the affair, but he informs us that Ruggles "did spit on the car in his own anger." We are never told what Ruggles was reacting to, what made him angry enough to spit, and thus he is left looking like an aggressive troublemaker. According to the eye-witness, Ruggles was most cooperative, most obliging, and initially willing to move his car to give the woman the space. Lauzon has the choice of seeing Ruggles as someone whose dignity was trampled upon and expressed his disgust by spitting on an inanimate object, or he can choose to view the spitting as an act divorced from its context. It appears he did the latter.

It is interesting that, although Ruggles' innocence was confirmed by his own police officers, Lauzon continues to characterize Ruggles as the "suspect" and describes Ruggles' daughter's gym as "the direction in which the suspect fled." The use of the word "fled" was totally unnecessary but effective in conveying a nefarious intention in Ruggles' actions. But Ruggles did not know at that time that the police had been called, therefore he could not have "fled." Fleeing implies attempting to get away from someone. Ruggles had merely gone in to pick up his daughter—information he had given the woman and information that was conveyed to the police by the eye-witness they encountered sitting in Ruggles' car. Throughout his letter, Lauzon accusingly refers to Ruggles as the "suspect" and to the woman as "the victim." He does not call her the "complainant" or even the "alleged victim." By choosing to see her as the "victim," even though all evidence points to the contrary, Lauzon shows us that his irrational prejudices blinded him.

Because Lauzon was prejudiced by his own assumptions, he actually misread his own police officers' report. The original police report, of which I have obtained a copy, actually refers to Ruggles as the "victim" and to the woman as the "suspect." Interestingly enough, even the police officers who filed the report and were seemingly convinced of Ruggles' innocence in the affair had trouble retaining the distinction as to who was the "victim" and who was the "suspect." In one part of the report they wrote:

The suspect held the suspect by the neck.

One wonders whether the picture of a Black man as a victim in an incident with a white woman was just too difficult for them to imagine. Was their inclination to vilify him so great that it could not be held in check even by contrary evidence? Was this merely an unconscious slip, an error made in the haste of filling out the report, or does it have greater significance?

One would assume Lauzon was not in a rush when he wrote the letter to the editor. He had time to read the police report and speak to his officers before making a public statement. One would assume that a man in his position of responsibility would have availed himself of whatever documents existed as evidence upon which to base his arguments.

Lauzon also chooses to inform the public that Ruggles was the "object of a criminal investigation which was warranted." This terminology, in the face of Ruggles' immediate vindication, seems highly inappropriate. I would suggest that perhaps the only reason Lauzon used this terminology at all was to cloud the issue and appeal to an association of Blacks with crime in the public's mind.

Another possible explanation for the victim/suspect confusion might be gender-related. What assumptions guided Lauzon's thinking with respect to gender? Did Lauzon have difficulty imagining a woman as the "suspect?" Is it because Ruggles was a man that Lauzon had difficulty envisioning him as the "victim"? This case defies common notions of who "assaults" and whom and what it is to assault somebody. It is highly likely that, if Ruggles had acted in exactly the same manner towards the woman as she had towards him, that is, if he had grabbed her by the lapels and hurled insults at her, there would be no question that some form of assault had taken place. But because it was a woman assaulting a man, because it was a reversal of roles, the situation is less clear. Usually physical aggression is associated with males and not females, and it may be this gender stereotyping that affected Lauzon's response. Ruggles acknowledges the role gender might have played in this affair when he wrote:

> She is a white, French-speaking Canadian female . . . well dressed, driving an expensive car with a cellular phone, with which she dialled 911.

It is also interesting to see how Lauzon downplays the presence of the eye-witness. He makes casual reference to a witness but does not say whether this witness corroborated Ruggles' story or not. One has to presume he did, because otherwise the police would not have considered Ruggles' story credible. Here is how Lauzon makes mention of the eye-witness:

> Mr. Ruggles also said he had a witness in his car. The policemen listened to Mr. Ruggles, took down his name along with his version of events.

This contrasts dramatically with Ruggles' account and with that of the eye-witness. Here is how Ruggles described it:

> When Harold insisted on giving his eye-witness account of the events, he was rudely told to be quiet.

Harold Spanier elaborated what happened in a letter to the editor:

> When I asked to know what was going on, the officers threatened to take me to the station and charge me as an "accomplice to the charge of

assault." When I asked to make an eye witness statement, they disregarded my request. I had to go down of my own accord to the police station and overcome attempts to dissuade me before being able to file my testimony.

Note the vagueness in Lauzon's reference to the eye-witness. Lauzon's statement, "Ruggles also *said* he had a witness," implies that it may be hearsay and not a verifiable fact. It is also not clear whether he means the police took down the eye-witness's name and version of events or whether it was Ruggles' name and version of the events they took down. It is made to appear that the latter is the case, but the former may also be implied. Once again, is this merely a grammatical mistake, or is Lauzon being purposefully vague so as to avoid confronting the charge that his officers may have acted inappropriately?

At one point in his column, Ruggles makes the observation that by calling the police under false pretences, the woman

wasted taxpayers money as well as valuable police time.

Yet Lauzon manages to misread this criticism, obviously directed at the woman, and interprets the comment to be a criticism of the police:

Mr. Ruggles complained of the formality of this dossier and the high costs resulting from police interventions.

Reading is not a neutral activity. It is a purposeful activity. We read with intent, and our reading is imbued with prior meanings and associations. How we read and what we choose to understand of what we read is a function of our prior conditioning and our worldview, as well as of our capacity to read critically, fair-mindedly and empathetically. Sometimes our worldview and our vested interests prevent us from reading correctly, and from perceiving clearly what we see and hear.

Let's examine how Lauzon further manages to devalue and ignore the viewpoint that informs Ruggles' perspective.

Lauzon shows no understanding of Ruggles' insistence on pressing charges against the woman. He tells us that "similar dossiers are usually filed without accusations and charges often not laid." He exhibits no understanding of the meaning and significance that Ruggles attaches to the incident, and he chastises Ruggles for inciting further trouble. Lauzon either ignores or trivializes Ruggles' concern over what might have transpired under a different set of circumstances as idle conjecture. "Instead of making alarming hypotheses" is how Lauzon reacts to Ruggles' concern with what might have been if he had acted any differently and had not been able to diffuse the situation as he did. Ruggles' concern was that a less articulate Black person, or one who wasn't able to make themselves heard, would likely have ended up in jail. Ruggles' "what if" scenarios are appropriate because they reflect the reality many Blacks confront when they interface with the police. Lauzon does not take into account the perspective of the Black person living in North America, who knows it is not at all unreasonable to feel terribly at risk in such circumstances. It can be argued that Ruggles' "what if" scenarios were very relevant in his decision to take the woman to court. He assessed the possible damage such an incident could have caused and it outraged him. He felt he had a responsibility to pursue the matter in order to sensitize the public and prevent such occurrences from happening again. The fact that he was able to convince the police of his own innocence does not negate his concern about the potential danger for other Blacks. He can envision someone becoming so angered or intimidated by the situation that he or she would be provoked to break the law. He is not merely engaging in idle conjecture; he is putting himself in the shoes of another.

Perhaps one of the most blatant of Lauzon's distortions is his claim that Ruggles was

> exaggerating about being brought to Station 31 to spend the night in a holding pen.

Lauzon does not understand the speculative nature of Ruggles' writing. Ruggles muses about what might have transpired under a different set of circumstances:

> I wonder how events might have turned out had I been less articulate, less controlled, if I did not have a witness who happened to be white and if I had dared to register an ounce of the outrage I felt. I tend to think that I would have spent the night in the holding pen at Station 31, if not worse.

Nowhere did Ruggles actually claim he was taken down to the station or arrested. After reading Lauzon's letter, anyone who had not read Ruggles' column would assume Ruggles had lied. Lauzon hopes to weaken Ruggles' position and discredit him in the public eye, to attack the individual rather than his ideas.

Highlighting the different ways Ruggles and Lauzon perceive the same event are their responses to Ruggles' refusal to get into the police car for questioning. For Ruggles, getting into the car carried the stigma of being treated as a suspect. Plus, he may have felt more comfortable being out in the open where his conversation could be overheard by witnesses, as opposed to being closeted in the police car where he might have been victimized. Is Ruggles being paranoid in not assuming good will on the part of the Montreal police force, or is he being reasonably cautious? In a previous column, "Growing up Black: The differences aren't always subtle," Ruggles (1991c) recounts numerous incidents of police racism directed at him:

> There had been some trouble in the neighbourhood involving some

black youths. I was on my way home from work when suddenly a police cruiser almost knocked me over while swerving on the curb to block my path. Two policemen jumped out of the car demanding to know what I was carrying. "Work clothes," I explained politely. One cop threw me against the car. The other wrestled the bag from my arms, emptying the contents on the sidewalk. Seeing there was indeed nothing intimidating in the bag, they shoved it back into my arms, got back in their car and sped off. No apologies were made. No effort was made to help me retrieve the contents of my bag. It made no difference to them that I was innocent. By virtue of my blackness I was guilty. . . .

On another occasion I was on a bus when a skirmish occurred between a black youth and a white youth. When the police arrived, they herded all the blacks off the bus and took them to the station. No questions asked to determine who was actually involved. Not one of the white youths was detained. Surely a few properly addressed questions would have solved the mystery as to who was indeed guilty. How necessary was it to arrest all the black youths? Was this a conscious or unconscious act of racism? Whatever the motivation, the results were the same. We were turned into suspects. We were guilty by virtue of our blackness.

In every facet of your life you are seen as undesirable, unworthy of the same rights and privileges as white counterparts. Colour sets the criterion for your interactions in the world. And it is the colour of your skin that condemns you.

And elsewhere in that column:

A white person grows up taking for granted that one has fundamental rights, freedom of speech and of assembly, that one is innocent until proven guilty. As a black person, the reverse is true, you live your life as a suspect. The police suspect you, store owners suspect you, school officials suspect you.

Ruggles' own experiences and the experiences of other Blacks were the evidence upon which he based his assessment of the situation in which he found himself. He had little reason to believe that he would be treated fairly once inside the police cruiser. Quite the contrary, Ruggles had every reason to fear. In the past three years, four black men had been shot by Montreal police officers, and relations between the police and the Black community had been particularly tenuous. Anthony Griffin is alleged to have been running from custody when he was shot; his offence was stiffing a cabbie on a taxi fare. Presley Leslie was shot while being subdued by a half-dozen officers inside a nightclub; he was alleged to have had a gun and to have fired a shot or shots inside the club. Marcellus Francois was shot by a SWAT team sergeant in a case of mistaken identity. Seymour Fletcher was alleged to have committed suicide by shooting himself in the head while being arrested.

From Lauzon's point of view, getting into the police car was "standard operating procedure." He sees Ruggles' insistence on remaining on the street as insubordination. He shows no sensitivity to how Ruggles may have perceived the situation. He reports that the woman cooperated by getting into the police car to give her statement, and he chastises Ruggles for his refusal to be as "co-operative." From the woman's point of view, getting into a police car had no negative connotations. She had nothing to fear. She was, after all, the one who had called the police and was herself part of the dominant culture. As Ruggles pointed out in this column, she was white and French-speaking like the police officers themselves, appeared to be well-do-do, as evidenced by her clothing and the expensive automobile she drove, and thus was positioned in a privileged social group. Ruggles felt like the "outsider" he was perceived to be.

One of the ways Lauzon tries to promote his own credibility is by repeating every nuance of information pertaining to the apprehension of the so-called "suspect," providing details about which police car responded at what time, and went in which direction. This presentation of detailed information succeeds in giving an aura of police professionalism to the whole affair, and in establishing Lauzon as a paradigm of objectivity. We tend to want to believe whatever else he says, because somehow he has established, by the presentation of these facts, that he is an authority in possession of all the relevant data pertaining to this case. He is the expert. It is ironic that he devoted several paragraphs to the exact details of the comings and goings of the police cruisers but did not provide any pertinent details about the verbal and physical assault on Ruggles or the comments his officers made to the eye-witness.

Lauzon was so preoccupied with defending police conduct that he failed to properly understand the intent of Ruggles' column or the tone in which it was written. Lauzon read selectively, paying attention to his own biases and rummaging for self-justifying evidence, noticing only that which reflected directly on the conduct of the police and entirely ignoring the actions of the woman, clearly the perpetrator of trouble in this whole affair. In doing so he ignored other issues at stake: the woman's attempt to abuse the law enforcement apparatus, and the harm to which her actions potentially could have led.

Conspicuous by its absence in Lauzon's response is the one criticism levied against his officers: that they came asking for the whereabouts of the "black guy." For Ruggles, this comment indicated that the police had preconceived notions about him that placed him in potential danger. Referring to him as "black" was to use a term that is not merely descriptive but carries a lot of baggage in this society. Transcripts of conversations that took place in the police cruisers just before the fatal shooting of Marcellus Francois, an innocent Black man who had no other similarity to a known felon other than also being Black, indicated that the police officers made many disparaging references to the suspect's colour. It was his colour they chose to focus on, to the exclusion of all other telling characteristics, including height and weight. There was actually a tremendous difference between the two men which went undetected because Blackness was the overriding concern, once again demonstrating that one uses information selectively, choosing not to see and notice what does not reinforce one's view and one's ideological perspective. Lauzon does make a vague reference to the fact that his police officers had a "mental picture as to what was possibly happening" when they received the 911 call, but this reference obscures rather than sheds light on the issue.

## Overcoming Prejudice

Overcoming prejudice is indeed difficult because, as Weinstein (1990) reports, even experiences that disconfirm prejudices are stress-inducing, because they conflict with one's prior belief system. To be proven wrong creates tension and anxiety and can damage self-esteem. This anxiety, Weinstein points out, is caused by prior expectations, and by relative unfamiliarity and lack of confidence in the reliability of those expectations to serve as predictors of behaviour. Lauzon's experiences told him that Blacks behave in certain predictable ways. Yet this particular case contradicted those experiences. To minimize cognitive dissonance and deal with this contradiction, he reconstructed the facts of the case to "fit" his preconceived notions.

This case exemplifies the problem articulated by Paul and Adamson (1990), that prejudice is more than an error in thinking, more than a deficit to be ameliorated. Paul presents two arguments: that prejudice is not an aberration of a logical mind, but the product of an illogical mind and that we tend to be prejudiced based upon what we believe. Complex personal, political and economic factors also enter in. Prejudices are deeply ingrained, the product of years of effective social conditioning. We tend to construct self-serving accounts of reality and see only those aspects of reality that reinforce our point of view, and we find it difficult to reason within points of view different from our own. We are emotionally attached to our prejudices and hold onto them even in the face of overwhelming contradictory evidence. We are experts in "selective perception," in constructing our self-serving version of reality, one that acknowledges only those perceptions that reinforce our point of view. Worldviews are powerful constructs that have a truth, logic and rationality all of their own making.

Selective perception distorts our thinking and creates barriers to effective thought. We have all had the experience of hearing some sounds but not others, seeing some events but missing others altogether. We imbue some aspects of an event with more importance than other aspects of it. Because of the way we have been socialized, some ideas simply will not dawn on us, and other ideas will dominate our brain circuitry, influencing our behaviour and our attitudes. Prejudicial thinking is very difficult to reroute once it has become habitual. Uncritical thinking becomes a way of life. We internalize the myths and values of the culture in which we were raised and we do not engage in ego- or sociocentric critiques. We echo the voices of our past. We take it for granted that our version of reality is the only correct one, that our way of interpreting the world is the one true and right way, and that all other ways are inferior to it. Our very identity becomes shaped by thoughts and experiences grounded in prejudices which were uncritically formed at an early age and that we retain and defend in our adult lives. Thus, as Weinstein says, prejudice is more than simply an error in thinking. Prejudice is not necessarily something abnormal or atypical, something outside the normal mechanisms of thought, desire and action. That is why it is so difficult to eradicate.

Prejudice can be seen as a form of cultural conditioning, a system of practices and a way of life that includes "maps of meaning" which make things intelligible to those who subscribe to them. These "maps of meaning" mediate the processes through which an individual becomes a social being and the manner in which reality is experienced, understood and interpreted. People tend to become emotionally attached to their prejudices and hold onto them even in the face of overwhelming contrary evidence, as we have seen in the case of Lauzon. Prejudice serves powerful motives and interests within ourselves and within our society. These powerful feelings often defy logic.

## Anti-racist Pedagogy

Anti-racist education requires exposure to diversity, particularly to diverse points of view that exemplify a multiplicity of responses and perspectives. Coming in contact with diverse viewpoints and understanding the meaning and significance that different cultural groups attach to their experiences may be a first step in a long journey towards overcoming a person's prejudices. Exposing others to some of the inconsistencies in their thinking may open a small door that, through further encounters, may open even wider. Anti-racist education can also help victims of racism to articulate the conditions of their oppression. In so doing, they can create "counter-narratives," as Giroux calls the testimonials of those who have been subjugated and marginalized.

Ruggles' account can be seen as an example of a counter-narrative, expressing, as it does, what it is to be discriminated against, and the significance he attaches to certain experiences that have helped form how he views the world and how he responds to it. Articulating the concrete terms of one's oppression can be an empowering experience and can provide valuable insights for others. Cultivating the skill of creating "counter-narratives" in oral or written form should certainly be part of "border pedagogy." Everyday life is fraught with experiences that could be articulated and problematized. Problematizing everyday life is a way of overcoming one's feelings of helplessness, a way of giving a voice to the otherwise voiceless and powerless, and a way of acknowledging that their perceptions have value and significance and are worth being communicated.

Henry Giroux (1992) has identified what he considers to be some of the necessary aspects of anti-racist pedagogy, which falls under the broader category of "border pedagogy." He believes that it should provide students with the opportunity to

> engage the multiple references that constitute different cultural codes, experiences and languages. This means providing the learning opportunities for students to become media literate in a world of changing representations. It means offering students the knowledge and social relations that enable them to read critically not only how cultural texts are regulated by various discursive codes but also how such texts express and represent different ideological interests. In this case, border pedagogy establishes conditions of learning that define literacy inside the categories of power and authority. This suggests developing pedagogical practices that address texts as social and historical constructions. It also suggests developing pedagogical practices that allow students to analyze texts in terms of their presences and absences and, most important, such practices should provide students with the opportunity to read texts dialogically through a configuration of many voices, some of which offer up resistance, some of which provide support (pp. 135–136).

According to Giroux, students should be taught how to deconstruct and critically interrogate the "master narratives of racism" and learn how these narratives contribute to the marginalization of certain groups in society and perpetuate oppression and human suffering. In Ruggles' account we see examples of what Giroux refers to as the ways in which "difference and resistance are concretely expressed," and in Lauzon's account we see the hidden ways in which "master narratives" construct their own self-serving accounts of reality that aim to exclude, subordinate and marginalize others. According to Giroux, a very important component of anti-racist pedagogy is making evident how "white domination colonizes definitions of the normal." Lauzon's letter is a superb example of how the dominant ideology redefines and recasts reality to suit its own ends.

Anti-racist education should help students discover how to critically analyze the "metaphors" that govern their thoughts and define their realities; how to interrogate the language, ideas and relations inherent in the logic of prejudice; how to understand the way in which their own particular worldview came into being and manifests in their everyday lives; and how meaning and knowledge are socially constructed and subject to multiple interpretations. Most importantly, perhaps, anti-racist education should, to use Giroux's (1992) words, teach students to understand how power as a cultural, economic and political set of practices works to define, organize and legitimize notions of "common sense" which we internalize under the auspices of rationality. Expanding our conceptual framework involves working through the framework of interpretations of the world we have uncritically amassed both logically and psychologically, and then generating and assessing our own perspectives.

The Lauzon-Ruggles case is important because it provides an example of a missed opportunity for "dialogue across differences." Ruggles' commentary could have been used by Lauzon to help broaden and enrich his own, and the police department's, understanding of the concerns of black males in Montreal. This knowledge could help them to take a more complex and multifaceted approach. This process, however, would also necessitate a critical look at the assumptions that underlie policing and would raise questions about the institution itself, whom it serves, how it serves them and why.

There is no doubt that dialogue is important because it can help address if not entirely reduce the misunderstandings associated with prejudice. However, not all dialogue is equally valuable. Honourable intentions alone are not enough to create the alteration of cognitive structures necessary to reduce prejudice. One must learn how to dialogue and one must learn the procedures that enable meaningful dialogue to occur. What does this kind of dialogue look like? Matthew Lipman's definition of critical thinking is applicable here (Lipman and Sharp 1980). Productive dialogue should incorporate the criteria one is using, it should be sensitive to the context in which the dialogue is occurring and it should be self-corrective, in other words, it should question itself. Dialogue for dialogue's sake is not enough because it will not challenge the prevailing modes of viewing a situation. Learning critical modes of dialogue can help to penetrate the logic of racism by challenging some of the bases upon which it is constructed. Dialogue is ultimately premised on the belief that reasonable thought is an ideal both worth pursuing and possible to pursue despite the obstacles facing it.

Case studies such as the one presented here can have some influence in making us aware of the ways in which racism manifests in subtle, non-obvious yet deadly ways. Case studies provide students with opportunities to understand how perspectives are constructed and how and why they differ. Being able to understand someone else's perspective can enable students to connect in a meaningful way with the views of someone they may not agree with. However, merely learning the skills of critical analysis is not enough to reduce prejudice, which, as I have stated before, is more than an error in thinking, more than simply a deficit to be ameliorated through proper instruction. Good thinking skills are important, but what is equally important is acquiring what Paul (1990) calls the intellectual dispositions associated with good thinking: fair-mindedness, courage and humility. Prejudice reduction begins with active, critical listening and with respect for the importance of accurately clarifying and understanding the views we oppose. Only when students have developed these dispositions are they able to engage in a detailed critical analysis that can begin to challenge the foundations of racist thought and practice.

Anti-racist education must occur in what Matthew Lipman (1980) calls a "community of inquiry," where "students listen to one another with respect, build on one another's ideas, challenge one another to supply reasons for otherwise unsupported opinions, assist each other in drawing inferences from what has been said, and seek to identify one another's assumptions."

Clifton Ruggles, when he was a teacher in an alternative school for high school drop-outs, established such a community of inquiry while teaching "Philosophy for Children" with his students. Ruggles reports an encounter that took place when a new student who identified himself as a "confirmed racist" joined the class, which was 40 percent Black. Instead of ostracizing him, the Black students began probing him about his racist beliefs. They asked him questions like "When did it first begin? Did you have any bad experiences with Blacks that might account for your racism? Were your parents racist?" What amazed the teacher was the fact that the student responded openly and honestly to the questions posed. This student sensed that the questions were being asked in good faith and he responded in kind. He was not being criticized, he was being asked to explain the views he held, and why and how he had come to hold them. There was something that moved him and made him respond favourably without the usual defence mechanisms. By the end of the semester he had developed a very close friendship with one of the Black students, and this experience, more than anything else, contributed to an alteration of his racist beliefs.

A certain level of trust is necessary in order for a community of inquiry to be effective in altering cognitive structures. If students don't trust each other, the teacher or the context in which the "community of inquiry" is held, they won't risk the kind of self-disclosure that prejudice reduction requires.

## References

Aronowitz, Stanley and Giroux, Henry. 1991. *Postmodern Education: Politics, Culture and Social Criticism.* Minneapolis: University of Minnesota Press.

Baldwin, James. 1990. *Notes of a Native Son.* Boston: Beacon Press.

Brown, Claude. 1966. *Manchild in the Promised Land.* New York: Signet.

Claude, Steele. 1992. "Race and the Schooling of Black Americans." *Atlantic Monthly,* April.

Ellison, Ralph. 1947. *Invisible Man.* New York: Modern Library.

Giroux, Henry. 1992. *Border Crossings: Cultural Workers and the Politics of Education.* Routledge Publishing.

hooks, bell. 1990. *Yearning: Race, Gender and Cultural Politics.* Boston: Southend Press.

Lauzon, Denis. 1991. "No Racism in Police Action." *Montreal Gazette,* November 14.

Lipman, Matthew and Ann M. Sharp. 1980. *Philosophy in the Classroom.* Philadelphia: Temple University Press.

Paul, Richard. 1990. *Critical Thinking: What every person needs to survive in a rapidly changing world.* Rohnert Park, Calif.: Centre for Critical Thinking and Moral Critique, Sonoma State University.

———— and Kenneth Adamson. 1990. "Critical Thinking and the Nature of Prejudice." in Paul, Richard, *Critical Thinking: What every person needs to survive in a rapidly changing world.* Rohnert Park, Calif.: Centre for Critical Thinking and Moral Critique, Sonoma State University.

Ruggles, Clifton. 1991a. "Police response to Ruggles a scary bit of distortion." *Montreal Gazette,* December 14.

————. 1991b. "How a parking dispute becomes something else when you're black." *Montreal Gazette*, November 7.

————. 1991c. "Growing up Black: The differences aren't always subtle." *Montreal Gazette*, September 5.

Spanier, Harold. 1992. "Director ignored woman's abuse" and other letters to the editor. *Montreal Gazette*, November 28.

Taylor, Charles. 1992. *Multiculturalism and the Politics of Recognition*. Princeton, N.J.: Princeton University Press.

Weil, Dan. 1992. "Critical Thinking and the Development of a Gifted Curriculum." Unpublished manuscript.

Weinstein, Mark. 1991. "Review of Postmodern Education: Policy, Culture and Social Criticism in Inquiry." *Critical Thinking Across the Disciplines*, December.

————. 1990. *Critical Thinking and the Psychologic of Race Prejudice*. Montclair, N.J.: Institute for Critical Thinking, Montclair State College. Resource Publication Series 3, No. 1.

# How a parking dispute becomes something else when you're black

November 7, 1991

The ink had barely dried on the column I wrote a little more than a month ago documenting the way in which blacks are often automatically treated as suspects by the police.

Well, it happened again, ironically right in front of the new headquarters of the Black Coalition of Quebec (BCQ) headquarters near the corner of Decarie Blvd. and Queen Mary Rd., under a sign that reads "We stand for human rights, stand with us."

It was during rush hour and my 6-year-old daughter was present.

It started out as the kind of encounter we've all had. Two cars, one parking spot. One driver gets the spot, the other is irate. Angry words are usually exchanged and the matter is dropped.

## Approached in a rage

But when you're black, a simple parking confrontation can turn into a nightmarish ordeal where you end up being falsely accused of assault.

I got the parking spot.

I hadn't noticed the dark car double-parked up ahead. There were no flashing lights indicating the driver's intentions.

As soon as I got out of my car, the female occupant of this vehicle approached in a rage, insisting I had taken her spot. I explained that I wouldn't be very long, that I was merely picking up my daughter from her gymnastics class.

The woman grabbed me by the lapels and proceeded to hurl racial insults at me: "Maudi negre, barbre, sauvage, chien sale."

She told me to go back to where I came from, that I didn't belong here.

I stared at her long and hard, but chose not to respond. I forced myself to walk away and went to get my daughter.

When we emerged, there was a welcoming committee from Montreal Urban Community police Station 31. The woman had called police and stated she was being assaulted by a black man.

While I was inside the gym, officers from two police cruisers descended on my colleague, Harold Spanier, a science educator working at my school, who happened to be waiting for me in my car.

"Where's the black guy?" the police demanded.

Harold explained that I'd gone to pick up my daughter. They asked Harold who he was, to which he replied, "I'm the Jewish guy."

The police officers could not appreciate Harold's pointed humour. His comment did not help them see the extent to which their language was racially charged. They didn't understand that the language they used was an indication of how they had perceived a person or a situation.

When Harold insisted on giving his eye-witness account of the events, he was rudely told to be quiet.

I appreciate that the police have to take every distress call seriously, but I do not appreciate the manner in which they handled the incident—seeing my blackness before all else and refusing to take eye-witness information that would exonerate me.

At first there appeared to be little doubt in the minds of the police that I was guilty.

Let's look at the facts:

I am a black male, and she is a white, French-speaking Canadian female. She was well-dressed, driving an expensive car, with a cellular phone, with which she dialled 9ll.

It was unthinkable to the police that the black guy was being victimized and the well-to-do white French lady was actually the aggressor.

When you perceive selectively, as the police officers who first arrived on the scene did, you construct an account of reality and see only those aspects that support your point of view.

Perhaps because of my experience as a crisis-intervention specialist, I was able to diffuse a potentially volatile situation. I was able to articulate to the police in a straightforward and intelligible manner that things were not as they appeared.

When they demanded that I get into their cruiser, I reminded them of the racial implications of doing so. I had done nothing wrong. Why should I be treated as if I had?

### Shaken and bitter

I wonder to what extent the manner of my self-presentation made them tread more carefully than they might have otherwise.

I wonder how events might have turned out had I been less articulate, less controlled, if I did not have a witness who happened to be white and if I had dared to register an ounce of

the outrage I felt.

I tend to think I would have spent the night in the holding pen at Station 31, if not worse.

I went home shaken, bitter, outraged. The more I thought about it, the more I realized I had been the one who had been violated. If anyone had been assaulted it was me.

The following day, I proceeded to press charges of my own. When I went to the police station, I learned that no formal charges had been laid against me. My account of the incident had been considered more credible.

Where will it go from here?

It's up to the judicial system to determine what happens now. As one police detective phrased it, if the case is to be tried, society would be taking this woman to court.

What is so frightening about this incident is that racists believe they can use the judicial system to reinforce their racism.

It is unacceptable to allow racists to abuse the law-enforcement apparatus. Any time someone makes false accusations and tries to manipulate the judicial system, he or she should be held accountable for the ensuing havoc and confusion.

This woman wasted taxpayers' money as well as valuable police time. She called police anticipating that my being black would result in my being harassed or even detained.

What if this lady had reported that I had a weapon? Would the SWAT team have been there, ready to shoot me as I emerged from the gym with my daughter?

And what if I had taken off—would

they have chased after me, endangering even more lives in their attempt to apprehend me?

The absurdity of it is that I could have been killed over a simple parking dispute.

Recent events involving racism in the Montreal area (as recently as last week, a black youth was held with a gun pressed against his neck when police mistakenly assumed he'd been the aggressor in an altercation) are disturbing enough.

Even more disturbing is Prime Minister Brian Mulroney defending Tory MPs who have made sexist and racist remarks in Parliament.

If the prime minister does not perceive anything wrong with Sheila Copps being called a slut, or Howard McCurdy being called Sambo, what can we expect of the police or the citizens?

By condoning these kinds of derogatory remarks, is the prime minister saying they are acceptable?

If this is so, then citizens of this multicultural nation have to let him know that they are not. If elected representatives are allowed to make disparaging remarks about sex and race, then this country has a serious problem.

And incidents such as the one I've written about will continue to occur.

# No racism in police action
## Station 31 director says ethnic groups need to co-operate with police

November 14, 1991

On Friday, Nov. 8, I read with surprise the comments of Clifton Ruggles in the West End edition of *The Gazette*.

After obtaining the information regarding the incident and having the investigating officer contact Mr. Ruggles to inform him of the procedures that would be taken, I was under the impression that Mr. Ruggles was satisfied with the investigation.

So that you can understand how astonished I was, I would like to inform you of the intervention that was undertaken by police officers of District 31 and of the results.

On Oct. 3, at 17:40 hrs., police officers assigned to Cars 31-2 and 31-7 received a priority call "for a man assaulting a woman" near 5185 Décarie Blvd. close to Queen Mary Rd. The information received by policemen via 911 was limited, yet gave them a mental picture as to what was possibly happening.

### Gave a description

Car 31-2 was on the scene first. They encountered the victim, who was very agitated.

She gave a brief account as to what happened to her and she gave a description of the suspect and the direction in which he fled.

At that point, the policeman relayed the information to the second police car on the scene via walkie-talkie.

The policeman in charge of the call asked the victim to sit in the rear of the patrol car where he took down the necessary information.

While the report was taken, Car 31-7 said he found the "suspect" and asked Car 31-2 what they wished to do since they were in charge of the call. They instructed 31-7 to stay with the suspect until they arrived to clear up this matter.

Five minutes later, Car 31-2 was with Mr. Ruggles and the policeman in charge of the call spoke with him in English. He asked him his account of the events. Mr. Ruggles admitted to taking the parking place of the victim and added, "She reacted very bitterly and adamantly."

Mr. Ruggles then told the policeman that he never pushed or hit her, yet did spit on the car in his own anger.

Mr. Ruggles also said he had a witness in his car. The policeman listened to Mr. Ruggles, took his name down along with his version of events.

At that time, it started to rain. The policeman asked Mr. Ruggles to sit in the back seat of the police car. Mr. Ruggles replied that he was not under arrest and that the racial implications of being seated in the back of a patrol car were too much.

At the end of the investigation, the policeman explained to Mr. Ruggles what was going to happen. He told him not to worry about this.

The officer was able to paint a good picture of what had happened there. The officer told Mr. Ruggles that he thought his story was not only plausible, but most probably what had happened and he wrote it in the report. He also told Mr. Ruggles a detective would contact him in the coming days to give him the outcome. The officer gave Mr. Ruggles the report number as well as his name and left the scene.

The station officer explained to Mr. Ruggles the procedures for investigating similar events, but Mr. Ruggles insisted that a complaint of assault be filed against the lady involved. A supplementary information report was forwarded to the detective with the added information.

Furthermore, Mr. Ruggles made a complaint to a municipal councillor in District 31 who later informed me of the situation. Meanwhile, the detective in charge of the investigation contacted Mr. Ruggles regarding the assault complaint and Mr. Ruggles clearly indicated that he had to consult his lawyer before confirming the complaint.

I forwarded this information to the councillor, who in turn informed me of his satisfaction regarding the police intervention.

Later, Mr. Ruggles confirmed with the detective that he wished to maintain his assault complaint against the woman and that he intended to testify in court.

**Seemed satisfied**

Furthermore, Mr. Ruggles's denunciation regarding his complaint was forwarded to the court and Mr. Ruggles seemed satisfied with the results and the procedures.

In conclusion, I would like to mention the following points.

• Mr. Ruggles was never ordered to get into the police car, but rather asked politely due to the fact it was raining. When he refused, the policeman complied to his wishes.

• Mr. Ruggles is exaggerating

about being brought to Station 31 to spend the night in a holding pen; in fact, he was never under arrest nor detained.

• Mr. Ruggles was not falsely accused, but, to be more precise, he was the object of a criminal investigation which was warranted.

• Mr. Ruggles complained of the formality regarding this dossier and the high costs resulting from police interventions.

It is to be noted that Mr. Ruggles is himself responsible concerning this incident and the judicial procedures occurred when he insisted that legal actions be taken.

Similar dossiers are usually filed without accusations and charges often not laid.

Finally, I must say that at no time was the ethnic origin of the persons involved the cause of the police intervention.

The conclusion comes more from Mr. Ruggles's presumptions to characterize this as a racist event.

Instead of making alarming hypotheses, I believe that Mr. Ruggles along with other ethnic groups, should make an effort to look for a way to achieve public peace by co-operating, among other things, with their police force.

I would appreciate it if you would publish this letter so that the population may be made aware of the police point of view regarding the incident incited by Mr. Ruggles.

Denis Lauzon
Director, District 31
MUC police
*Montreal*

# Letters to the Editor
November 28, 1991
## Letter painted Ruggles as instigator

Denis Lauzon, director of Montreal Urban Community police Station 31, responded to Clifton Ruggles's account of events involving himself, a disputed parking spot, a white woman and the police.

In this letter (*The Gazette*, West End Community Edition, Nov. 14) Mr. Lauzon continues to perpetuate the standard police line that blacks and other minorities are hysterically overreacting and labelling as racist what are in fact routine and unbiased police activities.

I could not but help notice a number of blatant discrepancies between Mr. Ruggles's version of events and the police director's account.

Nowhere in Mr. Ruggles's article does he admit to "taking the parking spot of the victim." It was, he explained, an empty spot legitimately taken, but immediately contested in openly racist and verbally abusive terms by the white "victim."

However, Mr. Lauzon goes on to describe Mr. Ruggles as being "himself responsible for this incident." Does this mean that black drivers must always yield their parking spots to white women?

I also found it quite odd that Mr. Lauzon points out that Mr. Ruggles did not spend the night in a holding pen. Mr. Ruggles, in his letter, never claims that he did. Rather, he muses on whether a less-controlled and articulate black person would not in all likelihood have been arrested.

Finally, Mr. Lauzon uses his letter as an occasion to lecture ethnic groups on good citizenship. How, I wonder, can a black person be expected to "co-operate with their police force," as urged by Mr. Lauzon, when he goes on to characterize Mr. Ruggles, who is the obvious victim in this affair, as the one who incited the whole incident?

Milan Kovac
*Montreal*

## Director ignored woman's abuse
### Response shows police have missed the point

I read Mr. Ruggles's article (*The Gazette* West End Community Edition, Nov. 7) and Mr. Lauzon's reply (West End edition, Nov. 14).

I was greatly disturbed by Mr. Lauzon's portrayal of the events. As the eye-witness, I would like to give my account.

Mr. Lauzon has given a distorted and, in part, incorrect account of the actual events. His letter is all the more troublesome because it is from a director of a police station.

There are several points that need clarification. First, Mr. Ruggles did not knowingly take the woman's parking space. She was double-parked and did not indicate her intentions. It is interesting to note that subsequently Mr. Ruggles even moved his car down the street to give the woman the spot.

Mr. Ruggles was most controlled, most obliging and never "instigated" the incident as Mr. Lauzon suggests. The incident was incited by the person who dialled 911 and made false accusations.

Mr. Lauzon fails to mention that the woman hurled racial insults at Mr. Ruggles, grabbed him and then proceeded to call 911 in a malicious attempt to gain revenge.

Mr. Lauzon leaves out this essential information. For those who did not read the initial article, it would seem indeed odd that Mr. Ruggles would be pressing charges against someone who merely "reacted bitterly and adamantly" after having her parking spot taken. In leaving out the woman's vicious, racist attack, the entire motive for pressing charges against her is lost.

Mr. Lauzon does not address the matter of the original statements made by his officers when they arrived on the scene.

I was in the vehicle when the police approached me, demanding to know: "Where is the black man?"

When I asked to know what was going on, the officers threatened to take me to the station and charge me as "an accomplice to the charge of assault." When I asked to make an eye-witness statement, they disregarded my request. I had to go down of my own accord to the police station and overcome attempts to dissuade me before being able to file my testimony.

Mr. Lauzon uses curious language in describing Mr. Ruggles's entrance to his daughter's gym as "the direction in which the suspect fled." The use of the world fled was effective in conveying the required nefarious intention to Mr. Ruggles's actions. Moreover, throughout his letter accusingly refers to Mr. Ruggles as "the suspect" and the woman as "the victim."

Why does he not call her "the complainant" or at the very least "the alleged victim?" Mr. Lauzon still chooses to see her as "the victim" while all evidence points to the contrary.

Mr. Lauzon's officers reported that they thought Mr. Ruggles's story was "not only plausible but probably what had happened."

In his letter, Mr. Lauzon says that Mr. Ruggles was "exaggerating about being brought to Station 31 to spend the night in a holding pen." In fact, what Mr. Ruggles wrote was: "I wonder how events might have turned out had I been less articulate, less controlled, if I did not have a witness who happened to be white and if I had dared to register an ounce of the outrage I felt. I tend to think that I would have spent the night in the holding pen at Station 31, if not worse."

Nowhere did Mr. Ruggles claim he was actually taken down to Station 31 or that he was arrested.

To be fair to Mr. Lauzon, it is worth asking to what extent the problems inherent in the letter are a function of translation from French to English. If this is the case, then I think more care should be taken in any document that is to become public.

Mr. Lauzon ends his article with a plea that "ethnic groups" should look for ways to achieve public peace by co-operating with their police force. As far as I witnessed, it was Mr. Ruggles who was most co-operative. Mr. Ruggles wanted to exercise his fundamental human rights.

Mr. Lauzon seems to have entirely missed the point of Mr. Ruggles's article, which was a general critique of a system that allows members of visible minorities to become the objects of discrimination.

It seems to me that the intent of this article was to alert the public to the dangers of a racist being able to pick up the phone and give false testimony to the police and of society's response to such behaviour.

The fact that this woman verbally and physically assaulted Mr. Ruggles seems of no consequence to Mr. Lauzon, nor does the fact that she gave false testimony.

The letter written by Mr. Lauzon is an example of the lack of sensitivity that still seems to exist within the police department regarding visible minorities.

Harold Spanier
*Montreal*

# Columnist lauded for showing self-restraint

After reading Clifton Ruggles's column (*The Gazette*, West End Community Edition, Nov. 7), I spent the rest of my day in a stupor, in utter disbelief. Is there any end to the insanity of racism? I sincerely hope so, but sometimes I am greatly discouraged.

I commend Mr. Ruggles for his control in a situation that would make most people explode.

I cannot think how he was able to contain the outrage at such blatant harassment. He has all my respect.

Unfortunately, the natural reaction to an unfounded provocation like that would be anger. For the "crime" of reacting to antagonism, I suspect that he would have fulfilled that woman's—and the police's—expectation, giving them reason to penalize him.

It is a frightening trap that happens much more often than is ever documented.

I hate to think how often racial harassment of this kind happens and the victim has no recourse. In Mr. Ruggles's case, he has *The Gazette*, and I thank him for broadening my perspective, helping me understand the extent of the problem.

Again, I am disgusted to think how often such events occur and only the victimized really know about it.

Christine Long
*Montreal*

# Article reminded reader of ugly incident on Métro

I read Clifton Ruggles's article (*The Gazette*, West End Community Edition, Nov. 7) and my heart breaks at what could have been, and all so easily.

Several months ago, I was on the Métro at Villa Maria station. It was 9:30 a.m. and the cars were not full. Besides myself, there were several other people on one car.

A well-dressed, middle-aged Caucasian woman walked on and chose to sit beside a young Oriental man. He was likely a student because he had a bag full of books, one on his lap, and he was reading.

The woman could have sat in many other seats, but no, she had to sit beside this boy so she could have an avenue for her venom.

As she approached him, she purposely jarred his knee and book with her heavy briefcase and in French told him to put both feet elsewhere.

She kept on knocking this boy's lap with her briefcase.

He asked her what her problem was and she said, cruelly, coldly and with a sneer on her face, "You, you are my problem. Why don't you ugly people go back where you came from and get out of my country?" etc.

I was seeing red, and all the other people who heard were also visibly angry. The poor boy was choking back tears. We all told the woman to be quiet, that no one was interested in what she was saying.

I fumed the whole day about this incident. She and I were the only Caucasians in that car that morning and she looked as if she couldn't believe what she was hearing when I spoke against her. I wished I could have physically removed her from the Métro.

The kid finally moved to make way for the woman.

Hana Cziment
*Côte St. Luc*

# Can't blacks press charges?

I read Clifton Ruggles's article of Nov. 7 (*The Gazette*, West End Community Edition) as well as the response (Nov. 14) of Denis Lauzon, director of Station 31 of the Montreal Urban Community police.

Mr. Lauzon tries to undermine Mr. Ruggles's grievances about racism in society and about police presumptions and a seeming tendency to abuse their authority.

Mr. Lauzon attacks Mr. Ruggles's credibility by appearing not to accept his own officers" view of the events that occurred before the police arrived at the scene.

He portrays Mr. Ruggles as the suspect who fled the scene and the woman as the victim.

He states what Mr. Ruggles did not do to her, but fails to mention that she had been physically abusive and had hurled racist insults at him. By so doing, Mr. Lauzon associated Mr. Ruggles in the reader's mind with acts of violence and associated the woman with nothing more than a "bitter and adamant reaction."

Furthermore, Mr. Lauzon chastises Mr. Ruggles for pressing charges against the woman and characterizes this as "inciting" an incident. This either means he views Mr. Ruggles with suspicion and doesn't believe the account of his own officers, or that blacks have no right to press charges against people who assault them.

Mr. Lauzon distorts the facts by making it seem as though the police dealt with Mr. Ruggles before dealing with the witness.

Mr. Lauzon conveniently ignores the initial exchange between the police and the witness in the absence of Mr. Ruggles, presumably to avoid the issue of the officers' racially charged language ("Where is the black guy?").

Mr. Ruggles is portrayed as a person of bad faith, who had made no effort to co-operate with the police, when obviously he had succeeded in opening a dialogue with the police, with the result that his version of the events was thought to be the only credible one.

To make Mr. Ruggles "along with other ethnic groups" guilty of not co-operating with the police is an instance of the racism Mr. Ruggles mentioned in his article.

Pascale Durand
*Montreal*

142

# Reducing Racism: The Role of Multicultural Education

# How education can fight racism

February 3, 1994

Multiculturalism is an elusive, much contested term that has sparked considerable controversy. It has elicited disapproval from assimilationists who believe in a "melting pot" theory of society which has little interest in acknowledging or in cultivating difference.

Emphasizing the distinctiveness of cultures is seen as counter-productive to national unity because it contributes to a lack of cohesiveness and a difference of values.

It also brings disapproval from cynics believing that official multiculturalism is nothing more than a way of placating resistance and buying ethnic votes. Cultural "power brokers" acting on behalf of the "powers that be", regulate the self-definition and struggles of the various cultural communities. From this perspective, official multiculturalism is seen as detrimental to the best interests of the cultural communities because it contains discontent and disarms opposition.

The very term "multiculturalism" has recently come under attack. Some people prefer terms like "cross-cultural" or "inter-cultural" because they do not carry the "baggage" that multiculturalism does. These terms imply a more interactive, dialogical approach as opposed to one that merely promotes "appreciation" of the cultural mosaic from a static position that does not transform in any way those individuals involved in the enterprise. Although I prefer the latter terms, I'm not as much concerned with terminology as I am with effective action.

Education has been identified as the appropriate site from which to promote multiculturalism. There are a number of approaches to multicultural education, many of them problematic. As it is presently practiced, multicultural education emphasizes respect for and appreciation of the diverse cultures that make up Canada as well as the cultivation of awareness and sensitivity towards cultural differences. This is reflected in visual images, stories and information disseminated within schools.

The "tourist approach" to multicultural education promotes the notion that exposing students to different customs will increase the students' tolerance of other racial and ethnic groups. This form of multicultural education promotes a superficial "surface ethnicity" marked by food, clothes and music and commodifies ethnicity in our consumeristic society by assigning to it a market value. The "tourist approach" decontextualizes ethnicity from its historical roots and renders it nothing more than a salable commodity.

Appreciation, without the necessary insight into the social and political struggles that embody a people is appreciation without substance. It is through an understanding based on an awareness of other communities' struggles, that empathy can develop toward people whose lives are embedded in different cultural realities. True multiculturalism must exist on the bedrock of understanding and empa-

thy. Because many of these struggles are reactions against systemic racism, the empathy I am referring to must embody a recognition of personal and collective responsibility. It beckons us to explore the extent to which the power and privilege some of us enjoy is directly responsible for the disempowerment and disenfranchising of others.

Another approach to multicultural education seizes the opportunity for marginalized groups to re-write history by presenting other versions of that history. Traditionally the teach-ing of history has excluded the experiences of women, workers, blacks and minority groups, thus skewing peoples' understanding of the past as well as the present. This approach however, is not without its own problematics.

The rewriting of history and the resurrection of ancestors has provided the "great person approach" to multicultural education. This approach is predicated on the notion that students naturally respond to and model their lives on "role models" identified by their teachers. This school of

145

thought holds that knowledge about great historical figures will have an empowering effect on young people's aspirations. Information alone, however is insufficient in altering those negative attitudes and low self esteem which are reinforced through systemic oppression within the society. Systemic oppression is usually internalized as self loathing by its objects, making the raising of self esteem by this method somewhat problematic. Multicultural education should not be reduced to anecdotal references to outstanding individuals. The purpose of historical study is not to glorify exceptional ancestors, but to understand how one's identity has been constructed throughout history and how it informs the cultural viewpoints of the present. Neither acknowledgment of individual achievement *per se*, nor descriptive accounts of a culture can deal adequately with the complex nature of cultural difference.

Another approach to multicultural education aims at altering formerly negative stereotypes of certain racial or ethnic groups by providing positive imagery in their stead. In order to present children of all races with positive self images, pictures are displayed of people in professional occupations from many cultures. A good indicator of whether a school is taking its multicultural mandate seriously is said to be the extent to which ethnic groups are positively represented in displays around the school building. While this strategy is very positive, especially at the elementary level, it sometimes leads to an exaggerated "positive" redefinition of history which denies the suffering and struggles of various cultural groups. For example, people who follow this line of reasoning often argue against teaching about slavery because it depicts blacks negatively.

Ignoring the realities of people's actual history can give students a false sense of their identities and a false picture of Canadian society, letting whites off with minimal guilt. A few years ago I submitted a manuscript on the subject of "Working in Canada" to a textbook publisher. The manuscript included pictures and interviews with black railway porters. Although the editor agreed to publish the work, she cut this particular section because it was considered politically incorrect to portray blacks doing menial labour. In so doing the editor was ignoring the fact that these were the only jobs available to black men during the 40s and 50s. In addition, the publisher did not want to suggest that there had ever been racial discrimination in Canada, thus contributing to a rewriting of Canadian labour history. The editor explained that rather than focus on the "negative", she preferred instead to include pictures of black doctors and black lawyers in order to convey a "positive" image about blacks. Perhaps it would have been more honest to explore why there were so *few* black doctors and lawyers, without pretending that the problem of racism in the workplace does not exist in our country. In addition, by omitting the section on the porters, the publisher rendered invisible an important part of Canadian labour history and the participation of black men and their families in the labour force. This hits very close to home for me, because my father was a railway porter and my family lived that history. My identity and very existence was hence denied and rendered invisible by this approach to "multiculturalism as fantasy".

What is often forgotten is that the black professionals paraded as the symbols of black success are often the offsprings of workers like my father whose struggles made our success possible. In addition, none of us would be here at all, without the strength exhibited in slavery by our ancestors who triumphed over the most adverse of human situations. These are narratives that need to be told in order for us to understand the formation of our identity as a people and in order for others to understand our history of struggle.

I believe that if multicultural education is done with integrity and courage it can help change attitudes in both black and white students. White students take the time to assess the diminishing importance of the white European culture in a richly diverse country with citizens from many other continents. Also, by becoming aware of their own ethnicity, white students might cease to see themselves as part of the privileged mainstream. By making visible their privileged positions in society might prevent them from perpetuating this domination in the future.

A transformative multicultural education must do more than simply "maintain" existing social relations. It must interrogate the existing discourse on multicultural education and develop effective ways of addressing issues of race and ethnicity. Merely focusing on the romantic celebration of differences is essentially trivializing and disrespectful; indeed it could be argued that it does more harm than good. Without examining the relations of power that create systemic racism, the "smorgasbord" strategy of multiculturalism attempts to obfuscate real differences and injustices.

In order to be effective and contribute to a much needed social change, multicultural education cannot avoid "unpleasant" realities which may still be reflected in current power relations. A multicultural education that challenges the status quo negotiates difference through a clear presentation of historical context, critical reflection, and the interplay of conflicting ideas and perspectives. This approach to multicultural education courageously renders palpable serious and potentially diverse issues rather than merely presenting culture, race and ethnicity as a melange of cuisine, song and dance.

# The Children's meets challenge of multicultural health care

January 5, 1995

How many West End residents have used the Montreal Children's Hospital and never for an instant thought what it would be like to take their sick child to a hospital in a foreign land where they neither understand nor are understood by the health-care professionals?

While working as a volunteer in a hospital some time ago, Milly Charon, author of Between Two Worlds—The Canadian Immigrant Experience, and Worlds Apart—Immigrant Voices, witnessed first-hand the problems that can arise when cultures clash and no one is on hand to mediate.

She recalls observing an Orthodox Jewish woman waiting in the emergency room with her son who had injured his arm. It was Friday afternoon and the woman was agitated because she had to get home before sundown. According to her religious faith, it is forbidden to drive after the sun sets on the Sabbath. Eventually, she told the staff she could wait no longer and would return when the Sabbath was over.

Charon wrote that the child need not have suffered and the mother need not have felt so distressed. One call to a rabbi would have set the matter straight. According to the Talmud, the health and welfare of the individual takes precedence over any religious observance.

Different customs, beliefs and values affect health care. Negotiating this foreign terrain can be frightening without a guide.

Enter the Multicultural Program at the Children's Hospital, which acts as a cultural broker, helping health-care professionals better understand cultural difference and helping patients and their families.

## Dramatic impact

Co-ordinator Heather Clarke said the cultural and racial diversity of Montreal's population is having a dramatic impact on our health-care institutions.

"Neither their formal training nor in-service program have prepared staff members for the challenges they now face," Clarke said.

Prompted by the staff, the Children's has been taking steps since 1986 to meet the challenges. They include a cross-cultural staff development program, interpretation services, consultations and referrals, organization of cultural activities and a multimedia library specializing in cross-cultural health issues.

A lecture series—on issues like racism, cultural influences on pain, different child-rearing practices and rites of passage for adolescents from different cultures—is open to the public.

"Racism can take different forms in the hospital," said Jonas Ma, who is responsible for education and staff development. "You might have a child saying nasty things to another child on the ward and the nurse may feel too uncomfortable to intervene, or may try to handle the situation by shifting the children around so they won't be

148

together, instead of trying to deal with the issue.

"Issues of race also come up in simple procedures like the detection of jaundice, which is more difficult to detect in people of color," Ma added.

I remember once being subjected to a test that was designed for white people. The technician kept waiting for my skin to turn a certain color, which it never did. The technician had no idea what to do to compensate for the difference in my pigmentation.

I've spent a lot of time in hospitals, both as a child and an adult and I've often wondered whether we receive the same care and attention as our white counterparts.

### Different beliefs

Racism is not the only problem, Ma said. There are different beliefs about health care that affect how patients react. In some cultures a hospital is the place where you come to die, so some families won't come for preventive or maintenance programs.

"Each culture perceives health, illness, disease, treatment, mental health and disability from different perspectives," Ma said. Ethnicity affects behaviour in both subtle and obvious ways.

It plays a role in determining how we feel about health and illness, how we express complaints and when and from whom we seek help.

To establish and maintain a good rapport with their patients, doctors

and other health-care workers need to understand their origins and cultural backgrounds.

Without consideration for cultural differences, health-care providers might actually contribute to a patient's problems.

One criticism that has been levelled

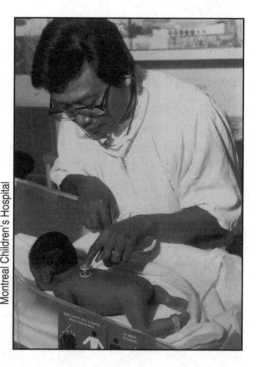

Montreal Children's Hospital

at programs like the ones at the Children's is that they stress differences between people rather than similarities. The other criticism is that they encourage people not to integrate and assimilate.

Ma replies that people from other cultures need support and acceptance—learning new habits and values takes a long time.

Here is a fictional case study given

to health-care professionals. See how sensitive you are in understanding the factors of the case:

"The Kims are from Korea and live as an extended family. Dongsoo, the 3-year-old boy, lives with his parents, grandparents, and two aunts. He was a premature baby and has been slow to develop physically and emotionally.

"Mrs. Smith is an occupational therapist who has been assigned to Dongsoo to assess and develop a home-care program for him. During her visits she notices that Dongsoo is always well-dressed and the family members carry him around with great affection. After visiting the Kim household a few times she designs a program.

"Dongsoo's mother, who speaks English, seems interested. The senior Mrs. Kim, on the other hand, refuses to co-operate. Dongsoo's mother then defers to the senior lady and tells Mrs. Smith that they are not interested in the program.

"Why do you think the Kims rejected the program?

A. They believed Dongsoo is disabled, can never lead a normal life and the program cannot help him.

B. They think they can train the child to look after himself.

C. They think it is the family's duty to take care of a disabled child.

If you chose C, then you are probably correct, according to a book on multicultural health issues from which this case study was taken. According to this book, among many Koreans, disability is regarded as a consequence of their own mistakes and wrongdoing. Therefore, instead of encouraging Dongsoo to be independent, the Kims try to meet all his needs.

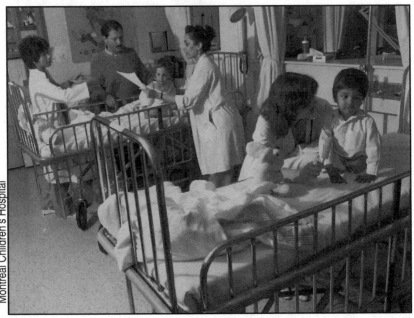

Montreal Children's Hospital

# Education, Access
# and Social Mobility

# Reading and writing are the tools to fight social injustice

December, 1991

Where I came from, reading was definitely not cool. If you happened to indulge in this anti-social behaviour, you did it in the privacy of your own home lest you be ostracized by your peer group.

I used to conceal books in brown paper lunch bags to smuggle them to and from school and still retain my tough street persona.

I didn't realize then that this passion for reading would open doors of opportunity that otherwise might have stayed closed.

Had I understood then that knowledge and the ability to use it is a form of self-empowerment, I might not have gone to such great lengths to disguise my attraction for the written word.

Why I was so determined to get an education when so many black kids from depressed communities give up before trying, I do not know.

But I do remember the tremendous effect it had when, as a teenager, I learned it was a crime for a slave to know how to read or write.

Slaves found reading were brutally whipped or even killed. A literate slave was a dangerous slave. He or she had the tools to organize other slaves.

Another profound influence was a passage I'd read from black activist Malcolm X's autobiography. Malcolm describes his relentless attempts at literacy while in prison, copying out virtually every page in the dictionary into the wee hours of the morning in the dim corridor light that cast a glow into his room.

What really got to me was his saying that becoming literate made him "free." I wanted to experience this freedom too.

The lesson was clear: to be voiceless was to be powerless. Literacy was the tool for liberation. In the rhetoric of the day, language was the gun and words were the bullets.

The newly emerging black rhetoric helped me achieve a new consciousness: a political consciousness, a social consciousness. It gave me the grounding and the impetus I needed to help me survive school. Without it I might not have seen the significance of my situation.

Growing up poor and black in the 1950s and '60s, I experienced firsthand a school system that failed miserably to develop the literacy skills of black students.

I watched black students streamed into practical classes and later into low-paying, dead-end jobs, watching their dreams dissipate in silence and despair.

The school system tried to steer me into the vocational stream, but I had witnessed too much to comply willingly. I saw the end of my life before my life ever got started. I saw myself buried in a factory for the next 40 years with no light at the end of the tunnel.

When I told my guidance counsellor I wanted someday to go to university, he tried to dissuade me, explaining that very few of my "kind" go to university, that it's much too expensive and that we're not "bright enough

Olivia Rovinescu

to make it."

Unknowingly, he did more to stimulate development of my literacy than any other human being.

I burned with a desire to prove him wrong. It was my sense of outrage coupled with my newly developing black consciousness that never let me give up on myself.

As circumstance had it, I was lucky enough to find my way out of the maze of hopelessness. But in far too many instances, individuals are not able to escape the oppression that entraps them, that renders them prisoners of silence.

But I don't want my personal account to give credence to the myth that anyone can make it if they try hard enough.

Equal educational opportunity is a popular myth in our society; that everyone can get an education if they really want to.

Not being able to do so is seen as an individual failing.

It simply isn't so.

There are many obstacles to this, including your own lack of self-confidence. Sometimes you give up the struggle because you do not believe it can be fought and won.

You are crippled by an all pervasive, all encompassing powerlessness. You are caught in a web and believe you cannot ever extricate yourself.

You believe you are at the mercy of forces that manipulate your life. You believe you'll never make it, whether you acquire these much-demanded literacy skills or not.

You've internalized society's attitudes about yourself. You become a victim of the "psychology of oppression," the "culture of silence" and their deadly, accompanying lack of self-esteem.

Mere access to education is not sufficient to guarantee school success. The fact remains that certain racial and socio-economic groups have never benefited equally from the educational system.

Achievement is not merely a function of students' choices and innate abilities. Complex social and psychological forces prevent the individual from exercising and developing natural talents and abilities.

If time and again we find that children who read poorly are almost always from certain oppressed groups, then we must ask why.

A Southam News survey conducted in 1987, showed 5 million Canadians cannot read, write or handle numbers

well enough to meet the literacy demands of today's society. Twenty-eight per cent of Quebec's population is illiterate—one-third of them high school graduates.

The dangers are stark: 10 per cent of Canadian adults can't understand dosage directions on a medicine bottle; 20 per cent can't correctly select a fact from a newspaper article; more than 50 per cent have serious trouble using bus schedules and nearly 60 per cent misinterpret key sections of the Canadian Charter of Rights and Freedoms.

The statistics tell us how many, but not why. It is the why that demands our attention.

Many literacy endeavours work on changing the individual, not the social order that produces the problem. It's viewed as an individual problem rather than a political, social and economic phenomenon.

Literacy is a social justice issue, a symptom of the inequality prevalent in our society. It is caused and perpetuated by poverty. Unless we change the social conditions that create illiteracy, we will never successfully stamp it out. Our efforts will be mostly Band-Aid ones.

Literacy is usually defined in mechanical and functional terms and reduced to the mastery of fundamental skills. It should mean more than knowing how to read and write.

Discussions about literacy tend to focus on the loss of productivity in the workplace and monetary costs to the economy. Its worth is defined and measured according to those standards.

Literacy becomes the admission ticket for the poor to enter the economy and nothing more. Economic viability is crucial for any oppressed group, but it should not be the sole end of the struggle. Literacy should mean more. It should mean much more.

The most profound, far-reaching

effect of literacy on people's lives is its empowering potential.

To be literate is to gain a voice and to participate meaningfully in decisions that affect our daily lives. It can help make us aware of our basic human rights, it can help us resist exploitation and oppression and enable us to have a greater degree of control over our lives.

As celebrated Brazilian educator Paulo Freire said, "To read the word, is to read the world." In being able to "read the world," one has the potential to transform it.

If literacy is to be responsive to a world in crisis, its goal has to go beyond merely turning out people who are "functional."

Literacy carries with it a moral imperative and a societal and global obligation.

156

# Sometimes it's the school system, not the dropout, that doesn't fit

February 13, 1992

My childhood buddy Gerry came over the other night, not to "party" as we used to do in our teens, but to get tutored in math.

Very early in his education, the school system labelled Gerry a failure. The label stuck until he finally quit school in Grade 10 at age 16.

Gerry always believed he failed the school system. He never considered that the school system might have failed him by not taking into account his learning style.

The prevailing view of dropouts is that they are deviant, lazy or inadequate. No one considers that dropouts are sometimes those who are unable to accommodate the rigid school framework.

At the prospect of turning 40, Gerry decided it was time to alter the direction of his life.

"Returning to school was the hardest thing I ever had to do. A thousand times I wanted to quit but I kept thinking of what my kids would think of me."

Gerry thought of what he'd say to his children should they one day dictate they wanted to quit school. That thought kept him on track.

At first, the return to school was painful. His head actually hurt when he came home in the evening. And there he was doing homework with his teenage children, knowing less than they did, asking his son for help.

And then one day, he experienced it—the thrill of learning.

"Euphoria, I think you call it," Gerry explained. "The time goes by so fast now. Before, I could never concentrate. My mind was somewhere else. The time would drag on and on. I'd ask myself, what am I doing here? I just wanted to escape, get out and be in a place where I didn't feel I was wasting my time."

Statistics Canada estimates that every year about 100,000 young Canadians quit school before graduating. In some communities, the dropout rate is as high as 80 per cent.

There is not one type of person who drops out of school. Dropouts come from advantaged as well as disadvantaged backgrounds.

Compared with high school graduates, dropouts make less money, have lower lifetime earnings, have problems finding and keeping jobs, are unemployed more often and longer, and marry at earlier ages.

Lower lifetime earnings will often mean a lower standard of living which might perpetuate the dropout problem within a family.

Dropping out also had medical and psychological effects. Higher unemployment is associated with higher death rates, higher rates of suicide, and higher rates of admission to mental hospitals.

Dropouts report that school is boring, that the courses are irrelevant to their needs. They tend to feel ignored or rejected by the school system.

Dropouts often complain that teachers in the regular high schools weren't interested in them, or that classes were so large they didn't receive any individual attention.

The need for money also drives dropouts into the workplace, which is attractive because it represents adulthood and freedom.

Strategies that have been suggested could be reduced or eliminated.

This might involve a combination of work and education, providing the students with the opportunity to earn some money as well as feel a part of the work force.

It's time we began to re-examine our curricula and guidance systems.

to reduce the dropout rate include "changing the school culture"—that is, altering the customs and rules.

It can mean anything from modifying the manner in which a student completes assignments, to developing different types of relationships with teachers.

Another strategy is providing a "significant other"—a person who displays caring and concern and who is in a position to develop an ongoing, one-on-one relationship with the student at risk.

A third strategy is to integrate the school into the community. By doing this, it is expected that the irrelevance that is often perceived by dropouts

Howard Gardner of Harvard University and Robert Sternberg of Yale University say that they believe human intelligence consists of more than the single dimension now used, which is almost exclusively based on verbal and mathematical abilities.

Since the high-school curricula is heavily weighted along these lines, students who are weak in these areas, though strong in others, tend to be at a disadvantage.

A curriculum that takes into account other dimensions of intelligence may help more students enjoy and learn in school and thus may end up lowering the dropout rate.

# Language laws can hurt illiterate youth
## Many English speakers are trapped in French schools until they turn 18

September 24, 1992

Darryl sat in front of me, his enormous hands clasped tightly, head lowered, staring intently at the high school application form in front of him.

He remained motionless for almost ten minutes. His younger sister sat next to him. She had already filled out her application form and was fidgeting nervously.

Eventually she leaned over Darryl's shoulder and began to read the instructions slowly to him. He mumbled a response. She picked up his pen and put it in his hand. He shook his head vigorously and gave the pen back to her. She began filling out his application form.

After the interview, she approached anxiously: "If you can only take one of us, please take my brother, he needs it more than me."

Unfortunately, we were not able to take either one of them because of their ineligibility under Quebec language legislation which states that new immigrants must be educated in French only.

Darryl had already spent three years in the French school system but was not able to read or write in either English or French. He came to our school looking for an opportunity to become literate at least in his mother tongue—English.

I wanted to help Darryl but I was powerless to do so. Imagine my distress when I learned that Darryl had bought a gun and had joined a gang. The chance of Darryl's photo appearing in a police file appears greater than it does of appearing in a graduation album.

Darryl represents a growing number of students who are dropping out of French schools and who are looking for ways to gain some basic literacy skills. They are legally trapped until they turn 18 and are eligible to enrol in adult education programs.

But what do they do in the meantime?

Jack's battle with literacy was of a different nature. He grew up in a household of academics, which isn't easy for any kid. You're expected to excel at everything—particularly reading and writing. But what if by some fluke of nature, you simply can't master the written word?

Everytime Jack looked at the page, the words seemed to be swimming. His eyes saw what they wanted to see and not what was on that page.

What Jack didn't know was that he had a learning disability know as dyslexia that prevented him from learning how to read and write in the same way the rest of his classmates did.

"I always felt people were thinking, 'your parents are so bright, what happened to you,'" Jack recalls.

In time he realized that his learning problems had nothing to do with lack of intelligence. But, unfortunately, intelligence is measured by one's ability to read and write.

When Jack went to school, people didn't know much about dyslexia. Consequently, Jack's teachers—as

159

well as his parents—accused him of being lazy.

Jack says he wanted them to think he wasn't applying himself. It was easier than letting them know that he had tried but had failed.

In order to cover up his inability to read, Jack had to learn how to manipulate the world around him.

He avoided going to restaurants where he'd have to read the menu. He avoided going to new places where he'd have to read a map.

Jack could razzle-dazzle people with his amazing memory and his ability to discuss almost any subject. No one suspected he lived in a world that could be as bewildering as living in a foreign country and not speaking the language.

In time Jack accepted that he was, to use the new jargon, "differently abled"—but not before the years of shame and frustration exacted their toll.

Drugs and alcohol helped him escape from the constant reminder that he was "different." But eventually he had to confront his demons and come to terms with them—or perish.

With the help of rehabilitation Jack was able to overcome his substance dependences and began learning how to accept himself.

With today's technology, people with learning disabilities like Jack's can be taught how to read and write. I know a person who suffers from dyslexia, albeit in a milder form than Jack's, who became a university professor and the editor of an academic journal.

There are many people who are not as literate as they might be but there are many reasons why they do not seek assistance.

Literacy is a complex issue that has educational, social, economic and psychological implications. It is the subject of a conference at Concordia University October 2–4.

What's different about this conference is that it attempts to broaden the manner in which literacy is conceived by extending the dialogue to include discussions about such issues as native and multicultural literacy, and seniors and literacy.

# How college doors opened for black kids
## DaCosta Hall provided inspiration and
## help to escape a dead end

June 25, 1992

It was the end of our senior year at Northmount High School. For the few black students who survived the school system (for there were many who were lost along the way) the spectre of graduation loomed forebodingly.

"Where to from here?" we wondered.

Now that we were armed with that much-sought-after High School Leaving Certificate, was the "sky the limit" or did class and race preclude the possibility of higher education?

I feared the worse. And like a child with his face pressed against the candy store window, I savoured the things I believed were outside the realm of possibility for a black ghetto kid like me.

College or university was a luxury few of us could consider in 1969. We believed we were destined to end up doing the same jobs that had frustrated our parents.

In the summer of '69, however, that destiny was changed by the creation of the DaCosta Hall Summer School Program, aimed at helping black students finish high school and giving them a chance at post-secondary education.

The DaCosta Hall program was named after Matthew DaCosta and William Hall. Matthew DaCosta was an interpreter for Samuel de Champlain and the first recorded black man in Canada. William Hall was the first black man to win the Victoria Cross,

for his bravery in the Crimean War.

DaCosta Hall was started by a handful of idealistic black educators: Leo Bertley, Garvin Jeffers, Ozzie Downes, Ashton Lewis and Clarence Bayne, just to name a few. They believed the time had come to make educational institutions look at the almost complete lack of black Canadian presence in colleges and universities.

On the sheer gut determination of these few individuals, an institution was created to help black students realize their full potential.

The organizers also found money through scholarship funds to send a limited number of DaCosta Hall graduates to university. I was lucky enough to be a recipient.

DaCosta Hall was located in the High School of Montreal on University Street and served two functions. It offered a program for those who already had diplomas and wanted to be better prepared for college, and it helped those who were missing credits and wanted to complete their High School Leaving Certificate so they, too, could go on to college.

Word spread quickly through the grapevine. This was the chance we'd been waiting for.

In the sweltering summer heat we cracked those books and lived and breathed the information they had to offer. Never before had we experienced such motivation, such commitment.

Terms like "prejudice" and "racism" often miss the full implications of the racial devaluation that occurs in our school system.

American psychologist Jacquelien Flemming has suggested that since many black students study in a hostile atmosphere, this arouses defensive reactions that interfere with intellectual performance. It's called "academic disidentification": students begin to believe they can't have an identity both as a black person and a scholar, and so they reject the values of the education system.

DaCosta Hall had a cultural element which gave us a grounding, a point of departure. It gave us a lens through which to examine black contributions throughout history.

It also gave us significant black role models. Many of us had never seen black professionals and we were inspired by their presence. These teachers got us to understand how the system had conspired against us and helped us see that through education we could begin to overcome some of the burdens of our oppression.

Gwen Lord, now a regional director for the Protestant School Board of Greater Montreal, said that teaching at DaCosta Hall was an incredible experience. "You were working with people whom you wanted to see succeed.

It was a win-win situation."

Every time we slacked off, Leo Bertley—an imposing figure of a man—would come storming into the student lounge, eyes bulging, nostrils flaring, bellowing at us that we were squandering our educational opportunity. He certainly had a knack for

My grandmother proudly holding my McGill University graduation certificate, 1976

clearing a room and getting us back on track.

DaCosta Hall is now located at Dawson College's old Selby Campus and is open to any student regardless of color.

DaCosta Hall gave educational opportunity to many black people. It affirmed our potential, credited us with our achievements, challenged us intellectually and inspired our dreams.

It has touched the lives of many of its graduates in a profound way. I know. It has touched mine.

# It's not just neo-conservatives who challenge affirmative action

September 9, 1993

I am a product of affirmative action.

Affirmative action was responsible for my going to university. My writing this column is probably an indirect result of affirmative action.

"Let the best man win," the saying goes. But that assumes the world is a fair and equal place. Best is in the eye of the beholder and for many decades "best" meant "white heterosexual male."

Hiring decisions have often been made on the basis of racist and sexist criteria and not on the basis of who was best qualified. In an ideal world, one can believe that each person gets a fair shake. But this world is far from ideal and women and visible minorities historically have been denied employment opportunities.

## Nothing personal

In my 20s, I worked as a dishwasher at the restaurant of the Ritz-Carlton Hotel. When a waiter's position became available, I told the manager I wished to be considered for the position. He told me very frankly that he liked me and thought I was a reliable worker but that being black was a big liability. None of their waiters was black, he explained. It's just the way it was.

Nothing personal.

Affirmative action tries to correct the damage done by years of discrimination. It attempts to redress some of the inequities by ensuring that employers hire more blacks and women.

On the whole, employment-equity programs for women have produced much more significant results than those involving visible minorities. Here in Quebec, in particular, employment equity has not had a very significant impact, especially in the civil service. There are few black faces on police forces, at the wheels of buses or behind counters in government offices.

For the black community, affirmative action means an attempt to eliminate poverty caused by years of uneven distribution of wealth, power and income.

Those who disagree with affirmative action claim it disadvantages other groups of people, creating reverse discrimination and new categories of oppression—such as white men.

Glenda Simms, president of the Advisory Council on the Status of Women, thinks this position is exaggerated. In a recent public appearance at Concordia University, she told white men that they have nothing to fear: "I checked with the House of Commons, I looked at the Senate, I looked at the rulership within the universities and banks and all the major institutions in this country. And I can assure white men, they are not an endangered species."

The backlash against affirmative action is not a white neo-conservative phenomenon. Afro-American writer Shelby Steele, author of The Content of Our Character, believes blacks now stand to lose more than they gain

163

through affirmative action. Steele believes that, under affirmative action, blacks earn preferential treatment because of an implied inferiority. Affirmative action indirectly encourages blacks to exploit their own past victimization, he argues.

According to Steele, it is impossible to repay blacks living today for the historic suffering of the race. "Blacks cannot be repaid for the injustice done to the race, but we can be corrupted by society's guilty gestures of repayment."

However, Patricia Williams, a University of Wisconsin law professor and author of The Alchemy of Race and Rights, doesn't see redistribution in the same way.

"If modern white man, innocently or not, is the inheritor of another's due, then the due must be returned," Williams writes. "If a thief steals so that his children may live in luxury and the law returns his ill-gotten gain to its rightful owner, the children cannot complain that they have been deprived of what they did not own."

Blacks have earned a place in this society, Williams argues, and they have earned a share of its enormous wealth.

People become what they can imagine themselves to be. Young blacks will begin to comprehend their own possibilities when they see other blacks in positions of power and responsibility.

This will not happen of its own accord.

It must be made to happen—by any means necessary, to quote Malcolm X's now-famous line. And if those "means" entail affirmative-action legislation to ensure a racially diverse workforce—so be it.

There are certainly some snags with affirmative action—especially when it comes to access to college and university for black students who are not prepared.

### Set up to fail

Shelby Steele reports that over 75 per cent of blacks who are admitted to U.S. universities under affirmative action drop out. If black students do not have the tools to survive or compete at college and university then, yes, affirmative action is setting them up for failure.

Tokenism is not affirmative action. Having just one visible minority in the workplace can be very difficult on that person and she or he will never achieve full potential. The psychological impact of tokenism can be devastating to self-esteem. Carrying the burden of their race exacts its toll—it's hard to be the measure by which other members of your race are judged.

Because we do not get what we deserve. Because the best man doesn't always win. And because the world is not a fair place. We have to struggle to keep it as fair as it can be.

# Reality check: CEGEP reforms could cause some real harm

March 25, 1993

Perhaps Jack Todd was just trying to fan the flames of debate when he suggested this month that we should shut down the CEGEPs.

"They were a bad idea to begin with," Todd wrote in his March 16 column. "They educate students who don't want to be educated for jobs that don't exist."

His suggestion to Higher Education Minister Lucienne Robillard is: turn the CEGEPs into "real" vocational training schools and turn the universities into "real" universities.

If we're going to talk about the "real" world, then let's talk about some of the very real implications of these suggestions. In the real world, those who are privileged will go to universities to become business persons, lawyers and politicians and those who are culturally, economically or racially disadvantaged will go into the trades. Those who are at a disadvantage will continue to remain at a disadvantage and decision-making will remain in the hands of a few.

People like myself, from impoverished backgrounds, simply will not have the opportunity to consider university. Inevitably, we will be streamlined into the trades.

CEGEP provided me with the opportunity to learn the academic ropes, find my talents and decide what career I wanted to pursue. At 18 years of age, deciding what to do with your life is not an easy matter.

CEGEP was the door to a world I did not know existed, a world of ideas, of possibilities, where my voice could be heard. My years spent in CEGEP, (all four of them, because I simply did not have the financial means to study full-time) were years in which I destroyed the ingrained belief that I did not have the ability to be an intellectual.

One of Robillard's proposed reforms to the CEGEPs is to penalize students who take longer than the prescribed two or three years to graduate. "Single parents and students who work will bear the brunt of these reforms," says Pat Powers, director of Dawson College New School, located in the Mother House at Atwater Ave. and Sherbrooke St. W.

## Clobbering those who are down

"It's going to affect those students who have been successful in doing their (diplomas) over longer periods of time. It's clobbering those students who are already down."

Powers says the face of the college is changing. "We are seeing more single parents, more members of minority groups, more people from disadvantaged backgrounds."

Joanne Deller, a humanities teacher at Dawson, points out: "The CEGEP system was originally set up to democratize education, giving more access to the economically disadvantaged.

"Universities have always been inaccessible to those who couldn't afford to pay the fees. The CEGEP is an educational equalizer—providing a space where all students, regardless of background, can receive opportunities to quality education."

Todd also recommended that universities be turned into "havens for the pursuit of real learning," that teach "real" subjects—the unreal subjects being sociology and psychology, use-

thought argues that such courses lower academic standards and prevent students from being "culturally literate."

This issue lies at the heart of the proposed CEGEP reforms. According to leaks of Robillard's plan for the CEGEPs, philosophy and the humanities would be reduced, redefined and standard-

Harvard Educator, Charles Willie

less subjects that promote political correctitude. For Todd, Hamlet may indeed be the "sum of all the psychology departments in all the world."

But there are other realities out there; other cultural perspectives that are equally important for students to know about.

Ever since colleges and universities started introducing courses on women's studies and minority studies in the mid-1970s, there have been critics who have expressed concern about altering the time-honoured "Plato to NATO" curriculum. This school of

ized. One example of what might be coming is a mandatory Western civilization course called the History of Ideas which Carl Witchel, chairman of humanities at John Abbott College called "a masterpiece of Eurocentric simplification." As Witchel so aptly put it in a piece he wrote in the Hour. "I would opt for teaching (the students) the danger of having the 'truth' determined by a centralized authority."

To behave as if we are a homogenous culture and standardize higher education based on Western notions of what is worth knowing is ludicrous. This is not to say that DWM (Dead White Males) have nothing to teach us. On the contrary. We do ourselves a great disservice if we cut ourselves off from intellectual traditions that have shaped us. However, the history of ideas is much broader, and should include other voices.

## Philosophies aren't relevant

Linda Collier, a humanities teacher at John Abbott College who teaches Native Studies, is leery of the benefits of Robillard's proposed changes.

"I have many native students in my class. If the proposed reforms go through I'll be teaching Descartes to Cree and Inuit students. Some of these philosophers are simply not relevant to these students whose life experiences are very different from our own."

Collier goes on to say that the proposed reforms are detrimental to the multicultural face of today's CEGEPs. The English CEGEPs have always been concerned with multiculturalism in terms of staff and course development, whereas the French CEGEPs have been much more homogenous. But the face of French CEGEPs in Quebec is now changing as the effects of Bill 101 are being felt."

It is in humanities that students learn there are many versions of "the truth" and people with different experiences perceive events differently. It is in the humanities that students learn how to think rather than what to think. It is there that they learn to consider viewpoints other than their own.

Because of the massive availability of information through electronic media, the humanities are more important than ever before. Individuals are confronted with a plethora of competing and conflicting claims and points of view. The humanities can help students to become autonomous thinkers and enable them to form intelligent judgments.

One would hate to think that all those police technology students in the CEGEPs will be getting fewer humanities courses. How is that going to prepare them to work in a multicultural society?

If Lucienne Robillard's reforms go through as they appear at the moment, we're going to be seeing more conflict situations between minorities and the police. We're also going to be seeing a society of people who can "do" things but who cannot "think" about the implications of what they do.

Get real, Jack Todd! Get real, Lucienne Robillard!

# A teacher can change your life forever—mine did

## Mrs. Gavras helped me believe in myself, giving me courage and confidence to go on

February 21, 1993

It was a tense relationship at first. I was an angry and defiant youth with a definite chip on my shoulder and a very short fuse. Arms folded, head cocked back, eyes glaring with that smug know-it-all look which said, "you can't teach me nothin' that I don't already know."

I knew the streets. I knew the score. No one was going to touch me or change me. I had my cool and that was my armour.

In class I'd throw my feet up on the desk provokingly and dare anyone to say or do something about it.

She tried to ignore me at first. But when I had succeeded in taking over the class and being constantly disruptive, she finally reached her boiling point.

I remember the day of the big showdown. She marched down the aisle, grabbed my feet and threw them off the desk and said: "You think you're real bad don't you? You come in here looking like some Black Panther. I bet you don't even know what they stand for."

She was probably right. I had the right look but there was nothing to back it up. I was angry and I wanted to make a statement about that anger.

But what could this white woman possibly know about me or the kind of life I led? She knew nothing of the hardship and degradation experienced every day of my life as a black person.

She knew nothing about the basement cold-water flat on Barclay St. where I lived with my eight brothers and sisters, crowded together like sardines.

No place to work. No place to think.

She knew nothing of my mother's bleeding knuckles from her hard work as a hotel maid.

What could she know about my father's bitterness after putting in 20 years of his life as a railway porter and then being laid off?

### Never gave up

What could she know of the despair I felt, of the hopelessness I felt, believing that no matter how hard I worked in school there was nothing out there for me?

I did everything I could to alienate her, but she never gave up on me. I would toss spitballs at her when her back was turned. I spent my time hanging out at the pool hall and never did any of my school work.

I'd show up to class late every day. I'd arrive without books or anything to write with, knowing that she would have to send me to my locker to get them, and I would be free to roam the halls at my leisure.

But no matter how obnoxious I was I could not discourage her continued efforts to reach me.

Again and again she would try to find out what was wrong, why I was so silent and bitter. But I would turn my back to her and walk out the door.

Eventually she succeeded in piercing my armour. I let her into my world and she let me into hers.

That was Freida Gavras.

What I didn't know was that she, too, had experienced discrimination. As a Jew growing up in southern United States, she had experienced the poison of anti-Semitism and it made her care and it made her want to fight against injustice wherever it manifested itself.

If she felt that an injustice had been perpetrated against a student she would storm into the principal's office demanding to know why that student was sent home.

She wouldn't back down from anyone. She'd get in the ring with Mohammed Ali if she had to. She had real class, that lady.

She started to bring books for me to read about the black liberation struggle. This became the turning point in our relationship. She had tuned me in and turned me on.

Here was this Jewish teacher telling me things about my own history, the history of black people, that I wasn't aware of.

After class we would sit and discuss the ideas presented in the books. When things were happening in the black community, she would ask my opinion.

She validated my knowledge, and my experiences through those questions and made me feel significant as a human being.

Freida Gavras did more than what was in her job description, more than what the collective agreement asked of her.

When things were falling apart for me at home, she opened her house to me until things cooled off.

When money was tight, she found a summer job for me painting houses. She was the glue that held me together.

Mrs. Gavras helped me articulate the anger and frustration that was within me and helped me put it in a framework so that I could work with it and grow not as an embittered person

but as someone with commitment and integrity.

She empowered me with the tools to take control of my own destiny. By radicalizing me, she succeeded in educating me.

She helped me understand that knowledge and the ability to use it as a form of self-empowerment.

Once l saw the need for education, I could not be held down. My appetite was insatiable. I was like a sponge assimilating new knowledge.

What Freida Gavras did was help me believe in myself. She gave me the courage and the confidence to go on. I

don't think that I would ever have had the courage even to contemplate going to university had I not met her.

I remember how proud she was the day I told her had been admitted to McGill University. She couldn't have been prouder had I been her own son.

She took me around the school and told everyone. They shook their heads in disbelief. But we showed them.

### Returned to school

As things turned out, I ended up going back to Northmount High School six years later, not as a student, but as a teacher, a colleague.

Mine is not the only experience that shows that teachers can make a long-term difference to the future success of their pupils.

Eigil Peterson, professor in the department of educational psychology in the faculty of education at McGill, and two colleagues conducted a study on the impact of the classroom teacher on children's adult status.

They focused on the enduring effects of one remarkable first-grade teacher at the now-defunct Royal Arthur School in Little Burgundy.

What the researchers found in their study was that on the average, this particular teacher's students reached higher levels of academic achievement and higher adult status than those of the other teachers.

What did this teacher have that the others did not? One of her former pupils said that she left them with a "profound impression of the importance of schooling", that she taught with "love" and that she gave of her time freely to those who needed it most.

That's precisely what Freida Gavras did for me.

She helped me understand the importance of knowledge. She challenged my curiosity and imagination and she shared with me her vision of a just society in the hope that one day I would share this vision with other young people.

I've lost touch with Freida Gavras. But if she is still around, I hope that she reads this.

# Crossing Cultural Boundaries

# In search of a forgotten heritage
## Art exhibit offers a glimpse into long-lost aboriginal family links

November 10, 1994

A part of my cultural background that has been lost is my native heritage. My great grandmother was full-blooded Cherokee but, since she did not live on the reservation, she was unable to pass on to my grandfather the customs and traditions of aboriginal people.

Hence I find myself without links to that part of my ancestral past. Many of my family members look native American, yet over the years we have come to identify ourselves as Afro-Canadian or black. It is only recently that I started looking into my native ancestry.

In my quest to find a link to my past, I went to an aboriginal art exhibit and book launching last month at the Red Cedar Gallery on Monkland Ave. in Notre Dame de Grace.

It was there that I realized I was not the only one trying to recover their Indian ancestry. Two artists exhibiting their work, Nick Huard and C.J. Taylor, had also found their roots later in their lives.

Huard, who is a member of the Bear Clan Micmac from the Gaspe region of Quebec, says his father left the reservation for economic reasons and adopted the ways of the white man—hence Huard knew little about his heritage. It was six years ago at a pow-wow that Huard became, what he refers to, as a "born-again Indian."

"At this powwow I saw an old man sitting there, weaving a dream-catcher for a young child and suddenly it occurred to me that this is what the creator wanted me to do with the objects I had been collecting for many years. And so I started making dream catchers."

Now Huard's dream-catchers can be found all over the world.

Dream-catchers are circular, web-like objects with animal skulls, beads, shells, feathers and anything else the artist decides to weave into it.

Oneida legend has it that when hung, the dream-catcher will draw in and catch all passing dreams. The good dreams, knowing the way, pass through the centre hole and slide down, off a feather on to the person below. The bad dreams become entangled in the web and stay there until the first light of dawn, when they melt away.

"The circle represents the circle of life," Huard explained. "The weave is the dream-catcher which is inside the circle. By incorporating the talisman, the skull of the animal, in the dream-catcher I'm giving the animal a second life as the guardian of dreams. I do not kill to make my art. I find remnants of the animals in the woods left by hunters.

### Different view of life

"Another purpose for the dream-catcher is to set things straight," Huard continued. "It is Indian mythology versus white ideology. Indian values signify a respect for nature and not its exploitation. My dream catchers are a way of educating people that there is

172

Nick Huard with one of his dream catchers

another way of seeing things, that there is a need for spirituality and that sometimes we should let our dreams guide us."

C.J. (Carrie) Taylor didn't know she was aboriginal until she was 6 years old. Despite this, she is rapidly becoming one of Canada's most popular Indian artist/writers, having published several children's books in little more than four years. She is also host of a weekly radio program called Earthsongs on CKRK FM, the Mohawk radio station in Kahnawake. Taylor

173

reviews books, plays songs by and about natives, tells stories and discusses ecological concerns.

The book-launching and exhibition of her paintings at the Red Cedar Gallery was for her latest book, Bones in the Basket, published by Tundra Books. Some of her other books include How Two-Feather was Saved from Loneliness, The Ghost and Lone Warrior, and Little Water and the Gift of the Animals.

Taylor, 42, who is a mother of three and a grandmother of one, was the daughter of a Mohawk father and a mother of German-British origin. Being interracial has not prevented Taylor from participating fully in native life and culture.

"I've always felt very accepted by the native community and have been fortunate in receiving guidance from elders who have helped me with the research for my stories."

Interestingly enough, it was from her mother, a history teacher, that Taylor first learned of her Mohawk roots. "My mother had more pride in my native heritage than my father. My father left the reservation when he was very young. He missed the culture, the language, the spirituality. He didn't know what it was to be native and he certainly wasn't white. He was a very unhappy man.

"Standing at the barricades during the 1990 Oka crisis, watching the effigies burn, I finally understood the pain my father went through . . . why he was so angry."

Much of Taylor's work is part of what she calls "a healing process."

Learning about her native heritage has been a great source of pride for Taylor, who feels she has become a better person because of it. "It has caused me to see the world differently. I appreciate the world that is around me and I want to share this vision with others, especially children who haven't yet been corrupted." Taylor travels across Canada telling her stories to school children.

The Red Cedar Gallery occasion was memorable for many reasons. The appearance of well-known native leader Elijah Harper (known for his role in scuttling the Meech Lake accord) was a surprise to everyone. I had an opportunity to talk to Harper, who emphasized the importance of the arts in promoting native culture. "The strongest tool we have right now in promoting native issues is through the arts," Harper said.

### Lost memories

Being amid the native artwork at the gallery, meeting Taylor, Huard and Harper, made me realize the richness of my heritage. But I was also saddened by the lost memories this experience evoked. It made me want to learn more about the native part of me.

Unlike Neil Bissoondath, the multicultural critic who has chosen to give up his Trinidadian heritage and who recommends that other ethnic groups assimilate as well, I believe that we empower ourselves by embracing the richness of our multiracial identities.

I am disconnected from both my African and my native American roots and cannot be so generous as to give up the little that I have.

# Blacks and Jews
## Ties between them are strong but strained

April 11, 1996

I was recently asked to animate a discussion at a symposium about relations between blacks and Jews.

The topic fascinated me. Not only because of the issues involved in building coalitions between the two communities but because of my own experiences.

Growing up in the 1950s and 1960s in the Cote des Neiges area, my childhood was influenced greatly by Jewish schoolmates and friends.

Black and Jewish kids would congregate in our Barclay Street apartment to hang out. We would play the latest soul records on my sister's pink portable record player, rehearse new dance steps or just shoot the breeze. In my house, the different cultures and backgrounds merged comfortably and border-crossing was a daily activity.

My first affiliation with a community organization was the YMHA on Westbury Ave. In those days, there were no black community organizations in the Cote des Neiges area and few facilities for children The "Y" opened its doors to the blacks kids who didn't have the money for memberships.

### Tears in her eyes

The relationships I formed in my community, both with other children and a few of my teachers who were Jewish, helped to develop my consciousness.

I remember one of my high-school teachers telling me that blacks were not the only ones who suffered from discrimination. She told me of her experiences growing up as a Jew in the southern Unites States. Tears welled up in her eyes as she recounted numerous stories of racism. Sharing these stories with me created a bond between us that would last a lifetime and gave me a deeper understanding and a more universal perspective on racism.

I learned that racial discrimination wasn't unique to the black race. This enabled me to understand racism from the perspective of the "other". What I took away with me from these encounters was the importance of a sense of identity, memory, a sense of community, and the importance of coalition building.

The March 24 symposium, by the League of Human Rights of B'Nai Brith and the Black Coalition of Quebec, explored the historical relationship between blacks and Jews. And it looked at ways in which the two communities can work together politically and economically in combatting racism and anti-Semitism.

Relations between the black and Jewish communities have in the past been very strong, yet strained in recent times. In the U. S. anti-Semitic comments made by black Muslim leader Louis Farrakhan and black politician Jessie Jackson have fuelled tensions. Jewish neo-conservatism and its opposition to affirmative action, and black anti-Zionism, all help to account for the break in black-Jewish relations in the U.S.

Last month's local symposium featured a keynote address by Julius Lester, a prominent African-American author and professor of Judaic and Near Eastern Studies at the University of Massachusetts at Amherst. (He also happens to be Jewish.)

According to Lester, what blacks and Jews have in common is the fact that both have histories that begin in slavery. Both have been subjected to stereotyping by the white majority. Both have been subjected to violence on an unimaginable scale — 6 million Jews exterminated in 5 years of the holocaust, 15 million blacks perished in the slave trade.

**Both groups in ghettos**

Both groups have been physically segregated — the word, ghetto was first used to describe the section of Venice where Jews were segregated in the 16th century. "Geto" is Italian for iron foundry — next to where the Jews of Venice were forced to live.

Although their histories share many similarities, Lester stresses that the differences are profound.

"Similarity of experience is not the same as shared experience," Lester explained. "Black-Jewish alliances are difficult because the similarities are not as great as the differences. Jews have a story of who they are and how they came to be and the Jewish narrative has been recognized by history. Whereas blacks have been denied both equality and their historical-cultural traditions."

Another factor that separates blacks and Jews is the fact that many blacks find it difficult to trust white-skinned Jews who have benefited from "white-skin privilege."

Black-Jewish relations in Canada have a long history, according to Concordia history professor, Stephen Sheinberg. Black men joined in defending Jews against a fascist attack at Toronto's Christie Pits riot before World War II. In 1953, when restaurants in Dresden, Ont., refused to serve blacks, the Jewish Labour Committee and the Canadian Jewish Congress joined a inter-racial coalition to fight back. According to Sheinberg, Jewish lawyers were the first to open their doors to black clerks and articling students.

**No time to fight**

In recent years, the League for Human Rights of B'Nai Brith has joined with black organizations to push for equal opportunities for Haitian taxi-drivers or protest the police killing of Marcellus Francois, a black man.

What does worry Sheinberg, however, is the growing interest in the Nation of Islam among young African Canadians. He fears that Farrakhan's anti-Semitic ideology will spread if unchecked by black leaders.

"With the increase in racism, anti-Semitism and xenophobia in Canada and abroad, this is not a time for the luxury of fighting within the family," Sheinberg said.

# Interacial relationships are demanding
## To survive as a couple, the partners must look racism in the face

September 10, 1992

She walked into the hospital waiting room. He followed. She was a tall white woman with blonde hair. He was a tall, dark black man. Their movements were awkward and they walked with their heads bowed, eyes staring at the ground.

The room suddenly became silent. All eyes followed them as they walked to a corner. The couple began to shrink under the oppressive weight of the atmosphere. It was as if they were trying to make themselves invisible.

Two women leaned toward each other, whispered and looked in the direction of the couple. One laughed, the other nodded.

In the short time it took me to jot down these notes, the couple had fled. Perhaps this event went unnoticed by most people but for me it was a haunting reminder of my own experiences as a partner in an interracial marriage.

Experience has taught me that when issues of racism are not addressed head-on, the individuals find themselves catapulted into a racial arena that they never anticipated and which they can't handle. The relationship collapses.

Not so with Bertha and Danny, acquaintances of mine who have been married for over 30 years.

Bertha was a white civil-rights lawyer and Danny was a black civil-rights organizer in Alabama during the early-1960s.

Their marriage provoked the KKK to burn crosses on their front lawn. Danny was beaten and left for dead and Bertha had her arms broken.

But after 30 years they're still very much in love. What's Bertha and Danny's secret? They had a common goal, a commitment to fighting injustice.

Sarah's case was the complete reverse. It came as a complete shock to her that after 24 years of marriage, Sarah's husband refused to attend the marriage of their daughter—because he didn't want his daughter's in-laws to know he was black.

What surprised his wife was that he'd never said a word about being black. Thus it came as a great shock to Sarah that he'd been wearing a mask all those years.

My own relationship of 18 years was, I suppose, a commitment to interracial understanding. It wasn't just a relationship, it was in some ways a political statement.

Even the songs and food we chose for our wedding reflected this commitment. We had everything from Romanian folksongs to soul music, from bagels to black-eyed peas and rice.

When I was in college, dating a white woman was anathema to the spirit of black solidarity.

Franz Fanon and other black writers warned of the dangers.

"To be loved by a white person," Fanon wrote, means "marrying white culture, white beauty, white

177

whiteness."

No self-respecting black growing up in the '60s wanted to be accused of this treason. When my wife and I began dating I was confronted by the president of the black students' union at McGill. Had I abandoned my responsibility to black women? Had I forsaken my people?

No, I hadn't. I had merely fallen in love with another human being and we were not about to let pressures of whatever variety deter us from making a commitment to each other.

Ian Cameron

Maybe because we understood the implications of what we were doing, we were able to weather the racial storms.

When we first moved into N.D.G. [Notre Dame de Grace] 15 years ago, we found what appeared to be a housewarming gift outside our apartment door. Inside were a white mouse and a black mouse, each with its neck broken.

We've had bus drivers refuse to let us on even when the bus was half empty. Landlords refused to rent to us.

A little boy, no more than 5 years old, stopped us in the street one day and wagged his finger at us. "You're black, she's white, you shouldn't be together. That's bad."

One employer told my wife that being married to a black man would hamper her career.

But these experiences didn't defeat us. They made us angry and with the anger came strength, understanding and a commitment to combatting prejudice.

I've often wondered whether relationships that are founded on ideological grounds have a greater bond and ultimately stand a greater chance of surviving. I'd like to hear from other people who have been involved in interracial relationships. What do your experiences tell you?

# Clashing colours

## Clifton Ruggles and Olivia Rovinescu

December 6, 1992

Our daughter Amy was 3 1/2 the Christmas she received her first black doll.

Later that day, we discovered she had scribbled over the doll's face with white crayon.

When asked about it, Amy confessed that she would have preferred to get "a good white baby" like her friends. We were shocked, but we didn't dwell on it. There would come a time, we knew, when these issues would need to be addressed.

As the daughter of a white mother and black father, Amy would have to face the reality one day of her own mixed-race status.

Meanwhile, the doll remained marked, unnamed and rejected.

A year later, we were watching a TV show called Black in White America. The program documented a study by Dr. Margret Field Spenser in which black children were shown images of black and white children who were dressed identically.

The children in the study were asked which image they preferred. They consistently picked the white children.

Amy was disturbed by their responses. "Why don't they pick the pictures of the black kids?" she asked.

A few days later, Amy said, "Brown kids should like themselves and not think that white kids are better."

That evening we found Amy furiously trying to scrub the white crayon marks off the black doll's face. When we asked her what she was doing, she said the doll's mother had been very bad to her but that from now on she would take good care of it.

"It wasn't that I didn't like the baby," she said. "It's just that I wanted to be

Gazette photo/Peter Martin

Olivia, Clifton, Amy, Ali and dolls

white like Mommy, but now I like being brown."

That was when she finally gave the doll a name.

What Amy was experiencing is not unusual.

Caught between two communities, mixed-race children feel the pull from both sides.

Parents face the dilemma of how they should raise such children.

Should they teach them to think of themselves primarily as black because that is how society is likely to view them?

Or should they encourage them to embrace all parts of their cultural heritage, not only the part that is black.

Experts don't agree on how parents should deal with this problem.

Child psychologist Jeffrey Derevensky says that parents of mixed-race children shouldn't do anything in particular to instill black pride in their children.

"Just allow children to develop naturally," says Derevensky, an associate professor in the department of educational psychology at McGill.

"Be sensitive to their needs. Studies have shown that black children often draw themselves as white. This doesn't mean that there is anything wrong with their sense of identity. Children often don't see color."

Derevensky says: "The more we emphasize the difference, the more self-conscious we can make them."

He adds, "Sensitize the child to the things that other people may be saying about him, but don't make a mountain out of a mole hill. Deal with things as they come up."

Another psychologist, Frances Aboud, says that to counter the negative images and the lack of representation of visible minorities in the media, parents should "go overboard" in emphasizing the positive qualities of visible minorities.

"Parents tend to emphasize the importance of everyone being the same. Appreciating difference is just as important as appreciating similarities," says Aboud, also a professor in McGill's psychology department.

According to Aboud, before the age of 5 or 6, children don't have the cognitive ability to understand the concept of prejudice. Therefore parents should simply make an effort to expose their children to different cultures and talk about these cultures with their children.

As a person of mixed race, Louise (who doesn't want her last name used), 40, who lives in Montreal, resented the emphasis placed on being black when she was a child.

"My parents tried to indoctrinate me with it. Because it was done in a negative way, it negated other parts of me. Their approach came out of a time when things were changing in the black community. Blacks were reclaiming their African heritage and ideas about black consciousness and black pride were very popular."

Louise says that today she isn't interested in instilling a black identity in her 9-year-old daughter, Rachel. "Rachel is mixed—part African-Canadian, part Jewish. I want her to figure out on her own who and what she is. If anything, I've tried to convey to her the importance of embracing all cultures she is part of."

Louise says that labelling yourself plays into the racist discourse. "I want Rachel to fight for everyone's rights, not just because they are black but because they are human beings, she says.

Florence Clark, 52, of Montreal is a woman of mixed race.

She remembers that, "My mother, who is white, taught me early on in my life that there is no such thing as being mixed because we live in a society that is inherently racist.

"She always told me, 'You are your father's child, because that is how society will see you.'

"I do believe you can have other heritages, but ultimately you are black," Clark says. "If you grow up believing you are something else and suddenly you find out you are not what you thought you were, it blows your whole sense of self."

Professor Joyce Lander of Howard University's School of Social Work in Washington, D.C., says that in order for mixed-race kids to grow up with a healthy sense of their own identity, parents must prepare them for the reality of life in a racist society—a society that will view them, despite their particular colouring, as black.

Lander, who wrote a book called Mixed Families: Adopting Across Boundaries, says it is crucial that mixed-race kids learn coping strengths rather than be shielded from unpleasant situations.

"Telling your child that everyone is a human being is tantamount to denial. The larger society makes distinctions which we may choose to ignore, but we are constantly bombarded with these distinctions. Parents need to realize that ultimately love is not enough."

When our daughter Amy ventures into the world with her dad, she experiences differential treatment. In recent months she has encountered at least three episodes where her father was the victim of racial prejudice.

His outrage became her outrage. His pain became her pain and has bonded them in their "difference."

It is this differential treatment that has come to define elements of her identity in this society, as it does that of other black people.

Ania and Bert Barnes of Notre Dame de Grace report that their teenage daughter Alexandra, who is mixed, has experienced being the only one among her friends to be stopped by the police when she and a group of her friends were loitering outside a store. Alexandra knew the reason was that she was darker than her friends.

"There was never any doubt that our daughters were anything but black," says Bert, who is of Jamaican heritage. "We never went out of our way to instill black pride. What we did was stress the importance of personal pride and self-esteem.

"Alexandra has that strong black-woman way about her," says Ania, who is of Eastern European Jewish descent.

"Having strong black female role models helped. Bert's sisters were very involved in the girls' lives."

Ania says the white parent in an interracial family has a special responsibility in reaffirming the child's black identity. The white parent needs to be knowledgeable about black culture and black history and establish good communication with the child.

"This is not to say that the white parent should sacrifice his or her own culture. We celebrate the Jewish holidays. The girls are black and Jewish," Ania says.

Denis, 39, (not his real name) who lives in Cote St. Luc remembers the first time he confronted his mixed-raced identity. He was passing out literature for the Black Action Party on a street corner in the Cote des Neiges area in the early '70s with a black friend.

Denis wondered if by being involved in black political activity he was betraying his francophone heritage and his mother who was white.

"I felt as much Quebecois as black. I was suddenly torn by divided loyalties. I turned to my buddy and explained by dilemma.

"My friend asked me, 'Do you feel that color has made a difference in how you've been treated?'

"I thought about this long and hard. I had to admit that I, too, had felt the sting of racism and because of it I was part of that struggle. And I continued to pass out that literature. On that day, I finally knew who I was."

Montreal filmmaker Shanti Thakur, known for her recent film Crossing Borders, is now completing a film called Domino which explores the experiences of adults who are products of interracial families.

Thakur, who is of East Indian and Danish origin, says she wanted to make a statement about a subject she believes has rarely been explored in a healthy manner.

"We are the minority within the minority. We are more faceless, more marginalized than the marginalized.

"In Canada there are no interracial support groups like there are in the United States or Britain.

"We are absent from the media and when we are included, questions of our legitimacy inevitably come up," Thakur says. "We don't seem to be portrayed as part of healthy, productive relationships."

"I wanted to document some of these success stories. I wanted to show that the problems faced by mixed-race children are not inherent in the mixture, but has to do with how society reacts to you," she says.

"It's society's problem. Race is a social construct. Racism isn't. It is real. We are not living in a multicultural mosaic, but rather within a racial hierarchy. The problem is not one that resides within the interracial family itself, but rather is imposed by external forces outside of the family."

Thakur's film examines the rites of passage of adolescence, the making of career choices and starting a family—which are turning points in the lives of mixed race children because this is where questions of identity come up. The film is being co-produced with the National Film Board of Canada and should be released sometime in the new year.

Amy, who is now almost 8 years old, is very aware of racism. It is this awareness that has prevented her from being devastated by racism. Last summer some kids at her camp chided her about being black.

"We're all white and you're black," they taunted her, to which she replied, "Oh yeah, well my daddy's black, too, so there!"

Today she seems to have established a balance and an appreciation for all her heritages.

For a school presentation, Amy dressed in costumes of her various cultural heritages and talked about her African and native North American roots as well as her Romanian Jewish roots. She sees herself as part of all these cultures but considers herself to be African Canadian.

Recently asked what she was, she answered, "Black of course, what do you think!"

# Heading gave impression of conflict
## Inappropriate choice for article about mixed-race children

Perhaps if the article we wrote on raising mixed race children published in last Sunday's *Gazette* was about color co-ordinating one's house or matching the colours of one's wardrobe, the headline "Clashing Colours" might have been appropriate. But given that the article was about raising interracial children, the headline was highly inappropriate.

Houghton Mifflin Canadian dictionary defines the word "clash" as: 1. To collide with a loud, harsh noise. 2. To conflict or disagree; to be in opposition. The dictionary also suggests other synonyms one can look up: discord, strife, dissension, conflict, dissonance, variance. Not exactly what I would call a friendly list of words.

The headline not only misrepresented the intent of the article, but inadvertently placed a negative value judgement on our family's experience and that of other interracial families quoted. This might not have been the intent, but the result is the same. There is no racist conspiracy here, only lack of sensitivity.

We have to be aware of the impact language has in transmitting certain kinds of values. Language has the power to affect in subtle and complex ways the manner in which we think.

Embedded in the word "clash" are associations about armies clashing, people at war, cultures at odds with one another and people in irresolvable conflict. The word "clash" sets up subtle, subliminal associations that subvert the positive message of the article.

If anything clashes, it is the intrusion of this headline. It is incongruous with the content of the article, which points to the possibility of people of all races coming together and being comfortable with the choices they have made.

The article could have been called "Blending Colours" or "Harmonizing Colours." Or, if one wants to use alliteration, "Breaking Boundaries" will do. Any one of these headlines would have expressed more effectively the content of the piece.

It seems that whenever blacks are portrayed in the media, no matter what the context in which they are represented, there is an association made with dissonance and conflict. Blacks are portrayed as being at odds with the society in which they live.

The headline is a graphic example of the media's lack of sensitivity to issues affecting visible minorities and cultural communities.

Clifton and Olivia Ruggles
*Montreal West*

I would like to comment on Clifton and Olivia Ruggles' article titled, "Clashing Colours," Dec. 6.

First, I'd like to commend *The Gazette* for devoting the space to the subject of interracial families—and specifically, written by authors with personal insight to the issues.

However, I was disappointed to read the editorial choice of the title: "Clashing Colours."

Having been a panellist on interracial families on such shows as Shirley and Newsworld, I see that *The Gazette* has made the same mistake I experienced with broadcast media.

Interracial families are interesting to look at as subject matters, but the media's unconscious beliefs still surface: namely that interracial families are problematic from the beginning.

The title, "Clashing Colours," denotes a sharp conflict between colours (and between races). Framing a feature article on interracial families with this in mind is not only dissonant to the Ruggles' photograph of a blatantly happy family, it also reaffirms uninformed readers that our questions and our ambiguity as interracial families are painful and to be avoided.

Researching for my film, Domino, I interviewed over 60 interracial men and women.

The common thread they voiced was that their experience was an enriching one. If the "personal is the political" and we're talking about racial politics, I hope that the media can portray a continuum of the possibilities we experience: cultural flexibility, empathy for other cultures and an understanding for the myth of "racial" difference.

I hope that in the future a word like "harmony" can be immediately associated with interracial families.

Shanti Thakur
*Montreal*

# Special people shape our lives
## A lifelong social activist,
## Dan Daniels of N.D.G. still going strong at 73

December 8, 1994

We have all been shaped by the special people we have encountered, people like Dan Daniels.

Storyteller, playwright, teacher, peace activist, environmentalist, labour organizer, social critic and more, the 73-year-old N.D.G. [Notre Dame de Grace] resident affected my life.

He has led not one life, but many lives. He has seen Canadian history unfold and has taken part in shaping it.

And he's still at it, having just finished his latest endeavour, a new book titled Waiting to be Buried, about people on the margins of society.

I met Dan 20 years ago while doing research on the Canadian labour movement and we developed a friendship that continues to this day. Age differences never seemed to matter. It was an intellectual relationship based on grappling with new and exciting ideas. I was always moved by his keen insights, his intensity and

his commitment. He made me feel like I, too, had something to contribute and that my voice should be heard.

Culturally we may have been miles apart, but intellectually and spiritually, we had a lot in common.

Dan Daniels is the son of Romanian Jews who arrived in Canada at the turn of the century, bringing with them radical working-class values that were to influence young Dan from an early age. He dropped out of high school to become a seaman, eventually becom-

Dan Daniels, union organizer and writer

185

ing a leader of the Canadian Seamen's Union and editor of its journal, The Search Light.

The Canadian Seamen's Union was formed in the Dirty Thirties to improve the abysmal working conditions of seamen on the Great Lakes, who had the highest death rate of any group of workers. They worked long hours in overheated conditions, breathing coal and cargo dust. Black lung was a problem.

### Strike was milestone

Dan was involved in organizing one of the most militant strikes, the general strike of the Seamen on the Great Lakes in 1946.

"We were grabbed off the picket line and thrown into jail without warrants," he says. "The employers hired goons to attack us, but we could not be held down. We brought into the struggle not only the seamen but many waterfront workers. The militancy of the seamen caught the imagination of the entire working class around the country. We had taken on the most reactionary section of society, the ship owners, and we smashed them, to the point that the government had to intervene and seize the ships."

The Canadian Seamen's Union was destroyed in the early 1950s by a coalition of ship owners, the government and a gangster-led Seamen's International Union.

Like many other labour leaders of the time, Dan joined the Communist Party [CP] but later grew disillusioned and quit. "I felt betrayed by the Communist Party, which I discovered was not really living up to socialist ideals. I continued to live my life as a radical person because I realized that the ideals that motivated me to join the CP in the first place were still there.

"I eventually became involved in the Peace Movement, which I believed better represented my values. I'm not sorry I joined the Communist Party. Those were very formative years. It was a form of education and I met a lot of extremely decent people who cared deeply about their fellow human beings."

Dan also became disillusioned with the labour movement, which in his opinion, ceased to have a social consciousness. "When we started organizing, trade unions were not merely organizations to get a raise in pay and shorter working hours, but had a vision of a new kind of society."

After he left the labour movement and the Communist Party, Dan's began to write full-time. But his radical affiliations were held against him. He was blacklisted during the Duplessis era and had his writings confiscated.

"The Padlock Law enabled the police to simply walk into your house and confiscate anything they wanted. Twelve of them came into my house with their muddy boots, went through my personal effects, read my mail and confiscated a book I had laboured over a whole year—the only existing copy 1 had. I felt very violated as a person. I have recovered much more easily from physical violence. I've been beaten more than once in demonstrations. That I could accept, but not this violation of my privacy."

During the 1960s, Dan's career as a playwright was launched. His play, The Audition, won the award for best

Canadian play at the Dominion Drama Festival in the 1965. A 1968 Montreal Star article said the play seemed to lure "audiences into an enticing labyrinth of entertainment and then leave them to find their way out—if they can."

Another of his plays, called The Inmates, attacked the rigidity of North American society and his Plot to Overthrow Peter Rabbit, which won a 1968 festival award, was a thought-provoking satire affirming people's right to live a more liberated life.

During the 70s, the high-school dropout returned to school, completing a Master's degree in environmental studies at York University in Toronto. He continued to write and taught for the Protestant School Board of Greater Montreal's [PSBGM] adult education department. He also worked as an animator at Tanguay Women's Prison, where he developed creativity workshops to help participants expand their creative potential. Eventually he called this workshop "Living Your Life as a Work of Art" and offered it to the general public through the Lacolle Centre for Educational Innovation of Concordia University.

Dan is the first to admit that he has lived an eclectic life and that he has paid a price for it. But it had to be that way, he says. "Social change involves a total change in consciousness—the way we treat the environment, the way we conduct ourselves in personal relationships, the way we treat our bodies. It was natural that at different times in my life I would become involved in each of these areas."

Despite his biting criticisms of our society, Dan is not a pessimist. In some ways, he's the eternal optimist, believing in the potential of humans to grow and change. "If I didn't believe this, I would not have been able to teach."

Dan has been so many things in the course of his life. I asked him which of his many roles he found the most rewarding. His greatest accomplishment, he said, is the influence he has had on individuals, through his teaching and personal encounters. He treasures the letters he received from former Tanguay inmates who wrote to tell him how profoundly he had affected their lives, enabling them to find the strength to change.

## No regrets

Dan is also particularly proud of the fact that he has been instrumental in helping young writers by establishing the Urban Street Writers Workshop, which operated out of his studio for many years. He was also one of the founders of the Playwright's Workshop, which helped develop local talent.

He is still very active as a writer and still looking for new challenges and still a powerful advocate of social change.

His advice to others: "Stay creative, stay involved, stay connected, live your life with integrity and attempt as much as possible to see the world from the perspective of others."

That's how he has led his life, he says, so that when the end comes, he will have no regrets. "When those doors close at the end, I don't intend to scream."

# Parenting across differences

Clifton Ruggles and Olivia Rovinescu

unpublished

When Gerry and Linda (not their real names) were told that they might not be able to keep the infant they agreed to foster because she was racially ambiguous, they were flabbergasted.

Even though the baby looked white the colouring on her vagina indicated that she might have some black blood and consequently there was discussion about placing her with a black family instead rather than with her foster parents who are white.

After further medical examinations however, it was decided that the baby may indeed stay with her white foster parents since it appeared that her black ancestry was three generations removed and thus not considered to be significant enough to warrant changing her caregivers.

The issue of transracial adoption and transracial foster care is a veritable hot potato in the social services these days. In the past, white couples have provided foster care and have adopted black children without considering their needs other than to offer them a loving home. Some of these children encountered problems with identity as they grow older.

Because of these problems there has been a backlash in recent years to allow white parents to adopt or even to foster black children.

For the black child brought up in a white family there is a risk to self-esteem because there are no black role models immediately available and no black family members on hand to deal with negative experiences the child may undergo. Black children do not often tell white substitute parents when racist comments have been directed at them by other white people.

Arguments against transracial adoption and transracial foster care rest on the belief that parent-child relationships can only work, or at least work best between biological "likes." This view reflects widespread and powerful fears that parents will not be able to truly love and nurture biological "unlikes"—the underlying assumption being that the parent-child relationship would be threatened by differences. Racial matching policies are designed to duplicate the "natural" biological environment so that the child could develop a "normal" family relationship.

Racial matching in adoption was initially developed in a historical context in which racial intermarriage was universally frowned upon and considered illegal. So much so that, in the early 1960s South Carolina's laws stipulated that neither a black nor a white couple could adopt a mixed race child since such a child was considered too black for white parents to adopt and too white for black parents to adopt.

A black man could not adopt his white step-child on the grounds that "the boy might lose the social status of a white man." Racial matching served to prevent racial integration in the intimate context of the family.

In the United States, the National Association of Black Social Workers (NABSW) takes a very strong stand against transracial adoption. The association argues that transracial adoption constitutes "an attack upon the black community" and that it "harms black children by denying them their black heritage and the survival skills needed for life in a racist society." According to this view transracial adoption is considered a form of "racial genocide," a part of a continuing pattern of discrimination against the black community dating back to slavery.

Proponents of this view believe that the black community has become merely a donor group to white middle class couples and that the dilution of identification that results from black children raised in white homes will

189

ultimately harm the black community. The NABSW issued a position paper in which it stated: "black children belong physically, psychologically and culturally in black families in order that they receive the total sense of themselves and develop a sound projection of their future. Black children in white homes are cut off from the healthy development of themselves as black people."

The association condemns the traditional screening criteria which emphasizes economic stability, marriage and middle class values as discriminatory against the black family. Social workers have in the past undermined, rather helped black families, causing unnecessary admission into the social services. These social workers often pathologize the black family, seeing only the disadvantages and deprivation of black people and frequently ignore the strengths of black families because they are not sensitive to cultural and racial differences in child-rearing practices.

The association also holds that mixed race children should be integrated within the black community so as to avoid mental confusion associated with his or her dual racial characteristics. This view holds that adoption by white parents would give the child a "white mask" and prevent exposure to the child's own self, leading to turmoil and pain that can only be offset if the child is assimilated into a black group.

There are others however that argue that bi-raciality provides insight into two communities and that, while it is certainly true that these children do have to come to terms with racial

discrimination because they will not be accepted as white, what is contentious is the argument that they will only find happiness with black parents and a black identity.

Supporters of transracial adoption and transracial foster care maintain that the delays involved in racial matching has deleterious consequences on the black children causing serious and lasting problems. Professor Barbara Tizard and Dr. Ann Phoenix, authors of the recent book *"Black, White or Mixed Race? Race and Racism in the Lives of Young People of Mixed Parentage"* don't believe that same-race parents is always best. In their view, what is important is that the parents, adoptive or otherwise, should be positive about a child's racial background. According to their research, the race of the parents was not significant in how positive the child felt about his or her identity.

Lawyer Elizabeth Bartholet has written extensively on the subject of transracial adoption and is the author of a new book on the subject. Bartholet, who is white and who is herself the mother of two black children says that studies show that transracial adoptees are more positive than blacks raised in all black households about relationships with whites, more comfortable in those relationships and more interested in a racially integrated lifestyle.

It is precisely these kinds of descriptions, together with their sense of comfort in the white world that is seen as evidence of inappropriate racial attitudes by the critics of transracial adoption. Although the studies show that black children adopted by whites appear to be surviving very well, critics argue that they are developing a naive and dangerous faith in their ability to get along in the white world, a faith that will serve them badly as they grow older.

Critics of transracial adoption question the criteria used for determining psychological health. As far as they're concerned, adjustment to their white families, indicates pathology, not health as some might think. From this perspective, the short term sacrifice of black children's interests are justifiable when weighed against the long term interests of the larger black community. They argue that black children will ben-

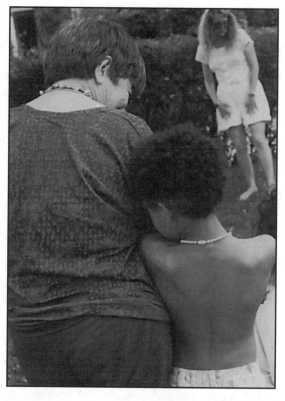

efit from efforts to strengthen the black community and that racial matching policies represent one such effort. It is argued that the preservation and promotion of a separate black culture and black community serves important interests.

Mike Godman, director of community services for Badshaw Family Services here in Montreal says that the placement of black children in white homes has been a contentious issue for many years and that Badshaw has recently developed a policy in regard to this issue.

"Essentially the policy is to place black children in black homes for the benefit of the child as well as the black community" says Godman. "However, when the child is of mixed race heritage, it's more difficult to assess what the placement should be. Some social workers believe that one ounce of black blood means the child should be placed in a black home. Others believe that the child would be better off in a white home and another group believes that they should ask the parents what they want. When we get ready to place a child, our policy is generally to first ask the foster family how they define themselves. Secondly we would ask the parents of the child what they want in terms of a placement. Thirdly, if we feel that the child may encounter certain difficulties because of colour, then we would make sure that that child has the necessary support during placement. We try to take it case by case because it's such a delicate situation. " No official policy has yet been created to address the issue of adoption of visible minority children into white homes, however a new policy has just been released respect to foster care and minority children.

Bruce Garside, also at Batshaw, explained that the need for the policy came as a result of studies showing that there was an over-representation of black youths in social affairs. Black children tend to be removed from their families faster and for longer periods of time than children of any other racial background and there are proportionately more blacks than whites in foster homes. Right now 40 percent of black children in substitute care are in homes of persons of a different race than their own. The study undertaken by Ville Marie Social Service Centre and Sawbridge Youth Centres, showed that black children were over-represented by nearly 400 per cent. They made up 23 percent of all youngsters receiving care, even though English-speaking blacks make up less then 6 per cent of Montreal's Anglophone population.

Vonnie Ruggles has been a foster mother to 38 children of different cultures and races over the years. Ruggles, the white partner in an interracial marriage said during a recent interview, " I truly believe that you can raise a child who is from another culture, love it, nurture it and give it a sense of identity. The foster parent has to be willing to go openly into the culture of the child they are fostering. I have seen terrible injustices done to children on the assumption that same race parenting is always better. I remember a case where the child had been with foster parents who loved it, nurtured it, made sure it played with children of the same race, fostered a sense of identity and the child was adjusting well. Yet five years later the social services found it in their wisdom to uproot the child and place it with black family on the assumption that this family can give it the identity that the white family could not. You can't tell me that in every black home they're thumping black culture."

Speaking to a group of social workers at Badshaw Youth Centre at the end of May, Harvard University professor Charles Willie said that he believes that the most urgent issue in the placement of black and mixed race children is their immediate happiness. Adoption and foster care should not be about parent or community rights and interests, but rather about serving the best interests of the individual child.

"What is important, " said Professor Willie, "is whether the white parent is aware of racism and committed to fighting it." This commitment to social justice and the willingness to give up "power and privilege" are, in Professor Willie's opinion, the key ingredients to successful interracial parenting. As he explained, it is not the skin color of the parents, but their commitment to the child and their willingness "to side with the oppressed" which will sustain the family that is raising an other race or mixed-race child.

# Race, Representation and the Arts

# Fame doesn't reflect talent for black artists

February 3, 1994

Here's a little quiz for Black History Month:

Name one prominent black Canadian artist. If no names come readily to mind, you are not alone.

Few black artists have gained any degree of notoriety in North America.

There are a few African American visual artists: Henry O. Tanner, Hale Woodruff, Aaron Douglas, James Porter, John Biggers, Charles White, Jacob Lawrence, Romare Bearden, Richard Hunt, Faith Ringgold, Hawardena Pindell, Lois Mailou Jones, Elizabeth Catlett—but they are not exactly household names (although Jacob Lawrence was featured in Time magazine last year).

For a long time, the boards of art museums, publishers of art books, owners of galleries rarely hired people of color in policy-making positions, positions that might have enabled our "voices" to be heard and our images to be displayed.

Throughout the 19th century, blacks were excluded from the academies, associations, and teaching institutions that were accessible to white artists.

Black artists were rarely able to attract and sustain dependable patronage.

Those who saw art as the highest manifestation of the human spirit did not believe that blacks could or should aspire to such heights.

Our collective failure to create "great art" was seen as a function of our being uncivilized.

But art always served an important function in the black community.

Many displaced African slaves brought with them an aesthetic based on the belief that beauty, especially that created in a collective context, should be an integrated aspect of everyday life, enhancing the survival and development of community.

These ideas formed the basis of an African American aesthetic. Performance arts like dance, music, theatre were the most acceptable ways to express our creativity.

Besides which, it was marketable because white people had no problem letting us entertain them. It was in keeping with existing power relations.

During the period of slavery when blacks were not allowed to read or write, black artists were not allowed to sign their work.

An effort was made to increase the cultural opportunities for free blacks in the mid 19th century. Abolitionists sponsored promising artists and there was a movement to include art in the curricula of all-black schools. However, after the Civil War, when blacks were fighting for their civil rights, interest in the arts was negligible.

The Harlem Renaissance of the 1920s was a period in which black culture flourished.

Second generation blacks began to seek inspiration for their art in black culture and started to express it artistically.

Despite this proliferation of artistic activity, for the most part, blacks continued to play an insignificant role in the world of the visual arts.

My own experiences reflect some of the reasons for this.

For a black ghetto kid, artistic production was not exactly on top of the preferred list of occupations. It was natural that my parents, who barely had enough to eat, would not enthusiastically support my interest in art.

I never felt I had the right to ask my parents for art lessons or art supplies. Eleven of us lived in a five-room basement apartment. I remember climbing on top of boxes used to store our winter clothes just to have a private space to draw.

If parental discouragement doesn't get you, peer pressure will do it every time. Artistic talent doesn't exactly make you the most popular kid on the block.

It was not until I achieved a certain measure of economic stability as well as maturity that I returned to doing art. At first my work was quite literal. When I started doing art I felt a deep need to represent black people in a way that I had never been represented.

Times are changing. Black artists are beginning to see their work displayed with more frequency. In 1993, the Smithsonian Institution of Washington D.C. set up an African American Museum.

Works by black artists can also be found at the Museum of African American Art in Los Angeles, the Studio Museum in Harlem and the Howard University Gallery of Art in Washington.

Insurance companies are even getting into the act—corporate collections include the Golden State Mutual Insurance Company and the Atlanta Insurance Company.

At the National Gallery in Ottawa, Helen Murphy, director of communications, said the gallery doesn't categorize artists according to race or ethnic group. "We don't file that way. If we did we'd have to justify purchases on a per capita basis, which would be discriminatory."

Murphy said she could not think of any black artists but promised she'd investigate the matter. She tracked down the names of five contemporary black artists with works at the gallery—Stan Douglas, photo-video artist; Julian Samuels, video artist; Time Whiten, sculptor; June Clark Greenberg, photo-artist; and Khadjeda McCall, textiles.

My quest continues. If you know of any Canadian black artists, particularly painters, please let me know.

# Seeking the limit
## Can black artist use white subjects
## to portray black experience?

cember 2, 1993

Can a white writer ever hope to
pict black life in the way that Afri-
American Nobel Prize winner
ni Morrison has been able to?

Who can comment on what is the
ject of much debate in artistic, lit-
ry and academic circles. The issue
a complex one with no easy an-
ers.

n 1992, the Advisory Committee
the Canada Council for Racial
uality in the Arts released its rec-
mendations, which dealt with the
ue of systemic racism in the arts.

Among the 12 recommendations,
2 of the items dealt with the need to
vent cultural appropriation.

### Claims story as own

What is cultural appropriation?
cording to aboriginal writer, Loretta
dd, appropriation occurs when
neone else speaks for, tells, de-
es, describes, represents, stories,
eriences or dreams of others for
ir own.

Appropriation also occurs when
neone else becomes the expert on
ur experience.

What I find objectionable is some-
e else's symbols of suffering being
propriated simply for profit. Black
istic expression has often been taken
er by members of privileged domi-
nt groups whose social advantages
ve them exposure and a venue for
tribution.

Our society has excluded minori-
s from the telling of our own stories.

We have often been excluded from
access to the funding which would
allow us to represent ourselves.

White artists have dominated the
artistic world. This is not a function of
artistic ability, but of political, economic and cultural variables at work.

Relations of power—who controls
the means of artistic production—are
at the core of the discussion about
cultural appropriation.

### Use stereotypes

Those who control the means of
artistic production define and represent "the other" according to their
own stereotypes and their own cultural imagery.

I do not want to be enslaved by
somebody else's notion of me. I want
artistic self-determination. It's part of
the process of reappropriating our history, which has been traditionally told
for us and about us, but never by us.

It is important for white artists to
acknowledge the degree to which color
has privileged them and how this privilege has influenced the perspective
from which they write or paint or film.

Historically our culture has been
the site of flagrant appropriation from
Al Jolston to Elvis Presley and beyond. Our art forms were subsumed
by white artists who were deemed
more acceptable than we were.

However, all art is a form of appropriation of one sort or another. Art
forms borrow from each other and
built upon each other. It would be
ludicrous to think that there is any art

197

form that is pure. We are a product of all that we have seen and experienced.

I do not hold on to the narrow view that people of other cultures or races cannot comment about us. Nor do I believe that the politics of identity should take precedence over talent, creativity and initiative.

Identity, in and of itself, does not produce insight. There are black artists who have exploited "blackness."

## Challenge status quo

And conversely, there are works by white artists who have challenged the status quo.

As a painter and as a writer, I have a serious problem with this. My life as a black person is equally influenced by my interactions with white people.

I may choose to paint white people and still be making a statement about the black experience. I do not want to be controlled by the simplistic aspects of cultural appropriation that ties me to a limited conception of art and a truncated notion of the human experience.

It is important to determine whether the artist is exploiting a situation or expressing an experience.

One way to make the distinction is to consider whether the work is respectful of the "other" or whether it reinforces stereotypes.

Ultimately, we can all only give voice to our own experiences. Sill, this shouldn't stop us from empathizing with others or depicting them artistically.

We must move toward considering a work's merits in terms that extend beyond the artist's identity, to the strengths of the work itself.

painting by Clifton Ruggles

# Black-and-white duo use dance to fight stereotypes—and have fun

May 5, 1994

Every Monday evening, the Centre Greene rocks to the beat of Special Blend, the unique interracial dance team of Jessica Goldberg and Eugene Poku, who teach children how to defy gravity as well as stereotypes.

Students Tamy Kozlov, Anna Bediako, Emily Orlov and Erin Laing described Special Blend as "outrageous, energetic, wild and funky" and said they "love the cool moves."

"Their style is very original," 13-year-old Tamy said. "It's more than gymnastics, more than acrobatics."

Some of the kids come from St. Henri, others from Westmount. Some are in it for the fun of it, others for the exercise; some do it for the cool image, while others want to experience a different cultural dance form.

Whatever race or class or gender, distinctions among the funk-dance students seem to vanish when they turn, spin, twist and bounce to the powerful rhythms being pumped out by the boom box.

And that, essentially is Special Blend's goal—to destroy barriers, challenge assumptions and communicate across cultures—and have fun doing it.

Beside teaching at Centre Greene, Poku and Goldberg also teach at Soul Impact Productions, the Westmount Recreation Department, the Point St. Charles YMCA and the Little Burgundy Tenants' Association.

In 1989, they created and performed in Youtheatre's Shades, which toured CEGEPS and high schools around the country. Shades tells the story of a cultural collision between two dancers who are forced to share a rehearsal space. In overcoming their preconceived notions about each other, they combine their training to expand their creativity.

He's Christian, she's Jewish. He's black, she's white. He's muscular, she's rotund.

But that's where the differences end. They both love dance and they both love kids and they both want to leave the world a better place than they found it. And they seem to be doing just that.

It is hard to categorize Special Blend's unique style. They call their style fusion, because it combines a variety of different styles, weaving elements from jazz, ballet, mime, breakdancing, martial arts and street dancing. Their choreography speaks to everyone, not only those literate in dance.

Poku, 32, was born in Ghana and began his dancing career as a street dancer in Montreal. He later decided to complement his dance training by studying ballet, acrobatics and martial arts. Before he met Goldberg, he had been dancing with his brothers and sisters under the name Shaka Dancers.

Philadelphia-born Goldberg came to Montreal when she was 3 years old and studied jazz and classical ballet in New York and San Francisco. Each has learned from the other and the combination is sizzling.

Jessie and Eugene, "Special Blend"

My daughters have been studying dance with Poku and Goldberg at the Centre Greene so I've had a chance to observe them in action. Both are natural teachers who communicate well with children.

"They know how to turn kids on," Tamy Kozlov said.

"They understand kids, they speak our language."

And they remember how to be playful and have fun. So many of us have forgotten how to express ourselves with our bodies.

In 1991, they choreographed and performed Taking Care of Business. The multidisciplinary performance deals with racism and sexism and expresses the energy that comes from breaking out of stereotypes.

The show is based on Poku and Goldberg's real-life encounter with each other and deals with confronting racism and stereotypes.

"He thought I had the wrong body type because I didn't fit the stereotype of the thin dancer," Goldberg said.

"And I thought he was insensitive and sexist."

Noomscape, another show created by the duo deals with drug abuse and peer pressure.

Through the use of mime and masks, they explore the changes that an individual with a drug problem goes through as he regains his independence from drugs.

Hip hop culture and rap music feature prominently in the work of Poku and Goldberg. According to Poku, some people have a problem with rap because they don't understand it.

"Rap has a bad reputation because some rap recordings are filled with foul language, violent lyrics and denigrating references to women," Poku said.

"It's important to keep in mind that not all rap is of this kind. There are many types of rap music—bragadosha, gansta, feminist rap, hard-core, conscious rap—and the list goes on."

In the ever-expanding world of rap, there are artists who rap about the eradication of violence and child abuse from the black community, rap that teaches black children about their history, rap that decodes the relationship between policing and the rights of individuals and even rap that gives the message to young black men on how to be a father.

"Some people are under the impression that it's rap music that makes people violent," Poku said. "If you're not a violent person, listening to rap isn't going to make you violent. That's too simplistic an analysis."

Poku and Goldberg believe that rap is a political expression of the times.

Hip hop has become a method of expression for black youth and offers a common literacy that provides a power in the face of nihilism.

Despite its focus on black urban resistance, rap is cross-cultural and appeals to middle-class white youth.

For those parents who think their children have never been exposed to rap, think again: Sesame Street does an alphabet rap.

Poku and Goldberg have shared their personal and professional lives for the past 12 years. For them, dance is a vehicle for social change.

They believe very strongly that creativity can help eliminate discrimination.

Their own racial and cultural differences are an asset to the message that underlies their work.

# An international language
## 'Dance is a tool to communicate a culture,'
## Selwyn Joseph says

April 12, 1995

The joint was really jumping.

But it wasn't Saturday night at the Apollo Theatre in Harlem and they weren't swaying to the pounding beat of James Brown. It was the World Gym in Cote St. Luc and the funky rhythms were those of Selwyn Joseph's Afro-Caribbean aerobics class.

"It's unlike any other aerobics class I've ever attended," said music teacher Carole LeDez Nonneman, 37, of Notre Dame de Grace.

"The music invites you to dance.

"There's more of a connection between the movement and the music. Some forms of music are more intrinsic to the human body than others.

"When I'm finished doing Selwyn's class I don't feel like I've done something unnatural to my body. Other aerobics classes are more mechanical and the music more aggressive."

"The fact he's a strong-looking black man sends a powerful message to the men that it's OK to participate in this sort of activity. I believe men in general need to shake their behinds a little more than they do."

Peter Howard, 56 is one man who is not afraid to shake his behind.

"The Afro-Caribbean rhythms make you want to move," he said. "Selwyn enjoys it and its contagious."

"The first time I took his class, it took me back to my teens and it brought forth a youthful burst of energy," Giuliana Pendenza said. "It's not just exercise, it's fun."

"The class lets you get rid of the demons inside you," said Laura DiLembo, of Cote St. Luc. "You get rid of negative energy and tension and you feel lighter."

Once I participated in one of Joseph's classes I understood what all the fervour was about. The gym floor was transformed into a gigantic drum and we seemed to become the instruments with which to beat that drum.

When you hear the drums it's like experiencing the heartbeat of Africa. It's a pounding that reaches into your soul and sets your blood on fire. Your body and limbs seem to have a will of their own.

With Selwyn's guidance our bodies moved in celebration of the voice of the drum. Sound, rhythm and movement became merged and one seemed to be moving in another space and time, connecting with something primordial in you.

Dancing links African Americans, African Canadians and Afro Caribbeans to their African past more strongly than any other aspect of their culture. Dance was not only a routine communal activity in West Africa but an integral part of ceremonies that bound people together. It linked one's personal identity to that of the group.

Dance also served as a mediating force between people and the world of the gods.

Joseph, who is nearing 50, is known as the "granddaddy of calypso" but has a schedule that a young man would have a tough time keeping up with.

Beside giving aerobics classes at the World Gym four times a week, he also instructs at the Westmount YMCA, the Women's YMCA, Le Sporting Club du Sanctuaire, Soul Impact, West Island Tennis Club, Caruso's Gym, West Coast Gym, Tennis 13 and at the Dance Factory, where he teaches professional dance. As well, he gives workshops in schools, coaches and choreographs and still performs with his own company, La Belle Caribbe.

The father of three, Joseph attributes his energy to the fact he's been dancing since he was 12 years old, professionally since he was 16, he's followed a healthful diet and he's never abused his body.

"I was always conscious that I was a dancer first and foremost and that affected the way I conducted my life," he said.

"If you were to categorize the type of music I play, it would technically be called 'soca' or the 'real soul of calypso.' Calypso music is very much a part of the African-Caribbean culture. It talks about a way of life, about opposition. It was the people's voice, it represented resistance. The slaves sang it in the fields as they worked.

"Calypso music is in my blood. My mother and grandmother were great calypso-lovers. They took me all over the country to hear calypso music.

"My aunt taught bele dancing, which is a Creole folk dance. It's my heritage, passed on from my grandmother and her grandmother before her."

Joseph came to Canada from his native Trinidad and Tobago in 1968. As a member of the St. Louis Dance Company he travelled to Venezuela and Suriname before being chosen to represent Trinidad and Tobago at Expo 67 in Montreal.

He has choreographed and danced in the halftime show at Olympic Stadium during a Concordes football game.

He has appeared with Maurice Chevalier at the Autostade in 1967, on Michel Jasmin's television show and on the Martha Howlett's dance-exercise show Looking Good.

He's also done many charity shows, such as for the Kidney Foundation.

"Dance is an international language, a tool to communicate a culture," he said.

"It makes people more comfortable with each other."

A home video of Selwyn Joseph's class will be available by the summer and will be available where Joseph teaches.

# Decorative or racist?
## Lawn ornaments can be offensive

August 11, 1994

Browsing through a Montreal antique store recently, I came across a collection of racist artifacts.

Among the more offensive items was a 4-foot-high wooden ashtray.

It was a figure of a redcap, with black face, large white eyes, thick red lips and hand outstretched.

The ashtray was part of his hand, and I imagined people butting their burning cigarette right in his palm. I also saw a lawn ornament/watering device that was a black man with wide-open eyes, thick lips and a long black hose running suggestively from his pants.

I assumed the objects had been produced somewhere in the southern U.S. because of its long history of racial discrimination. But the antique dealer told me they were "homegrown products of Quebec."

And they're bought by white and black people alike. He called the objects "black collectibles" and said they are in popular demand both in Canada and the U.S. I guess he thought that because they had achieved the status of antiques, displaying them in his store window was perfectly acceptable.

Every summer as I drive through the Quebec countryside I am reminded of people's fascination with little dark beings perched on their lawns. I've never quite figured out the attraction.

I've made it my personal mission to try whenever possible to make eye contact with owners of these lawn ornaments. I don't know whether this was the reason one disappeared from the lawn I often passed, but I like to think so. One down, thousands to go.

### Systems on alert

When I'm driving through the countryside my radar is out and all systems are on alert. Even my 9-year-old and 4-year-old daughters participate in the sightings.

Sometimes we make a game of it. We see how many we can spot in a given period of time. We spotted none as we drove through little towns between New York City and the border but counted 25 just this side of the border.

Taking in the scenery on a leisurely drive through the Eastern Townships a few weeks ago, I spotted, prominently displayed in the yard of a lawn-furniture supplier, six or so little black figures perched on a water fountain.

I asked the owner whether he was aware that these figures are racial stereotypes and offensive to some people. He was surprised by my question but willing to discuss it. As far as he's concerned, he said, they're decorative lawn ornaments—just like the others that he sells.

### Supply and demand

If people didn't buy them, he wouldn't be carrying them. Can't argue with the principle of supply and demand.

Are black lawn ornaments public declarations of racism or benign displays by people who just don't know any better?

Refusal to know is no excuse. They've made a choice to stay within a certain framework of thought despite the history of the civil-rights movement and other events of the last 30 years.

I suppose one can argue that these lawn ornaments don't do anybody any harm and that they are, after all, on private property. But that argument doesn't hold any weight with me. The homeowner's right to display these figurines interferes with my right to be free from painful reminders of the subjugation of my people.

These are images that clearly come out of slavery. To think of them as cute or harmless is to accept the past to which they are linked.

Unlike the Blessed Virgin, which is an object of worship, or endearing figures like ducks and deer, these aren't benign images devoid of meaning. Removing these objects from the his-

torical context that produced them obscures their original purpose, which was to reinforce racist beliefs and attitudes.

The fact that such ornaments continue to be displayed makes a statement about what people will tolerate. Racial politics are not always clearly stated but are woven into the social fabric, and shape the values, the behaviour, and even the aesthetic sensibilities of people.

I decided to do a quick check of my own neighbourhood—N.D.G. [Notre Dame de Grace]—to see whether racist ornaments are a rural phenomena and how the tastes of urbanites differ. I found the usual array of ducks, cats, and Blessed Virgins, but found no trace of plantation ornaments, except for one I noticed that had been repainted white—standing as a reminder of the unacceptability of these images and a symbol, I hope, of the changing times.

Eric Ourique

# Played out
## Makeup perpetuates stereotype

January 6, 1994

The Moor doll burst out of the gift box and on to the stage as he probably had done many times before in the history of the Nutcracker Suite. Wielding a massive scimitar, he looked dark and sinister. Had he not been painted a shoe-polish black, were his lips and eyes not so exaggerated, I would have focused on his graceful movements rather than on his racial connotations.

My 8-year-old daughter Amy, who was performing in the Ballet Ouest version of the Nutcracker this December, had mentioned that she thought that something was wrong with the portrayal of the Moor doll, but I guess in all the commotion over her involvement in the ballet it didn't quite register.

My wife and I stared at each other in disbelief at the Al Jolson lookalike who exploded on to the stage on opening night.

We spoke to the artistic director, Margaret Mehuys, who thanked us for bringing the matter to her attention. In subsequent shows, the dancer was painted white rather than black. We were most impressed with Mehuys's sensitivity and with the speed with which she made the changes.

Changing the makeup generated a variety of responses from some members of the cast and parent volunteers. Some said they couldn't understand what was wrong with the original and thought the doll didn't look as frightening with the white makeup.

One of the parent volunteers, Susan Van Gelder, said she was very glad to see that the makeup had been changed. "An image of a golliwog in this day and age is definitely not appropriate.

"Just because a stereotype existed when the ballet was made doesn't mean we have to perpetuate the stereotype."

Maurice Lemay, a professional dancer who played the Moor, said he was simply trying to render what he thought was an accurate portrayal of a Moor. "When you do period pieces such as the Nutcracker, stereotypes are inevitable. I believe it's up to the parents to discuss these stereotypes with their children."

After the show, I lamented the fact that the art education course I'd been teaching at Concordia University this semester had come to an end because I could have used this as an example of how important cross-cultural sensitivity is in the arts.

I had tried to explain to my students that cultural sensitivity enters into a variety of different decision-making situations in the arts—and could include anything from makeup to costume design to set design.

In the course, we had explored how cultural images contain definitions of groups of people and that blacks have, to a large extent, been negatively stereotyped and rendered into caricatures over the years.

Cultural images contain inherent assumptions regarding the physical, emotional and social characteristics of the people being portrayed, and as

Dolls on display. Shelbourne Museum

such, reinforce negative cultural attitudes.

The issue is a complex one. We can go too far in our zeal to rid the world of stereotypes. I don't think that it is to our advantage to totally rewrite history.

I want to know what the dominant stereotypes were and I want to understand how they evolved.

On the other hand, I know that some people accept stereotypes in the arts at face value. We don't want to promote the perpetuation of negative stereotypes. But could these images not be discussed and used to re-educate the public?

Discussion periods could be organized after a controversial performance. The issues could also be raised by including articles dealing with controversial subject matter in the programs handed out at the time of the show.

I would agree with Mr. Lemay that it's the parents' responsibility to discuss stereotyping with their children. However, for these kinds of talks to be effective, parents, like the rest of the general public, must have access to the information that can help to facilitate these discussions.

207

# Defining art—and racism
## Painting controversy could have generated useful debate

April 2, 1992

Recently, the Concordia Women's Centre refused to display a painting by a white woman depicting a black woman carrying bananas on her head. They said they feel Lyne Robichaud's "Femme aux Bananes" is "stereotypical and racist."

Robichaud maintains the image was intended to exemplify the dignity of the working woman and pay homage to a simple way of life.

She challenged the centre's right to censor her work.

The issue received wide media coverage because it appeared to be yet another example of "political correctness" trying to curtail freedom of expression.

The media tended to focus on the censorship issue rather than provide an opportunity to discuss how visual images can be interpreted.

Such a debate could have examined the influence of visual media and given a clearer understanding of what constitutes a stereotype.

The painting raised important questions about the role and responsibility of the artist in society; whether society should impose restrictions on artistic expression; and how race, class and gender have been and should be treated in art.

My reaction to the painting was strongly divided.

As a visual artist myself, I was uneasy about the restriction on freedom of the artist. I do not believe that we should restrict artists' rights to represent another culture.

### Why bananas?

Art should not be produced to fit someone else's political agenda, even a politically progressive one.

But the bananas kept getting in the way.

Why bananas of all fruits? Surely the artist should have been sensitive to how bananas could be perceived as an insult to blacks who have often suffered the humiliation of being likened to monkeys.

In her homage to the simple life, the artist failed to take into account that for the slaves who worked on plantations, this simple life was neither simple nor was it freely chosen. The image is painful to many successors of those slaves.

Not all black people, however, would respond in the same way to this image.

### Highly problematic

The issue raises many questions: Can one use a stereotypical image without it necessarily being racist? Does racism always involve racist intent or can it be accidental?

A painting like Femme aux Bananes might not be racist, although the artist's vision might have been formed by an unexamined world view that has roots in racism.

Still, I wonder whether reality can be represented without the use of recognizable images or stereotypes.

Historically, blacks have been an oppressed people. Images of people of color tend to be highly problematic because, inevitably, the images are linked to notions of power and domination.

Would the image have been any more acceptable without the bananas? According to some feminists, any image of women bearing fruit can be viewed as an oppressive stereotype (whether the woman is black or not).

These issues are not new.

When Gauguin's paintings of Tahitian women were first produced a century ago, they were met with outright ridicule because they elevated the uncivilized to unprecedented heights. Never before had women of color been accorded such beauty, which challenged Western notions of esthetics.

While Gauguin might have been challenging these prevailing notions, he also exploited his subjects by presenting them as primitive creatures of passion and desire.

The day for painting the "noble savage" is over, along with images of Aunt Jemima, Little Black Sambo and racist lawn ornaments.

This is not to say one cannot take these stereotypes and integrate them in a critical fashion. There's an important distinction between doing work about racism and doing racist work.

Nor is it to say that a white artist can't comment on the black experience, for to say that is to close a very important cultural door.

Several years ago, I brought one of

my paintings, of a despondent white woman, to an art course. It was a study of a childhood friend who had recently committed suicide.

As soon as I displayed the painting, I was met with a barrage of criticism—questions about what I, as a man, could possibly know about the female experience to depict it.

I explained that pain is a universal emotion, not gender-specific or culture-specific. I remember wondering whether the professor would have had less problem if the painting were that of a despondent black woman. I wonder whether color takes precedence over gender.

On another occasion, I was criticized for promoting stereotypes when I submitted a painting depicting aspects of my life as a black person in a white society. I included images of a railway porter (my father) and domestic worker (my mother).

What the professor failed to see was that these were not caricatures but real people.

Art that attempts to be politically correct might cease to challenge our notions of what art is all about.

It was unintentional, but this painting became a catalyst in a debate about racism, stereotypes and freedom of visual expression.

For this reason alone, it should have remained in the exhibit.

The organizers of the show could have arranged a discussion of the complex issues generated by the painting. Then individuals could determine for themselves whether the painting had any artistic or social merit.

# Reader—especially parents—beware
## Popular children's story, Tintin au Congo, is rife with racist stereotypes

September 15, 1994

From the expression on her face, my 9-year-old daughter Amy had picked up something at the library that she could not wait to show me. "Wait till you see this Dad, you won't believe it," she said, thrusting a copy of Tintin au Congo at me.

She had picked out certain pages she wanted to draw my attention to, pages with images of blacks made to look like monkeys; blacks bowing down before Tintin, insulting images of tribal chiefs mimicking European royalty by wearing pots and pans for crowns and rolling pins for sceptres.

Even a seasoned veteran of racism like me was unprepared for the racist representations contained in Tintin au Congo. It emphasizes the old racist chestnuts of black stupidity and laziness.

One sequence had Tintin intervening in a fight between two black men who are arguing over the ownership of a straw hat. Tintin saves the day in a Solomonesque decision to cut the hat in two and give each man a half of the hat. The men walk away satisfied, each wearing a portion of the hat and wondering why they hadn't thought of such an ingenious solution.

Another equally disturbing sequence has Tintin crossing a railway track and having a collision with a train filled with black passengers. In an attempt to get the derailed train back on the tracks, Tintin instructs the blacks to "get to work" but is told that they are "too tired."

### Dog gets involved

Tintin's little white dog Milou then gets into the act, valiantly pushing against the train in a single-handed attempt to get it back on track and calling the blacks "lazy" for their lack of effort.

Milou is presented as smarter and as having more rights than the natives.

In one sequence Milou is helping Tintin teach a group of natives and snitches on those who are not paying attention, drawing attention once again their shortcomings.

On nearly every page we see the white man solving problems and taking on leadership roles and on nearly every page we see the black man portrayed as lazy, lacking in character and intelligence and needing and even wanting to be dominated. The last page of the book has the natives so saddened by Tintin's departure that they have erected a monument of him.

### Equally racist

As I turned the pages I could feel my blood pressure going up. How could such racist books still be found in libraries—in this day and age, with all the rising public awareness about racist stereotypes.

As it turned out, many libraries in Montreal carry Tintin au Congo and other Tintin books, which are equally racist. I decided to investigate the situation in local West End libraries.

The children's librarian at the Fraser Hickson Library, Jane Toward, said she checks books for racist and sexist content and has a stack of books in her office that she has taken out of circulation.

She keeps them around for historical purposes, saying that she believes it's important to understand how racial and sexual representation in books has changed over the years.

When she heard about the article I was doing, she invited me to see her special collection. What a find for anyone doing research on the subject! What was particularly interesting was the updated versions of the same books which had deleted some of the more racist parts.

One book, The Rooster Grows, had been edited so as to omit an image of a barefoot black child and a rhyme about the "frost gwine to bite my toe."

Another book in Toward's collection is a 1923 version of Dr. Doolittle's Post Office by Hugh Lofting. In one passage that was omitted in subsequent editions, Dr. Doolittle makes reference to the weather in Africa in the following manner: "A climate? Well, I should call it a Turkish bath. In England we like variety in our climate. And we get it. That's why Englishmen 'ave such 'earty red faces. 'Ere the poor creatures turn black."

When she was children's librarian at Westmount Library, Maria Varvarikos dealt with racist books in much the same way as Toward. Varvarikos remembers a man once asking why he could not find Tintin au Congo in the stacks.

Varvarikos explained and the man asked to see it so that he could determine for himself whether it was racist.

When the man returned the book, he said that he didn't find it racist. Varvarikos asked him if he would feel the same way if he were black. After thinking about it, the man agreed that indeed, he wouldn't, and admitted that he'd never thought about it that way.

## Pressure works

Public pressure can affect change. Herge, the author of Tintin, has been criticized for anti-Semitism. Subsequent editions of a story depicting a big-nosed Jewish businessman named Mr. Blumstein was changed to Mr. Bulwinkle, so as not to offend the Jewish community, which had protested.

No such changes were ever made to Tintin au Congo even though nearly every page is offensive to people of African descent.

Tintin has been, and continues to be, tremendously popular. The Tintin series has been in publication since the early 1940s and has been translated into 28 languages.

What should be done with books that are deemed unacceptable because of their racist or sexist content? Should they be relegated to the garbage heap of literature?

I like Toward's approach of keeping them around so that they can be subjected to critical analysis.

It's important to understand the literature that has affected generations of children.

I'd like to see more children with the skills to recognize racial and sexual stereotypes when they appear in books.

## Book analyzed

In a conference last May called Diversity: Challenge and Response, the Quebec Library Association dealt with precisely this issue.

The racist text and images contained in Tintin au Congo were subjected to critical analysis and librarians from across the province discussed the role that literature plays in shaping world views and inculcating values.

I don't believe that every book that has a questionable depiction of a black person should be banned.

Books like Mark Twain's Huckleberry Finn and Joseph Conrad's Heart of Darkness are significant pieces of literature and should be understood within the historical context out of which they were produced.

On the other hand, teachers and librarians should make available to children books written by people of African descent that provide other perspectives. Insight is developed from this juxtaposition of ideas.

A friend of mine had a great suggestion—why not have stickers on the front of books warning readers that the book they are about to read includes racist content. Reader beware!

# Combatting Social Problems/ Making a Difference

# Bureaucratic tunnel vision
## Black health-care workers stand to be hit especially hard by plan to cut hospitals

July 27, 1995

Being a sickly kid I virtually grew up in hospitals. The same small community hospital that I was born in also nursed me back to health after a near fatal car accident. My weekly visits to the hospital for allergy shots was a constant in my life. The only person I trusted to administer these shots was Nurse Loftess. The needle somehow hurt less when she gave it.

Neighbourhood hospitals are an integral part of a community. The technological efficiency is essential but an important part of getting better is how comfortable you feel. This, one would think, is basic common sense.

But reason doesn't always prevail. Neither does public outcry, it would appear. Despite the protest from the public and the medical community, the bureaucrats in Quebec city are still suffering from myopic vision and are barrelling ahead with the closing of the Queen Elizabeth hospital in N.D.G. [Notre Dame de Grace] like a bull in a china shop.

Dr. Robert Weinman, who works in the Family Medicine Unit at the Queen Elizabeth Hospital argues that the decision to close the hospital at this time makes absolutely no sense at all given that a committee, le Groupe Tactic d'Intervention set up by the Ministry of Social Affairs to investigate emergency rooms in Montreal hospitals has recently assessed the Queen E to be one of the best models of care delivery in this province.

For Rosalie Johnson who is the assistant head nurse in the orthopedic unit at the Queen E the prospect of leaving is shattering, "I spent a good portion of my life at the Queen E. It's not just a hospital, it's like a family. Everyone's working together and it makes for a very strong community based hospital. It's a comfortable feeling to work in an environment where you have all that support".

I talked to many doctors who expressed similar views about the Queen E being a model of what a community based hospital should be. They were concerned that the larger hospitals simply could not provide the same personalized services.

I have yet to talk to anyone who sees any benefits to the closing of the Queen E. Most people foresee impersonal treatment, big line-ups, decline in services, unemployment, and a host of other problems arising from the fact that no other structures have been put into place to absorb the services that will be lost. But the bureaucrats stand firm on their reasoning, such as it is.

Doctors I interviewed were skeptical of the suggestion that patients could be absorbed by the CSLCS and other hospitals explaining that there would simply be more people than jobs—downsizing by its very nature means jobs will be lost. They had little faith that even the unionized employees could be absorbed or that the government would pay indefinitely the salaries of those that can't be relocated. As soon as the current contract ends, they predict there will be massive job cuts. Observers say that the idea that doctors and nurses will be easily transferred to other hospitals is ludicrous since these other hospitals do not have the budgets to absorb these additional salaries. They have not been mandated to expand in order to make use of the services of the surplus personnel.

According to Alliance Quebec, hospitals who do not have special status to communicate in English are under no obligation to absorb Anglophone personnel who do not have a sufficient working knowledge of French.

Black and visible minority hospital workers feel particularly threatened. Hospital work has been one of the few areas that has provided blacks and other people of colour with well paying stable employment. There was a time in Montreal's history when blacks were prevented from getting work in hospitals. Black women who wanted to become nurses were forced to go to the United States. It took many years to break through the racist hiring practices of Montreal hospitals. Hospital closures mean unemployment for everyone, but the black community will be particularly affected because job discrimination is, unfortunately, still a lived reality for many blacks.

Many of the highly skilled technical staff who perform much of the lab work are recent immigrants who will be particularly hard hit because those positions are already filled. Unlike nurses and doctors who can work in places like CSLCs, technical staff can't be absorbed in the same way.

The implications are far reaching because this will also impact on the technical training programs at the CEGEPS as well as the nurses' training program both at the CEGEPS and universities. If there are no jobs, then there will be no need for technical training or nursing programs.

I fail to see how a government who claims it is concerned with the unemployment problem in Quebec goes about terminating already existing jobs instead of generating badly needed new jobs.

We can't afford to compromise our health system. We have to look for more creative ways of solving our health care costs. To take away something as essential as hospital services is ludicrous.

The bureaucrats in Quebec City are suffering from a common affliction— its symptoms are short sightedness and tunnel vision.

For a government that prides itself on its connectedness to the people of Quebec, this disruption of hospital services indicates that it is totally out of touch with the reality.

# Heartbreak
## We couldn't keep our promise to a sick mother

October 3, 1991

We all make promises. Some we can keep and others we come to realize are impossible to keep.

This summer, my family and I faced the dilemma of whether or not to honour a promise we had made to our mother years ago. We had promised never to put her away "in one of those places." We had promised not to let her "die among strangers."

This was her greatest fear about growing old—being separated from the people she loved and cared most about.

This was a promise, however, that we could not keep.

My mother was suffering from an Alzheimer-related disease known as frontal lobe syndrome and we found ourselves unable to provide the constant care and attention she required.

Like most working-class families in our society today, we had neither the available time nor the financial resources with which to honour our promise to care for her at home.

In the days in which my mother grew up, that kind of promise might have been easier to keep, although no easier to do. Fifty years ago, most women worked in the home, there were larger extended families living in closer proximity, and extended care for the elderly in the home became a realistic possibility. And there were fewer facilities available.

My mother had looked after both her mother and her mother-in-law when they were unable to care for themselves. She naturally assumed we would do the same when her time came.

That's why, she often told us, she had so many kids.

The disease seemed to strike almost without warning. The signs were there, but we didn't pay attention, we didn't want to believe anything was seriously wrong.

We thought of logical explanations to account for her peculiar behaviour: wandering the streets late at night, befriending strangers, absentmindedness and inattentiveness.

In the early stages of the disease, she became preoccupied with making preserves. We attributed her behaviour to her loneliness, the loss of her husband, her children moving away, the natural effects of the aging process.

We even explained the fixation on preserves as a manifestation of the need to exert some kind of control over her aging.

We engaged in psychobabble of the worst kind to explain her altered behaviour, her lack of reasonableness, her relentless insistence on acting out her second childhood.

We did not want to believe the obvious. So we were caught unprepared, having not made arrangements for her eventual placement. We preferred to think of our mother as idiosyncratic. We were still in the stage of denial.

### Married at 17

After the denial comes the angry

painting by Clifton Ruggles

"Why?" stage. Why her? Why my mother? Hasn't her life been hard enough? She spent her childhood living in a depressed area of Nova Scotia, in a shanty less than 10 metres from the railway tracks.

She married at 17 only to see her young husband go to war while she carried and gave birth to their first child.

She raised nine kids in a cold-water basement flat on Barclay St. and was widowed at 48 when her husband drowned in a fishing accident, leaving her the family's sole supporter.

Is there no justice in this life? Why should this woman, whose life has known so many burdens, have to face still another hardship—aging with an affliction that slowly strips away her intellectual and physical abilities?

It wasn't fair and we were outraged.

The anger subsided and we entered into the third stage—that of acceptance. In this stage, you start thinking about what needs to be done.

How were we going to manage? Knowing very little about Alzheimer's, we had to become more informed about the disease, its symptoms, its rate of progress and what resources were available.

My sister took it upon herself to join an Alzheimer's support group, to learn more about the effects of the disease on the family and how to deal with one's feelings of helplessness, of guilt, of inadequacy, and of despair.

But more important, it taught us how to appreciate those moments when we could communicate or experience things with our mother.

In time, my brother Hilton, the primary care-giver with whom my mother lived, came to the realization that he could no longer give her the round-the-clock care she required.

There was no alternative. She would have to be placed. We would have to renege on our promise.

Good facilities for chronic care patients are hard to find, especially when you don't have a lot of money. Her name was added to a huge waiting list and we were told it would take six months to a year, if not longer, before a suitable placement could be arranged.

The situation became desperate.

Reputable sources in the medical community told us that if we couldn't get her placed, we should simply drop her off at the emergency department of any major hospital and refuse to take her home. When I first heard this advice, I was appalled. It meant abdicating all our duties and obligations.

### Many not so lucky

Within a few months, however, the disease had wreaked such havoc in our lives that the advice seemed less distasteful.

Luckily, we were able to get her placed before resorting to this last, extreme measure. I am told that 10 years ago, you'd have to wait five years for placement. Today, the wait is down to six months to a year.

My mother is one of the fortunate ones. She had people who loved her and cared for her. She now has a place to stay, a bed and qualified people to take care of her.

There are many others who do not. They are destined to continue to walk the eerie and bewildering streets outside the fringes of reality, shuffling back and forth, like used playing cards ready to be discarded before the last hand can be played.

Alzheimer's disease now affects at least 300,000 Canadians and causes 10,000 deaths a year. As demographics shift over the next few decades, the incidence of Alzheimer's disease will increase dramatically and will affect the lives of many Canadian families.

It's time we started to examine the way our society chooses to allocate its scarce resources and start putting a higher premium on the needs of the elderly. After all, we shall soon be among them.

# 'Lifetime of dying slowly'
## Domestic violence doesn't affect only the victims— it must be seen as problem that hurts us all

March 5, 1992

After many years of enduring the physical and mental abuse of herself and her children, Linda finally decided she'd had enough and walked out on her 30-year-long marriage.

"My husband would beat the children unconscious with his belt, fill their mouths with hot peppers and tie them up," she recalled.

"He made me out to be a failure— that I couldn't do anything right, not even keep the house clean. He'd have me scrubbing walls at midnight.

"He didn't want me leaving the house so he'd take away my shoes.

"I lived in terror of that man. I don't know how I managed to live through it. Now it seems like a horrible nightmare."

What made Linda stay all those years? What would make anyone endure such an ordeal?

As hard as it might be to believe, Linda says she did it for the sake of the children—to provide them with a roof over their heads and food in their mouths.

"I couldn't give them all the material things my husband could. I really thought I was doing the right thing.

"I felt guilty for bringing them into the world. I thought, 'what could I possibly offer these children on my own?'"

### Beg for forgiveness

And she always held on to the hope that he might change some day. Every time he had an abusive episode, he'd cry and beg for forgiveness, promising never to do it again.

"I thought I was doing what any dutiful wife should do," Linda said. "I took my marriage vows very seriously: in sickness and in health, until death do us part.

"I made so many excuses for him— it's because he's sick, it's because he's insecure, it's because he was abused as a child."

Linda says she believes people in abusive situations become creatures of perpetual hope. "We hope that things will get better—if I'm a better mother, if I'm a better wife, if I'm a better housekeeper and if I can just keep things quiet and calm, everything will be all right.

"I wasn't angry at him. I was disappointed in myself because I couldn't change him."

Another woman with a violent husband, Clara, told me about the emotional scarring of her children. Her youngest daughter was in therapy by the age of 3. The girl was afraid to grow up. She couldn't go to sleep at night. She'd get to her bedroom door and scream, and scream.

Another child threatened suicide when he became frustrated and couldn't solve problems.

"My oldest son, who had experienced the worst of my husband's violence, became an armed robber by the age of 16," Clara said. "It was his way of dealing with the powerlessness he felt because of the constant abuse."

219

Historically, the nuclear family has been romanticized, yet we know that for many women and children, violence and the threat of violence have been parts of everyday life.

There are some estimates that one in every 10 women in Canada—that is, one million women—are abused by their partners each year. In 1988, 15 per cent of Canadian homicide victims were women killed by their male partners.

The Canadian Centre for Justice Statistics reports that in 1988, 76,000 men were charged with assault of their wives.

There are no social, cultural, religious, financial, geographic or occupational barriers to abusing or being abused.

Some believe that wife abuse occurs because, historically, women have not been valued as equal partners in marriage or society. Males in this society learn through a process of socialization and sex-role stereotyping to hold power over women and encourage their submission. As a society, we condone and even value aggression.

Family abuse is often bound up in a sense of powerlessness on the part of the abuser. Men often start abusing when they feel they are failing financially or their self-esteem is in jeopardy. The abuse is a response to a perceived power deficit.

## Emotionally scarred

Victims suffer not only physical injury but emotional scarring. They commonly see themselves as having provoked the abuse or deserving it.

This distortion of reality and self-image is one of the most damaging effects of family violence.

People unfamiliar with the dynamics of family abuse are often shocked that the abused are unable to extricate themselves from the relationship. In fact, in many instances they go to great lengths to protect their abusers from outside intervention.

The long-term effects of family abuse are devastating: depression, suicidal feelings, self-contempt and inability to develop intimate relationships. One woman referred to it as "a lifetime of dying slowly."

In learning to recognize, understand and cope with domestic violence, victims need to have a greater awareness of what constitutes abuse and how it manifests itself in relationships, as well as community resources that are available to help them.

Preventing abuse has to go beyond individual initiatives and must be seen as a larger societal problem that affects us all.

Often children who have been abused abuse their own children— and the cycle is perpetuated.

It is imperative that we learn to live together in non-violent, non-oppressive ways.

# Child's illness creates heartbreaking choices

January 9, 1992

Life on this planet is being profoundly affected by our rapidly growing medical technology. New powers that can cure or injure, preserve life or destroy it, bring into question our very conception of life and death and the worth of human existence.

One of our most difficult questions is when to use our amazing medical technology—should we try to keep everyone alive just because we are able?

It was this kind of dilemma my neighbours experienced when their first child, Jason, was born eight years ago.

Jason was born with an unusual malady, the result of possible genetic incompatibility, medical advice which might have been unsound and pure old-fashioned bad luck.

The hormone shots Jason's mother took to prevent what she feared would be her fourth miscarriage appeared to have caused some of Jason's abnormalities.

## Born premature

He was born premature, with a head large in proportion to his tiny body. He was diagnosed as having congenital heart problems, ambiguous genitalia, and other problems which kept him in the premature nursery for four months.

At 6 months, Jason was admitted to the hospital after a bout of diarrhea which resulted in a near total breakdown of all body systems. He experi-

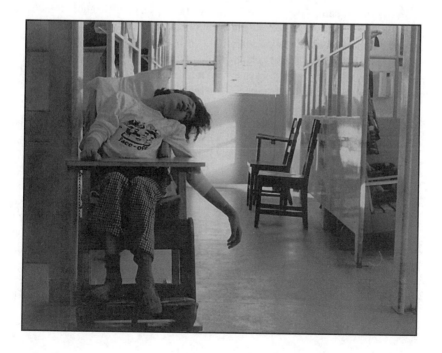

221

enced renal failure, his immune system was practically non-existent, and he suffered irreparable brain damage as a result of an epileptic seizure.

He was plugged into every conceivable machine—respirators, catheters, mainlines for fluids, monitors for his heart.

Even when Jason's situation appeared hopeless, his parents fixed what was fixable, treated what was treatable and coped as best they could with the rest. They were determined their baby should live.

"We never for an instant hoped that he would die," Jason's mother recalled. "Every little bit of progress was magnified a thousand times. When he succeeded in touching my face, it was pure exhilaration."

Despite formidable odds, Jason survived. Over the years, his health improved. Still, he required an inordinate amount of care.

Looking after Jason became an all-encompassing activity that exhausted his parents physically and emotionally, tapping into the strength of their relationship and unravelling it.

Jason's parents are getting a divorce. Neither can look after him alone, so he had to be institutionalized. It was not an easy decision.

### Raises questions

Jason's plight raises many ethical questions. Is it right to save a baby's life when his future appears hopeless? And how do we assess what quality of life really is?

What factors should be taken into account in deciding whether an ill child should be kept alive? Should the parents' capacity to cope enter into the decision? Should parents be forced to fulfil their obligations to offspring they do not want? Does an infant have a legal right to life?

The questions go on and on, but the answers are not easily forthcoming. There are two equally compelling arguments here.

One holds that the weak and defective must be cherished and protected, otherwise we risk corroding our humanity, the start of a slippery slope that would make it easier for our sense of humanity to become corroded even more.

Ill children are a natural part of life and should be accepted as a possible consequence of the decision to have children. We cannot play God and decide to terminate a life we do not consider "normal."

The other perspective holds that modern medicine has the ability to sustain misery which otherwise would not have existed.

Some ethicists go as far as to say that if the infant's life is judged to be intolerable, if it involves greater suffering than happiness, not prolonging the life is the morally correct thing to do. The right to die is seen as equally important as the right to life.

I asked Jason's parents whether any conditions existed under which they would have refused to allow aggressive intervention to continue. Jason's father said they would have refused treatment if it appeared that Jason would be hooked to machines for the rest of his life, or if he would be a vegetable with no chance of ever getting better, or if he were wracked with pain.

"Jason is a very happy child. We can always make him laugh. He loves to cuddle. We feel that we have maximized his quality of life, which is more than acceptable.

"Jason progresses each day at his own rate of development, optimizing the abilities he does possess, charming every caregiver who has ever had any contact with him."

The divorce rate for couples with severely handicapped children is in the 90th percentile. Jason's mother is not surprised by these statistics. It requires superhuman qualities to care for a handicapped child and still retain a good relationship with one's spouse.

### Little support

Part of the problem, according to Jason's mother, is that there is very little support available to parents who want to keep their severely handicapped children at home. It costs soci-

ety five to eight times the amount to keep a child institutionalized than it would to subsidize parents who want to keep their handicapped children at home.

Only minimal government subsidies are available to individuals whereas institutions get much more substantial subsidies per child. Jason's upkeep now costs society about $50,000 a year.

Jason's mother is sad that after all she has gone through with Jason, she has had to institutionalize him. "Our entire lives revolved around Jason. Now there is an immense emptiness."

While Jason seems to have adjusted well to his new home, she has yet to adjust. Both parents realize the price they have paid both emotionally and physically in order to bring Jason to where he is today.

# Intellectually handicapped enrich the workplace, employers say

Clifton Ruggles and Olivia Rovinescu

June 17, 1993

It's a workday at the Peel St. offices of the law firm McCarthy Tetrault and Heath is making his rounds, picking up and delivering mail.

Heath's a popular worker in the high-pressure atmosphere of the law office—cheerful and diligent. He was McCarthy Tetrault's "most improved" employee in 1991.

Like Benny, the office clerk in television's L.A. Law, Heath is intellectually handicapped. He's also one of the success stories of Summit School's unusual job-training and integration program for the intellectually handicapped.

There is a philosophy that drives the program at the St. Laurent school, principal Gloria Cherney says: "Employment opportunity for the intellectually handicapped is a right."

And along with this right comes society's obligation to provide handicapped persons with opportunities.

### 'Every person has a place'

To make this possible, Summit School runs a job training-integration program that makes students employable upon graduation. And then they find them jobs.

"We believe every person has a place in society. Our job is to find out where that place is," said Gurit Lotan, psychologist and director of the vocational program.

This does not mean, however, that all intellectually handicapped persons are employable. It depends on the severity of their disability and the extent to which they are trainable.

The Summit School experience has shown that if schools for the mentally handicapped change their curriculum in specific ways, even persons with severe disabilities can be trained to become part of the regular work force.

Integration can work as long as it is started early enough so that the students pick up the social skills necessary to function in a work environment, Lotan said.

"We've had to rethink our entire curriculum," she said. "Before we used to do a lot of busy work, but now we focus on what the students are actually going to need to make it in the work force.

"Our goal is to prepare them for the future. They're no longer just biding time. They've got a purpose."

The students need practical skills, like how to take a bus, how to cross a street, go to a bank or a grocery store. They have to learn things that we take for granted.

The program begins at the school with individuals assigned responsibilities like photocopying, collating or helping younger children. Learning responsibility is a major part of this experience.

In the second phase, 16-year olds are exposed to a variety of jobs. Teaching takes place outside the school, in various companies. It's important to learn job skills in a real workplace so that the student experiences working with other people, Lotan said. The students are matched with a job that suits their interests and abilities.

This integration takes place under the supervision of a job coach supplied by the school.

The third phase of the program is actual job integration. When students reach the age of 18, the school looks for long-term employment, based on their skills and interests. The job coach also helps employees learn about working alongside the handicapped person.

Gradually the job coach withdraws and the students' ability to function on his or her own is evaluated by the coach, the program's director and the employer.

"Employers are worried that we're just going to dump these kids on them," job coach Franca Baratta said. "But we don't. We're there until we're not needed any more. It could take anywhere from two months to five months.

"We guarantee the work. So if the kid can't get it done for some reason, we have to do it for him. We have faith that eventually the student will pick up the slack. We know exactly what the student is capable of."

And Baratta added: "Sometimes an employer will be afraid to give a handicapped person a chance because they're afraid that if that person doesn't work out then they're going to have to fire them and then they'll feel guilty.

"And nobody wants to be put in that position. We reassure them that we will know before they do if a situation is not working out and we have to pull the student out."

Over 50 companies have provided work-study opportunities or jobs to Summit School students since the program began in 1985. Banks, hotels, law firms, restaurants, pharmacies, libraries and government institutions have participated. Twenty-two handicapped people have been hired to date.

The benefits can be two-way.

"Heath has enriched our lives," said Rita Apa, director of human resources at the law firm McCarthy Tetrault. "He continually reminds us to be curious and to take pleasure in achieving new goals, no matter how small. He has humanized this fast-paced environment."

Joe Amiel, owner of Cumberland Drugstore in Westmount, has had four Summit School students doing "stages" or job training at his store.

"These kids deserve a break," Amiel said. "If I had an intellectually handicapped child, I would want someone providing him with an opportunity to have a meaningful life.

"As far as I'm concerned, it's a duty, a must."

Gloria Cherney says integration is more natural in the workplace than in schools.

"It's natural to develop friendships with people who share similar interests. Schools are not necessarily the best place for these intellectually handicapped students to experience integration."

The workplace is another story. "It's a more equal place because people are all there for the same thing—to work. The students experience a great deal of pride and satisfaction."

Michael, for example, works at a pharmaceutical company as a packer and says he loves his job.

Michael's parents never dreamed that their son would hold a job, let alone travel to and from work on his own. "He's made such tremendous progress," Michael's mother said. "I can hardly believe it. His vocabulary seems to be increasing daily. And he's so much happier."

The school administrators say Summit's success lies in the staffing. With 280 students, the school uses four psychologists, four social workers, an occupational therapist, a nurse and a speech therapist.

The average ratio in each class is eight-to-two, with each teacher working with an aide. But numbers alone do not explain the success of Summit School.

The enthusiasm, commitment and dedication of the staff plays a key role, the school officials add.

A major problem confronted by the school is money. It is expensive to run a program of this calibre. Consequently, Summit must do a lot of fundraising.

The other problem is finding the companies that will integrate mentally handicapped individuals and pay them. Quebec government wage subsidies are available for up to five years. But Cherney says five years is not enough: the government should be guaranteeing lifelong subsidies.

Otherwise, five years down the road some of these handicapped individuals will find themselves unemployed and unemployable, she argues. It is not fair to let them taste independence then take it away.

That's why the school argues that the handicapped have the same rights to employment as non-handicapped people: if they work hard and do their share, they should be given the opportunity to do the work and be paid equitably for it.

# The Illness that is killing U.S. cities already has hold here

August 5, 1993

Despair, outrage, powerlessness. Those were the emotions that flooded through me when I read the series of articles in The Gazette last month on the United States' crumbling cities.

What became painfully clear from the articles is that black neighbourhoods in cities like Miami, Detroit and New York are becoming wastelands and combat zones.

Reporter Linda Diebel drew haunting images of shattered neighbourhoods and shattered families, mindless violence and deteriorating buildings, escalating class inequalities and a consumer culture which spawns addictive personalities and passive citizens.

Commentaries in The Gazette and the Mirror about these articles revolved around the questions of whether "it can happen here," "why it hasn't happened here already" and "what we can do to prevent it from happening"—all very worthwhile questions.

But discussion has to go beyond that—to acknowledge it is already happening, albeit in a much lesser form.

Less is better, to be sure. But less implies some, and some is still too much, as far as I'm concerned.

It means the social conditions that spawned the erosion of some American cities have their poisonous roots firmly in our soil as well.

Surveys conducted in the Jamaican and Haitian communities of Montreal reveal that more than 40 per cent of persons of Jamaican and Haitian backgrounds between the ages of 25-35 are without jobs. For those under the age of 25, the unemployment rate rises to 70 per cent.

These figures are three times the national average. The school dropout rate for blacks is almost double that of the provincial average, which stands at 36 per cent.

The over-representation of black youths in the penal system in Quebec is alarming.

It is imperative that we learn from the mistakes of U.S. cities. However, we must not only look to the government to solve our problems because the problems are not just economic and political ones. They go much deeper than that.

## No more hope or meaning

What must be addressed is what writer and scholar Cornel West has called the "eclipse of hope and the collapse of meaning" in black America. According to West, who is professor of theology and director of the Afro-American studies program at Princeton University, the most dangerous enemy in the black community is nihilism within. The threat is not simply a matter of economic deprivation and political powerlessness. The real threat, in West's view, is psychic depression brought on by years of living with systemic racism.

Systemic racism attacks black intelligence, black ability, black beauty and black character in subtle and not-so-subtle ways. It also contributes to black students' "disidentification" from the school system.

According to psychologist Claude Steele, economic disadvantage alone does not explain the underachievement of blacks in school. It's just that black students can't believe school achievement can be a basis of self-esteem and a passport to a life with good prospects.

The black student no longer regards achievement as important to his self-esteem.

I've had students tell me that they see no hope, no life for themselves in this society.

Lewis was 17 years old and had returned to school to try to get his high-school leaving certificate. He already had a young family he desperately wanted to provide for. He applied for countless jobs but somehow never got them. He finally came to me and said, "Cliff, there ain't nothin' out there for me. I got ambition. Ain't no dummy. But the doors are closed wherever I go."

Traditionally, the black community had certain buffers to ward off the nihilism—churches, civic organizations.

Growing up in the '60s, we had hope that things were changing for the better. The civil rights movement gave us a measure of hope. There was a sense of solidarity in the streets.

What is needed today, West says, are more grassroots movements that generate "a sense of agency" which promote self-worth and self-affirmation.

In June, I attended Concordia University's Summer Institute in Management and Community Development at the Loyola campus. The insti-

tute offered 22 workshops in areas like community economic development, community empowerment, recruitment of volunteers and training new leadership.

### First-hand knowledge

Lance Evoy, the institute's director, expressed strongly the need for grassroots movements: "If the governments aren't going to address community economic issues for us, who the heck is? If anybody knows what solutions there should be, it's the people who are marginalized, the people who are poor and out of work."

One of the most interesting ideas described at the summer institute was the community revolving loan fund for community development. This involves putting together those with financial resources, those needing financial resources and those providing technical assistance to groups starting businesses.

Another interesting session involved the community land trust which addressed the lack of secure and affordable housing and which explored new land-use models.

Evoy said it was inspirational to hear the testimonials of people who have participated in a community land trust project: "People get to redefine concepts like profit and capital. Fundamental changes take place because suddenly people have a stake in their neighbourhoods."

The major concerns echoed by the conference participants was the need to develop community-based structures to deal with the complex issues of unemployment, housing, education, racism, class exploitation, environmental abuse and economic development.

I walked away rejuvenated and feeling there is hope as long as people from all communities come together to work on common problems.

We need to become involved, each in our own way, taking our civic responsibilities seriously, not just sitting back but giving back. We need to become aware of the initiatives going on out there and how we can get involved—doing volunteer work as literacy tutors, helping in after-school programs at community centres, becoming mentors or Big Brothers and Sisters, providing work opportunities to young people, doing fundraising.

In other words, it's time to draw upon our skills and expertise to make a difference where we can, to make this city the kind of place our children will be proud to inherit.

# Wanted: A new way of thinking
## Black men caught in cycle
## of violence, hopelessness

March 10, 1994

Recently, I took part in a panel discussion in Westmount, as part of Black History Month.

The subject was "Issues for the Black Male."

Participants in the panel, organized by the Association of Black Human Service Workers in co-operation with Ville Marie Social Services, spanned several generations, the youngest member being in his 20s, the oldest in his 80s.

Some of us were seventh-generation Canadians, others were newly arrived.

We talked about the education of black males; immigration and how it affects job status; discrimination in employment and housing; the effects of stereotyping on young black males; and the need for black male role models.

Olivia Rovinescu

### Many contradictions

The black male is riddled with contradictions.

On the one hand we're the products of a patriarchal, sexist society that expects us to be aggressive and dominant in our relationships with women.

On the other hand, we're the products of a society that sees us as unworthy of the same rights and privileges as our white counterparts; a society that views us with suspicion and renders us invisible.

Sherrie Elder, an executive of the Association of Black Human Service Workers, said the association considers the black male a priority: "We need to understand what effects the mainstream institutions have on the black male and by extension on the family and the community."

Right now, our community offers black men—especially young men—very few ways to learn how to understand themselves and the forces that shape them—racism, sexism, violence.

The N.D.G. [Notre Dame de Grace] Black Community Association comes the closest with its Changes program, which addresses the concerns of black teens.

They explore issues like teen sexuality, male-female relationships, police-youth interaction, young offenders, parent-child interactions, drugs and alcohol, staying in school vs. dropping out.

### Successful program

Girls meet Wednesday nights, boys meet on Thursday nights. Both groups meet on Friday nights for special activities.

"The program is very successful because it gives kids the opportunity to exchange ideas and to express their feelings more effectively," co-ordinator Egien Scotland said.

Beyond that one program, the West End appears to have little available.

As the youngest of five boys and the third-youngest of nine children, I had the opportunity to witness, first hand, gender politics at work.

painting by Clifton Ruggles

Olivia Rovinescu

My father fit the mold of the patriarch. He was the provider, disciplinarian, and "king of the castle." He was a World War II veteran and he ran a "tight ship" modelled after his army training.

The boys had their jobs to do, the girls had theirs.

Being a male meant learning to be tough.

My father was very proud of his role as the breadwinner and when, in his mid-40s, he was laid off from his job as a railway porter, his world began to crumble.

The more powerless he felt, the more power he tried to assert over us—especially the boys.

Because I was younger than the rest of my brothers, I hung out with my sisters, who undoubtedly affected the way I viewed women and consequently treated them.

My older sisters educated me, the younger ones provided me with the opportunity to be a caregiver.

Despite these positive influences, I was shaped by a society where the masculine ideal dominated.

I picked up the attitudes at Kent Park, in the pool halls, in the locker rooms and everywhere the boys hung out.

Our role models were Shaft, Superfly and a whole array of blaxploitation movie heroes. It was the pimps and the con men who set the tone in my neighbourhood—the smooth-talking dudes who wore the nice threads.

### 'Political kool'

Competing with this form of "kool" was the "political kool" of the activists involved in the black liberation struggle, with their Afro hairstyles, battle fatigues and clenched fists.

One thing I always had tremendous difficulty with was their treatment of women. Members of both groups referred to women in the most sexist and derogatory terms.

Still, while I may have been sensitive to women thanks to my sisters, I was not impervious to the unwritten male code of violence.

The first principle: "If someone starts a fight with you, it's your right and even your obligation to retaliate."

Honour was everything.

I no longer feel I have to defend my honour through physical violence. I've learned other ways—my writing, my teaching, even my paintings have become the tools with which I wage my war against racism.

Most black males have not been able to participate in legitimate use of power, but rather attempt to mirror it in other less acceptable ways, hurting themselves, their wives, their children—and the black community as a whole.

Black males physically inflict more harm on themselves than on anyone else.

### Frustrating experiences

Black men "shout" louder than anybody else, it seems. We shout because we don't have a language to describe the torment and frustration we feel: frustration at being denied job opportunities; at being turned away from apartments; at being perceived as suspects by police.

We're frustrated by our school experiences where many of us receive less attention, lower grades, harsher punishment and fewer rewards.

If violence is one pervasive effect of that sense of hopelessness, we have to look at attitudes of sexism, too.

Many black men refuse to acknowledge the extent to which sexism provides them with forms of privilege and power. They do not want to surrender any amount of power in a world where they feel powerless.

There is a conspiracy of silence about black men's physical and emotional abuse of black women. African-American writer Audre Lord called it "a disease striking the heart of black nationhood."

We have to construct a new black masculinity.

We have to learn a new sense of honour and a new code—one that is premised on notions of caring, sensitivity and support. We have to develop a new model of a black male who does not need to behave in an oppressive fashion.

But how do we get there from here?

# Defiant, angry and filled with bitterness
## Young people learn to hate because they see themselves as powerless

April 29, 1993

Defiant, angry and filled with bitterness.

That was Marcie. Shaved head, home-made swastika tattooed on the back of her hand, glaring blue eyes that challenged you, dared you, mocked you.

Marcie was one of the angriest students I have ever worked with. She could poison the atmosphere in the classroom with one look.

Marcie was the product of a dysfunctional family and was so angry at her parents that she would do anything to evoke their disapproval.

She had a profoundly divisive effect on the class, orchestrating conflicts between students that gave her a sense of power non-existent in other areas of her life.

Young people learn to hate because they perceive themselves as being powerless. That anger is redirected toward others or select groups of people, especially minorities.

Through her identification with the right-wing skinhead movement, Marcie found a way of legitimizing and expressing her rage.

Marcie was hurting. But she could not articulate her hurt, her pain, her despair. At every opportunity, she lashed out. Her attraction to the skinhead movement gave her a focal point to express that rage.

Psychologist Rollo May believes that power and powerlessness are at the root of violence.

"Power is essential for all living things," May writes in Power and Innocence.

We see the emergence of power as soon as a baby is born into the world—in his or her demand to be fed and noticed. The first three years of a child's life are crucial.

If a child's cry of hunger or discomfort is not responded to, that child will learn not to trust his caregiver and will come to distrust all social attachments.

It is those who suffer attachment disorders who turn to violence. The individual is saying, "I'm going to ruin your life the way my life has been ruined. I am going to do to you what has been done to me."

Michael Chervin, lecturer in McGill's faculty of education, believes that children learn to hate not so much because they don't get enough love from their parents, "but rather because they feel profoundly devalued as human beings."

"You can love your child and still devalue her or him," Chervin said.

"Love is not enough. It is those who feel the most profoundly devalued who end up hating themselves and perpetrating acts of violence, both to themselves and to others."

According to Chervin, what needs to be changed is how children experience the world.

Young people also learn to hate by experiencing hatred directed at them. They learn to hate through their interactions with the world.

I remember taking a group of black high-school students to the Centaur Theatre for what was their first theatre experience. It was an experience, all right, but not the kind I had intended.

The people sitting next to us were extremely annoyed by the presence of these students and expressed their views by making angry, racist remarks.

The students did not respond but instead came to alert me about what was happening. My advice to them was not to talk to these people.

After leaving the theatre, the female students were approached by a male member of the party who had made the comments.

Once again, he complained that their presence had interfered with other people's enjoyment of the play, adding that schools should not be permitted to bring "these types of students" to the theatre.

Still, the students would not be provoked. But when the guy told one of the girls she should go back to Africa, she snapped.

A fight ensued during which she apparently bit his hand. She just couldn't handle another derogatory comment. That man provided her with a focal point for her anger and her rage.

Discrimination evokes violent reactions. When you treat someone like they're nothing, like they don't belong, then you're going to get a violent response.

Individuals need to feel they are contributing members of their society.

The moment comes when you can no longer repress your anger, and an explosion occurs.

According to black psychologist Franz Fanon, author of Wretched of the Earth, violence is like a cleansing force. It frees the oppressed from "his inferiority complex and from his despair and inaction; it makes him fearless and restores his self-respect."

This helps explain why in our society, the young urban poor, with no legitimate prospects for the future, engage in acts of violence.

Any sense of personal merit quickly comes to mean being stronger, meaner and better-armed than the next person. Gangs provide camaraderie, safety in numbers and some degree of control.

They give estranged youth something meaningful to which they can belong, an identity they lack.

Because black children will experience racism, it is important that we teach them how to handle it without allowing it to become crippling or provoke them to violent outbursts.

It's important to teach black children to have pride in their cultural heritage and to help develop in them a strong sense of self-esteem.

As parents and teachers, we must strive to help black children understand the nature of racism so that it does not cripple their development.

We must teach them how to respond to injustice in concrete, empowering ways.

# Confronting violence
## Parents must teach children
## how to handle aggression

September 1995

They descended like a swarm of locusts, pushing, shoving, shouting, taunting the young kid in the centre of the pack who was the focus of their aggression. They threw off his hat, scattered his book bag, mussed his hair.

Harmless fun? Rite of passage? Male ritual? It was horrifying to watch young boys, in proper school uniforms, behaving like barbarians on the corner of de Maisonneuve and Decarie. It looked like a scene from William Golding's book *Lord of the Flies.*

I honked my horn and they scattered like sewer rats.

Kids are notorious for expressing themselves in physical ways when they get frustrated or angry.

If they're very young we don't call their behaviour violent. But at what age should we draw the line?

This summer I had to ask myself this question when my ten year old daughter came home from camp with a puffy eye—a boy her age punched her because she would not relinquish the swimming board she was using.

He let her have it, right there in the middle of the pond.

I remember my sister Joan once beat up a boy who called her a bad name. We watched in fascination at her wizardry of fisticuffs and footwork.

Despite her small, lithe body, she was more than a match for any of the brutes who inhabited our neighbourhood.

And when this boy's family, outraged by their son's humiliation at the hands of this wisp of a girl, came down to defend his honour, we Ruggleses were poised, ready to take up the challenge.

We saw no harm in defending our sister's honour. It was character-building. It showed we had "moxie." No one would mess with her again, if we had anything to say about it.

It's now 30 years later and I'm the parent now. Do I want my daughter engaged in a slugfest with her aggressor?

Part of me wanted her to fight back, defend herself, but the other part of me didn't want her involved in this behaviour.

What do I, as a parent, tell her? Hit back or turn the other cheek? Physical retaliation is not a solution. Neither is allowing oneself to be victimized.

Amy explained that she didn't hit back because they were in the water and she thought it dangerous. I'm glad she was able to think clearly and did not allow anger to overcome her good judgement.

Girls, for the most part, seem to be better at this than boys. Quite frankly, I don't know whether I would have been capable of restraining myself.

I wonder whether there isn't some response other than the "fight or flight" that we can teach our children.

The way the camp director handled the incident was disappointing.

Rather than speak to the boy and my daughter, she chose to lecture the entire camp about violent behaviour. She was convinced that after her talk, the boy would feel badly and apologize to my daughter. He never did.

Children must have lines clearly drawn for them, to understand that violent behaviour is simply not acceptable and that there are consequences.

For the boy who punched my daughter in the face there were no consequences. He wasn't reprimanded. He wasn't asked to consider his behaviour. He didn't learn any ways of dealing with anger.

The experience taught him very little.

If anything, it might have reinforced his aggressiveness since he did get the swimming board he wanted.

It seems like society only responds when the violence results in someone getting seriously hurt or killed. Then we wonder why nobody saw the signs sooner.

Everyone involved with children has a duty to be much more vigilant .

We must be models for children.

We have to start working with children at a very early age and teach them to respect the rights of others. We must teach them to be assertive and help them learn to cope with their feelings and negotiate to resolve conflicts.

We must pay attention to their choice of music, video games, television shows and movies.

And we should encourage them to become involved in physical activities that allow them to redirect aggressive feelings like frustration and anger into more positive ones.

# Fighting violence with LOVE
## After her husband was slain by teen, woman starts group to help youth
Clifton Ruggles and Olivia Rovinescu

June 12, 1995

On a cool evening in the fall of 1972, Twinkle Rudberg's life was irrevocably changed when her 37-year-old husband was killed trying to stop a 14-year-old purse-snatcher.

After experiencing what violence does both to its victims and the victimizers, Rudberg founded LOVE—Leave Out Violence.

Its 50-member board is committed to involving young people in creative and challenging projects.

Rudberg, 59, believes in the African proverb that "it takes a whole village to raise a child."

But then, she notes: "These villages, as our ancestors once knew them, no longer exist.

"Ordinary citizens must get involved, hands-on, in their communities in order to help raise a generation of children whose world is not threatened by violence."

LOVE members include Montreal Urban Community police chief Jacques Duchesneau; Quebec Court Judge Andree Ruffo; former Quebec justice minister Herbert Marx; Appeal Court Justice Michel Proulx; Rabbi Ira Grussgott; social-work professor Jim Torczyner; and singer Ranee Lee, who also teaches music at McGill University.

One LOVE project, a photojournalism program for high-school students, started in January. The kids are directed into the program by a youth-squad officer, a social worker, a community organization or by their school.

They're working on a book of photographs on violence and its prevention, for which they're writing about police officers, rape victims, the impact of violence on their lives, the need for role models, and the effects of violence on TV and in movies.

Working at Dawson College, the participants are guided by the interracial team of Stan Chase, technician at the Dawson Institute for Imaging, Arts and Technology, and Brenda Zosky-Proulx, a Concordia journalism teacher.

It's the ideal learning situation, Chase and Zosky-Proulx said.

"It's not school and nobody's making them do it," Chase said. "They've chosen to be there, so most of them show up regularly."

Chase, who grew up in Little Burgundy, believes it's important for inner-city kids to have access to resources and trained professionals.

The students were as enthusiastic as the project co-ordinators.

"It's a new adventure," said Michael Filion, 15, who's been working on articles about hockey players as role models.

I've hung around the Forum and interviewed people, including hockey stars. The program has made me more assertive in approaching people, getting them to talk to me and taking their photograph."

Junie Desil, 17, enjoys the opportunity to voice her opinions. "We get the

238

chance to dispel some of the stereotypes society has about teens," she said.

She has written an article about the hidden effects of violence, another about a utopian society without violence, and is working on one about violence in the media.

The photojournalism project is just one of the creative programs LOVE is interested in developing.

An inter-generational choir, directed by jazz singer Ranee Lee, will bring LOVE board members together with some of the young people involved in its programs at a June 14 fundraising performance at Dawson. Photographs and writings by the photojournalism students will also be shown.

A gardening project, being carried out in co-operation with the city of Montreal, is designed to provide youths with summer employment by forming a landscaping company, with each of the youths a part-owner.

"If LOVE is able to help just a few young people, then I will feel it has been worth it," Rudberg said.

There are indications that the Dawson photojournalism course is doing what it was designed to.

I think the photojournalism project is absolutely terrific for kids who have potential," said Constable Ron Durand of Station 24's youth squad.

The youths I have referred to this program have changed their attitudes and behaviours—they're enthusiastic and co-operative. Their parents have also seen tremendous changes.

These are kids from areas of town where there's more than ample opportunity to get into criminal activity. This program lets them see there's something else out there, not just the streets."

Leave Out Violence
Centre: Stan Chase, Brenda Proux, Twinkle Rudberg and the photojournalism team.

239

# Get involved: You can make a difference

July 14, 1994

It grew out of a black single-mothers' support group three years ago in N.D.G. [Notre Dame de Grace]. The mothers said their sons needed black men that they could spend time with, look up to and emulate.

Enter Black Star.

The Big Brother-type organization will match black male role models with boys between the ages of 8 and 14 who live in single-parent black families that are headed by women.

Volunteers will be matched with boys with similar interests and backgrounds and will share activities for at least one year.

Although Black Star is intended to serve the black, English-speaking community of N.D.G., its organizers hope to cover the entire black anglophone community of Montreal eventually.

Responding to criticism from the black community that youth-protection authorities remove one-third more children from black families than non-black families in similar difficulties, the N.D.G. CLSC decided to launch Black Star in the hope of reducing this number and stopping problems before youth protection gets involved.

Black Star has obtained a $245,000 grant from Community Action Project for Children, a federal government initiative.

Jim Olwell, the CLSC community organizer responsible for the project, said he hopes the experience will increase the boys' self-esteem, improve school performance, promote better behaviour and improve the relationships between mothers and sons.

Olwell notes that single-parent black families doesn't necessarily refer exclusively to families headed by black women.

There are also white mothers raising black sons. These children all need black male role models—perhaps even more so—because in many cases the children do not get exposure to black life and culture.

Project co-ordinator Michael Baffoe said:

The response from mothers and social workers has been overwhelming. However, Black Star needs more black male volunteers."

Of those who apply, Olwell is anticipating that one-third will be accepted. "Just because someone wants to be a Big Brother doesn't mean that they're appropriate," he said.

## Training provided

"They'll be asked to fill out a 10-page application form and will be subjected to a 1 1/2-hour interview with a black social worker who'll be asking some pretty intimate stuff."

For some people, being a mentor or role model is second nature, others need guidance. For that reason, Black Star will provide training to those who are selected. Workshops in active listening and child and adolescent development will be mandatory.

Workshops to make children aware of sexual-abuse issues will also be made available.

What if a white man is interested in becoming a Big Brother to a black youth? Olwell said that would defeat the purpose of the program, which is to provide black role models.

"The program doesn't discriminate against anybody, it's just saying that what the boys need right now is ethnic and gender identification."

I certainly agree. Programs like Black Star are long overdue.

However, I also think there are benefits from encouraging cross-cultural relationships as well. Such relationships can be instrumental in breaking down barriers and allowing black youths to navigate both worlds comfortably.

I have been effective in working with white and black youths with equal success.

Maybe it was because I already had black role models at home—my father was a presence in my life until he died when I was 20 years old and my four older brothers provided guidance and support.

And at every stage in my life, it seems there were significant people who took an interest in me, spent time with me, provided me with advice and a chance to talk things through and, most important, helped me believe in myself.

Although most people in the black community would agree that boys need mentors, not everyone is enthusiastic about Black Star.

Michael Gittens, director of the Cote des Neiges Black Community Association, said he doesn't believe that the CLSC should be setting up programs for the black community.

"We've seen what happens when social services get involved running programs for the black community," said Gittens, who argued that the black community should be running its own programs.

He said he believes social services are already far too involved in people's lives. "Black parents have allowed social-service institutions to walk into their lives and tell them what they should be doing with their kids. Black parents need to take more responsibilities in the guidance and education of their children and not relinquish that responsibility too readily."

Olwell, who is white, replied that as community organizer at the CLSC, he works with many different cultural communities to get projects off the ground but he will not be the one delivering the services.

All those affiliated with Black Star are black—the advisory board of professionals from the black community, the co-ordinator, the social workers and the consultant.

Olwell said he consulted several black community organizations, which supported the idea. In addition, Olwell said, the plan all along has been to transfer the program to the black community.

In fact, Olwell first approached the Montreal Association of Black Business Persons and Professionals with the project, because of its pool of potential mentors, hoping that association would run it.

### Will be transferred

"Transfer to a black community organization will occur in time," Olwell said, "after activities have been put into place and are stabilized. The advisory board will decide which black community organization is best suited to take over operations."

The program is about the survival of the black family. It's about providing youths with the opportunity to grow and learn. It's about hope and change. It's a program that the black community needs.

We're always asking, "What can I do?" Well, here is something tangible. Here is something that can make a difference. Let's get involved.

# AKAX Destructive young radicals? Here's what they're really doing

June 3, 1993

A couple of months ago, I was asked to speak on radio station CJAD on the topic "why children hate."

The discussion touched upon pathological behaviour in children and why they perpetrate acts of violence.

As we were talking, host Jim Duff suddenly brought up AKAX, introducing them as a black youth group that had recently urged the black community to refuse to co-operate with police until the officer responsible for the killing of Trevor Kelly was punished.

Duff chastised AKAX for "pulling bridges down" at a time of great racial unrest.

Coming during a discussion about hatred and violence, the comment left listeners with the impression that AKAX is a group of black militants interested in promoting violence and hatred.

Nothing could be farther from the truth.

AKAX, which stands for Also Known As X, (referring to the rejection of the names blacks were given during slavery and a commitment to the teachings of Malcolm X) is a group of university students concerned with the welfare of the black community.

Its motto is "education in the service of liberation."

I wandered into the AKAX offices on Decarie Blvd. in Notre Dame de Grace one Saturday morning in February not knowing exactly what to expect. I was immediately swept up by the enthusiasm and commitment of the organizers and the quality of the tutorial programs they were running.

The place was bustling with activity, with young and old alike participating. It was education as a community activity.

The young seemed eager and keen to learn. Gone were the bored expressions I was used to seeing in the classroom. I could not help but be moved— I felt I was part of something special.

Ariel Deluy, one of the organizers, explained that AKAX came into being as a response to fragmentation in the black community and what young people perceived as a lack of effective leadership.

"We noticed that there was a lot of animosity between the different black student groups," Deluy said. "The black-consciousness movement of the 1960s had died out. The Caribbean and African associations had split up and then the Caribbean association split even further, with the Haitians having their own association.

"Brothers were fighting with brothers." For example, an African student belittled a Caribbean black, saying he was the son of a slave.

"That comment started a whole new black-consciousness movement in the universities."

A first meeting between two associations found "that they had more in common than they thought.... Instead of putting the blame on each other, we decided to come together and start organizing."

This was around the time of the killing of Anthony Griffin. On Remembrance Day, Nov. 11, 1989, AKAX had its first massive rally, to remember Griffin.

"The dynamic within the community changed with that demonstration," Deluy said. "We began challenging the position of certain community leaders, demanding that they be more accountable to the community."

AKAX became visible.

And with that visibility came the charge that it was "radical."

What people thought, Deluy explained, is that AKAX is made of young people who really don't know what they want and are tearing down what is there for the sake of destruction. That is not the case.

"We have a political agenda and that agenda is to bring the community together and to work toward social change."

AKAX members have the expertise and knowledge to press for change, and more education than older people now running community groups, he said.

"Yes, we do take an activist position, and it's about time that somebody did."

The people at AKAX are anything but armchair revolutionaries. Members go door to door, play music in the park—anything to get people out and talking to each other.

They set up a boycott at the club where Presley Leslie was shot because they believed that the club owner had acted irresponsibly and they wanted an investigation into violence in clubs.

Other activities sponsored by AKAX include public rallies, lectures, concerts, poetry readings and even fashion shows.

Every Friday, AKAX holds what it calls "rap sessions," where it brings black people together to discuss is-

Marcos Townsend

AKAX Demonstration

Marcos Townsend

AKAX Demonstration

sues confronting their community. An important part of their work is trying to integrate the English- and French-speaking black communities.

The organization also publishes and distributes a newsletter.

The weekend AKAX school is based on the philosophy of empowering learners—not "teach" them as such, but rather providing them with skills to survive and do well in the school system. Students learn organizing, problem-solving and networking skills.

"If they have a problem with homework, we teach them to set up a study group and learn how to help each other. Our goal is to make the student take responsibility for his or her own learning."

AKAX encourages parent participation in the weekend school and helps parents understand how to get the most out of the school system for their chil-dren. "Having parents actually attend the weekend school with their child has tremendous psychological benefits for the child."

At the beginning of the program, AKAX offers an African history course which includes the contributions of blacks in North America. Deluy explained: "We make sure the students understand that we as a people are very capable, that we are strong, because we have a glorious past."

High on AKAX's list of priorities for this summer is tackling the problem of black-on-black crime, by organizing a retreat, in neutral territory, of gang members who agree to look for a way to reduce violent confrontations.

Last weekend, AKAX held its second annual East-West conference. This conference focused on the division in the black community along lines of nationality and language.

The hope is that black francophones

245

and anglophones will come together, get to know each other and work together.

Egbert Gaye, editor of Community Contact, a black community newspaper, was impressed by the conference, which he says helped bridge the gap. He added that he is excited by the new vision of community promoted by AKAX.

"We have new blood and a new perspective," Gaye said. "They are in the process of creating a strong, mature and proud black presence in Quebec."

AKAX represents the finest our community has to offer—forthright young people who are committed, idealistic and not only "talk the talk, but walk the walk."

It is time we started listening seriously to what they have to say.

# Unitas' program, which started in Bronx, might work in Cote des Neiges

June 1, 1995

Something in all of us wants to relive our childhood—no matter how difficult it was—and it is for that reason, I suppose, that I often find myself driving down Barclay Ave. when I'm in the Cote des Neiges area.

There is a rush of memories: I can hear the excited chattering of my brothers and sisters as we watch our father fixing our bikes; I can smell the mountains of fresh laundry waiting to be hung up—and mountains they were with 11 people in the house.

I hear the sounds of children playing, radios blaring out rhythm and blues sounds as my brother and his friends practice their dance steps, the smell of exotic foods emanating from nearby apartments.

In the 1950s and '60s, Barclay St. was a smorgasbord of nationalities.

## Belonged to 'notorious' gang

The notorious gang, in which it seemed everyone who lived on my block was a member, and to which I was proud to say I belonged, was composed of kids from many different cultural backgrounds. The friendships and loyalties that were created crossed racial and cultural boundaries and sustained us through some very difficult periods in our lives.

It wasn't a gang in the sense in which we think of gangs today (although we did manage to induce some measure of fear in the hearts of our opponents).

There was a real sense of community. If you were hanging around the streets too late at night, you could expect a neighbouring parent to ask you why.

The Barclay avenue development was built for the veterans who had come home after the Second World War. The apartment afforded my family the opportunity to get cheap but relatively decent housing. Because of the difficulty of those times and because we were such a large family, the apartment provided a welcome relief from the St. Henri dwellings that my family members occupied when they first arrived from Nova Scotia.

The Barclay St. area of today faces many of the same problems that plague other inner-city urban communities—poverty, unemployment, illiteracy, crime, violence, lack of opportunities, teen pregnancy, isolation, racism.

In looking for alternative ways to address community problems, the Montreal Urban Community [MUC], along with the police department, invited Dr. Edward Eismann to Montreal in mid May. Eismann is assistant professor in the Department of Psychiatry at the Albert Einstein College of Medicine and supervisor at the Lincoln Community Mental Health Centre.

Eismann discussed the Unitas Therapeutic Community, which operates in the Bronx in New York City, an area that has become a nationwide symbol of economic and social decay.

## Pilot project being considered

It is hoped that such a therapeutic community can be adapted to the

Barclay Street Home Boys

word of a psalm Eismann heard as a young boy "how good it is and how noble for people to live in unity."

The hub around which everything goes is a "tribal circle." The circular structure that is used during tribal meetings consists of a number of sub-groups consisting of older and younger children.

### Circle is forum for discussion

The circle is the forum for discussion of problems, sharing information, communicating rules of order, establishing boundaries, resolving conflicts and giving affection.

Montreal area. A pilot project is being considered for the Barclay St. area with the black, Hispanic, Filipino and Korean populations.

Recognizing the power of the natural influences that children have on each other, Unitas teaches young people how to nurture one another by creating a new sort of family in which older children parent younger children through "symbolic families."

Dubbed the clinic of the street, Unitas limits itself to an eight-block radius so that the kids involved deal only with kids from their own neighbourhood.

There are presently 500 members in Unitas between the ages of 5 and 35. The name Unitas comes from Latin and means unity. It is also the last

Story telling is a major vehicle used within the circle. It helps children think through alternative solutions to problems. Fables, folklore and fairy tales are used in contemporary terms.

A cadre of caretakers 16 years and older take neighbourhood children under their wings, so to speak, and become the symbolic mothers and fathers. They are the heart of the system because it is through them that the love, esteem, and value of Unitas is channelled to the constituency of children, molding their attitudes, equipping them with parenting skills and nurturing them in order for them to be able to nurture children.

Why did he start Unitas?

Eismann recounts how he sat as a clinician in a community mental-health centre in the South Bronx, an area considered the most disastrous area in the United States.

I waited in my office for the client to come. The client never came. So I went out into the streets in desperation. I stood on street corners and on rooftops. I watched what was going on."

"What I saw in the street was wonderful," Eismann explained.

"It wasn't the pathology that was spoken about in the books. What I saw were children helping other children. The teenagers in the neighbourhood were the street heroes and heroines, who intervened in breaking up fights and resolving conflicts.

That's what I did in the summer of 1967 and the response was overwhelming," Eismann continued. "In the fall the children brought me to their schools and they brought me to meet their religious leaders. So I joined forces with the education system, with the police systems, the religious system and the street system made up of the teenagers who have a tremendous influence on the kids' lives."

The success of Unitas, according to Eismann, can be seen in the intensity of the commitment people have made to the program. Some of the original beneficiaries are now in their 30s and are still involved in Unitas as group leaders. They are now considered the grandparents and that's how the cycle continues.

One of the most moving parts of Eismann's presentation was a video of a young man by the name of James who expressed what it was like not having a mother or father and what it meant to him to be involved in Unitas and having the power to change someone else's life.

## Crime statistics down

Michael Gittens, director of the Cote des Neiges Black Community Centre, was surprised that Cote des Neiges was targeted for this project. "Crime statistics in the area have dropped in recent years and existing programs are doing well and need continued support," said Gittens, who also expressed concern that it was a "top down" initiative from the MUC.

Noel Alexander, director of the Jamaica Association, felt the Unitas program presents concrete strategies for effective parenting in the community. "Teaching young people to care about each other is something the community desperately needs," Alexander said.

One of the major concerns echoed by several people was whether community groups would be able to work together in the development and management of such a program.

Some were apprehensive because unlike the Bronx the diverse population in the Cote des Neiges might be a major stumbling block.

Although I share some of these concerns, I also believe that the Unitas project offers exciting possibilities.

It seems to be a very flexible model and one which can, with some creativity, be adapted to the Montreal scene.

# Teacher introduces kids to the empowering effects of art

November 16, 1995

Getting out of my car, I caught a glimpse of them through the window. Even before I could hear what was going on in the Grade 5 class at Coronation School, I knew something special was taking place. The students were turned on and tuned in. The person who had fired their imagination was New York artist/teacher Tim Rollins.

He was in the process of telling the students the story of the Red Badge of Courage, written by Stephen Crane. The Civil War story, he told them, was a metaphor for survival, a metaphor for their lives. The students were to create a personal mandala, their own "badge of courage." Rollins talked about the beauty of going through a struggle and surviving and the beauty of making history by making art with an empowering and lasting effect.

Rollins was in Montreal recently to give a public lecture at Concordia University. The members of the university's art-education program that sponsored the talk did not merely want to hear what Rollins had to say; they also wanted to see Rollins in action—hence the workshop at Coronation School.

Rollins founded a highly successful after-school studio art program known as Kids of Survival, or KOS, for at-risk black and Hispanic kids in New York City 12 years ago. Rollins began teaching art to junior high school special education students in the South Bronx in 1980. Two years later, with a shoe-string budget and while still teaching at a public school during the day, Rollins and a small band of his most dedicated students founded the Art and Knowledge Workshop, which developed the KOS program.

The Kids of Survival program gained attention in the art world as a pioneer in collaborative works that draw parallels between themes in literature and the daily realities and concerns of participants. The youths read books together, discussed them and attempted to render them artistically as a group.

I visited Rollins in his studio in New York City last year and I was most impressed with what I saw. In a spacious and sunny studio looking out on New York's skyline, I saw a group of young, dedicated inner-city youths deeply immersed in their artwork. They had just finished reading Animal Farm and were treating an artistic interpretation of the work using caricatures of modern-day politicians.

At the time of my visit the work of KOS was being shown at the Whitney Museum as part of an exhibition on the black male. The team's critically acclaimed paintings, drawings, prints and sculptures have been exhibited internationally, entering many private and museum collections.

"The kids have been to Europe several times and have dealers in places like Germany, North Ireland, and Zurich," Rollins reported. "They've developed marketing skills as well as artistic skills, on a world-class level.

The kids know that this is for real, not like most school art programs, which are like dress rehearsals for plays that are never produced."

The kids that Rollins works with were the so-called "unteachable ones." They had few academic skills and very limited basic knowledge. Art gave them an awareness of what was happening in the world and a voice for expressing their own social commentary. Several of Rollins's students have gone on to major universities and art colleges. Many come back and become mentors for the younger students.

"Because the students work together, the combined creativity of these voices has a unifying power," Rollins explained. "Making art becomes a metaphor for making life. Today's youth culture is based on immediate gratification so it's important to create something concrete and that has lasting value. Using art as a means to knowledge really works. The students' reading skills went up dramatically and so did their self-esteem."

Rollins believes art has a special role to play in education and in community-building. "What's wonderful about art is that it is a non-linguistic way to exchange symbols and signs and ways of working. It crosses cultural boundaries and has a unifying power. Through art we find out that we have much more similarities than differences."

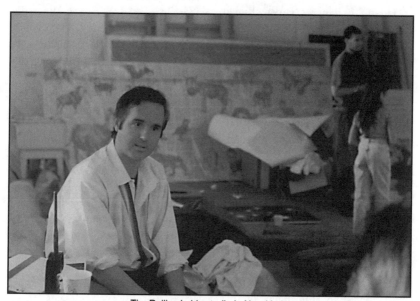

Tim Rollins in his studio in New York

# Referendum blues continues to plague us in the new year

February 8, 1996

The prospect of starting the new year with the spectre of another referendum looming on the horizon is not exactly encouraging.

The sting of the disparaging remarks towards "ethnics" made by the Parizeau-Landry team after learning that the "yes" side lost, has not dissipated with the coming of the new year.

If anything the arrogance and total disregard for public opinion demonstrated by these comments have had time to really sink in. The politics of intolerance, like a festering wound, has been exposed for all the world to see.

Had these remarks never slipped out, white anglophones and francophones could continue to bury their heads in the sand and go on pretending that Quebec is a fair and just society.

Anglophones were quick to denounce these statements as xenophobic and racist. Yet my own experiences in this country tell me that the sentiments expressed by Parizeau and Landry are shared by many people in the francophone as well as the anglophone community.

These comments, coupled with the post referendum acts of vandalism directed against anglophones and members of cultural communities, have created an atmosphere of fear and distrust.

Over the holidays I was struck by the number of comments friends and acquaintances in the cultural community made to me about the degree of insensitivity and intolerance among some separatists towards "ethnic" Quebecers.

They expressed a profound disillusionment with the hostile political climate directed at them. They have chosen to come to Quebec to make a better life for themselves, have learned French, sent their children to French schools, made every effort to integrate socially, contributed economically to the development of this province—yet they've been made to feel like second class citizens.

The October 30 referendum has shown them that there is no place for them in a separate Quebec. When you are devalued, excluded, when you're told that you *are* the problem, when you feel your rights are being violated and you feel you are at the mercy of a government that doesn't really represent you, then you don't see a future for yourself in this province.

In the many conversations I had over the Christmas break, people expressed a tremendous sense of despair and powerlessness. Many newcomers to Quebec are talking about pulling up their roots and leaving—again. Something they are not looking forward to doing, something they'd rather not be doing at all...if they had a choice.

Part of the disillusionment comes from watching businesses close, friends leave, families uprooted. Under the present political regime, you can't make any plans for the future. Relationships are transitory.

Every time my children make a new friend, they up and leave. We're constantly saying good-bye to someone.

As a visible minority I'm already being penalized for the color of my skin—despite the fact that my ancestors have been here for seven generations. As an anglophone I am being penalized for the language I speak.

The issue is how can we in the cultural communities have more of a voice in the decisions that affect our lives.

Perhaps this is where a group like Alliance Quebec, a linguistic lobby group, can play a role. At their post-referendum conference at the end of November, Alliance Quebec attempted to strengthen its links with the cultural communities.

President of Alliance, Michael Hamelin, said, "It's important that Alliance Quebec recognize that our community is changing and that the traditional circles that has put Alliance together in the English speaking community are not a majority any more. The English speaking community is much more diverse than it used to be. There is a need to build broader coalitions."

Speaking in a panel discussion at the conference, black community activist Alfie Roberts expressed the view that the issues in the black community are much more immediate than simply one of language rights. People are primarily concerned with employment, discrimination, housing, education. He recommended that if Alliance Quebec wanted to reach out to the cultural communities it would have to address these basic issues of survival

that are a daily reality for individuals in the black community.

Dan Philips, director of the Black Council of Quebec, hopes that "Alliance can help in articulating the problems plaguing the black community and that this involvement will have a positive effect in making people of color feel that they are a part of this society and that their rights are being protected." The problem, as he sees it, is not just one of English language rights but of the perpetuation of uncorrected stereotypes about black people.

Phillips went on to say that "unless Alliance Quebec can address the problems of the conditions of black people in this society, then we will always feel alienated from the objectives of Alliance Quebec."

"Reaching out to the black community must be in concrete terms in making the community feel part of these exercises. The black community has a high unemployment rate which exceeds 50% and affects young people between 18 and 35 and when young black people can't find jobs they lose hope in the system and then they become victims of this hopelessness," said Phillips.

These sentiments are reminiscent of the fundamental friction between the white anglophone community and the black community prior to the formation of Alliance Quebec when there existed a coalition of groups called the Quebec Council of Minorities. The two agendas—language rights and racial discrimination—were in conflict with each other. That caused a split in the group, out of which Alliance Quebec was formed, whose mandate was to protect English language rights in the Province of Quebec.

Because of the political climate in Quebec, white anglophones now identify with the discrimination that black people already know. They have begun to realize and experience for themselves what it's like to be a minority. These experiences offer a window of opportunity to enter into a coalition building process which is built on empathy and understanding. One of the most important aspects of coalition building is that people need to have common agendas and there must be support for each other's agendas. The fact that we are all minorities means that we have to support each other.

# Biographies

**Clifton Ruggles** was born in Montreal on November 20, 1951. Clifton's ancestry is mixed African Canadian and Native with roots that go back to the Black Loyalists who settled in the Annapolis Valley, Nova Scotia, in the late seventeenth century. His parents, Harold and Mary Ruggles, left Nova Scotia in the late 1940s and moved to Montreal where they raised nine children. Clifton's father worked as a railway porter and his mother as a domestic. While attending university Clifton worked as a sleeping car porter, during which time he interviewed and photographed many of the porters with whom he worked.

Clifton has a Bachelor of Education degree from McGill University and is in the process of completing his Masters degree in Art Education at Concordia University. Clifton has been writing a monthly column called "Perspectives" for the *Montreal Gazette*, West End Edition, since 1991. He has been a teacher with the Protestant School Board of Greater Montreal since 1976 and has also worked as a part-time lecturer in the Department of Art Education at Concordia University and at College Marie Victorin where he taught courses on creative thinking and problem solving in the Special Care Counselling program.

Clifton is also an exhibited visual artist (painting and photography) whose area of interest is documenting the Black experience. He is co-author of *Words on Work*, a language arts textbook for senior high school. He was also at one time co-editor of the *Sentinel*, a magazine published by the Provincial Association of Protestant Teachers.

**Olivia Rovinescu** was born in Bucharest, Romania, on November 16, 1952 and came to Canada in the early 1960s. She has a Masters degree in Education from McGill University and is presently the Associate Director of the Centre for Teaching and Learning Services at Concordia University. Olivia has been the director of the Lacolle Centre for Educational Innovation at Concordia for 12 years and has taught in the Faculty of Education at McGill University. Along with Clifton, she is co-author of *Words on Work* and has written several articles on the subject of critical thinking and prejudice reduction.